LAWYERS GONE BAD

PHILIP SLAYTON studied law at Oxford University as a Rhodes scholar. He taught at McGill University and the University of Western Ontario (where he was dean of law) before becoming partner of a major Canadian law firm. Since leaving practice in 2000, Slayton has commented on legal matters in newspapers and magazines, and on television and radio. He lives in Toronto.

LAWYERS GONE BAD

MONEY, SEX AND MADNESS IN CANADA'S LEGAL PROFESSION

PHILIP SLAYTON

PENGUIN
CANADA

PENGUIN CANADA

Published by the Penguin Group

Penguin Group (Canada), 90 Eglinton Avenue East, Suite 700,
Toronto, Ontario, Canada M4P 2Y3 (a division of Pearson Canada Inc.)

Penguin Group (USA) Inc., 375 Hudson Street,
New York, New York 10014, U.S.A.
Penguin Books Ltd, 80 Strand, London WC2R 0RL, England
Penguin Ireland, 25 St Stephen's Green, Dublin 2, Ireland
(a division of Penguin Books Ltd)
Penguin Group (Australia), 250 Camberwell Road, Camberwell,
Victoria 3124, Australia (a division of Pearson Australia Group Pty Ltd)
Penguin Books India Pvt Ltd, 11 Community Centre, Panchsheel Park,
New Delhi – 110 017, India
Penguin Group (NZ), 67 Apollo Drive, Rosedale, North Shore 0632, New Zealand
(a division of Pearson New Zealand Ltd)
Penguin Books (South Africa) (Pty) Ltd, 24 Sturdee Avenue, Rosebank,
Johannesburg 2196, South Africa

Penguin Books Ltd, Registered Offices: 80 Strand, London WC2R 0RL, England

First published in a Viking Canada hardcover by Penguin Group (Canada),
a division of Pearson Canada Inc., 2007
Published in this edition, 2008

1 2 3 4 5 6 7 8 9 10 (OPM)

Copyright © Philip Slayton, 2007, 2008

Epigraph from Sybille Bedford, *Quicksands: A Memoir*
(London: Hamish Hamilton, 2005), used with permission.

Excerpt from Kelly Toughill, "Intimate politics allows for some hard truths,"
Toronto Star, 2 October 1999, reprinted with permission
—Torstar Syndication Services.

Manufactured in the U.S.A.

LIBRARY AND ARCHIVES CANADA CATALOGUING IN PUBLICATION

Slayton, Philip
Lawyers gone bad : money, sex and madness in Canada's legal
profession / Philip Slayton.

Includes bibliographical references and index.
ISBN 978-0-14-305610-2

1. White collar crimes—Canada. 2. Lawyers—Canada—Bibliography.
3. Lawyers—Canada—Discipline. 4. Practice of Law—Corrupt
practices—Canada. I. Title.

KE415.S58 2008   340.092'271   C2008-900674-7
KF345.Z9A1S58 2008

Visit the Penguin Group (Canada) website at www.penguin.ca

Special and corporate bulk purchase rates available; please see
www.penguin.ca/corporatesales or call 1-800-810-3104, ext. 477 or 474

For Cynthia

"What does any of us know about one another?
And what does a writer know?"

—Sybille Bedford, *Quicksands: A Memoir*[1]

CONTENTS

ONE

MONEY, SEX AND MADNESS

Most of the stories in this book are about dishonest lawyers. These lawyers (so a tribunal or court found) seized opportunities to behave badly, opportunities offered by legal practice.[1] They broke trust with their clients, or law firm, or both (often stealing money or abusing fiduciary relationships); they had sex with clients or others they met in the capacity of lawyer and who, arguably, were susceptible to their influence and power; or they participated in schemes that used the law to cheat the public or deceive the government.

Only a few lawyers are dishonest. Most behave honourably, serving their clients, profession, and community well. My stories of dishonest lawyers are about a handful of people in a profession that now, in Canada, has over ninety thousand members. Nonetheless, the stories of that handful give insight into the legal profession and legal practice, into how lawyers band together and govern themselves, and into how the law itself can fail or be perverted.[2] They imply reforms of the legal profession and the law, and I suggest in the final chapter what some of these reforms might be.

I started getting interested in lawyers gone bad in the earliest days of my first legal job. In September 1969, back from studying at Oxford University in England, I began a year as law clerk to Justice Wilfred Judson of the Supreme Court of Canada. The first case on the court's list that fall was that of Sam Ciglen, a Toronto lawyer appealing a criminal conviction of conspiring wilfully to evade income taxes.

Eager to make a good first impression on my judge, I worked hard to master this highly complex file. Finally, Justice Judson summoned me to his chambers. "What have you been doing?" he asked. "Reviewing the Ciglen case," I said, enthusiastic to explain at length the matter's difficult facts and complicated law and present him with a carefully nuanced conclusion. "Oh, Ciglen," he said with a dismissive wave of his hand. "Just another crooked lawyer!" Later the Supreme Court rejected Ciglen's appeal and he went to jail.[3]

After working at the Supreme Court, I taught law full-time for thirteen years, first at McGill and then at the University of Western Ontario (where I was law dean for a time). During those years as teacher and dean, I looked over the lectern at hundreds of young men and women eager to practise law. Did I and my fellow law professors say much to these students about the ethics, dangers, and responsibilities of their chosen profession? No, we didn't, if only because virtually none of us had ever practised law, and we knew little or nothing about its temptations and difficulties.

In 1983, I turned to practising law on Toronto's Bay Street, becoming an associate and then a partner of Blake, Cassels & Graydon (known as "Blakes"), one of Canada's oldest and biggest law firms. This was shortly before the cases of Martin Pilzmaker and Bob Donaldson (a Blakes partner), described in Chapter 2, ushered in what I call the "new age" of lawyers gone bad. I practised corporate law at Blakes for seventeen years, watching the Canadian legal profession from a fine perch, and seeing first-hand what I had not seen as a law professor—how a lawyer could get into big trouble. It was during this time, as I gained experience and collected information about life in the front lines of law, that the idea of writing a book about lawyers gone bad came to me.

A 2004 Leger poll found that only 44 percent of Canadians trust lawyers, a dramatic fall from the 54 percent reported by the same pollster two years previously. (Firefighters headed the 2004 poll, with the trust of 97 percent of Canadians, while politicians were at the bottom with 14 percent.)[4] A 2006 Harris poll in the United States found that only 18 percent of Americans trust lawyers completely; 50 percent trust doctors completely (top of the poll), and 6 percent trust stockbrokers completely (the bottom).[5] In 2002, according to records of the Federation of Law Societies of Canada, Canadian law societies received about fourteen thousand complaints about lawyers, about the same number as the year before, and the year before that.[6] (The federation apparently has not compiled comprehensive discipline statistics since 2002.) That's approximately one formal complaint for every five lawyers, year in and year out. Quietly considered, statistics such as these are hugely troubling. They imply that little trust exists in a relationship where trust is essential.

The most common negative belief about lawyers is that they are greedy[7]—so greedy that, given the chance, they may steal. Perhaps people believe this because they know temptation stares lawyers in the face. Lawyers are often entrusted with other people's money; in the febrile public imagination, they cannot always be counted on to move that money along to its rightful destination. But, when money in a lawyer's hands goes missing, the simple notion of greed often seems inadequate to explain what happened. Some lawyers whose stories I tell in this book took other people's money to pay for what they could easily afford themselves. Bob Donaldson (Chapter 2) carelessly used clients' funds for unrelated business trips that could have been billed to someone else, and for trivial personal entertainment expenses. Dan Cooper (Chapter 3), earning almost half a million dollars a year in the late eighties, put his professional and personal life in high jeopardy for less than half that amount, stealing to pay for entertainment and buy art.

Even when simple greed appears to explain sufficiently what happened, on closer examination the truth may seem more complicated or different. Martin Pilzmaker (Chapter 2), a Toronto immigration lawyer and central figure in the Lang Michener scandal, who committed suicide when faced with charges of theft, fraud, forgery, and conspiracy, had a chauffeured Rolls-Royce and wore a $20,000 fur coat. But what motivated the tortured Pilzmaker seems not to have been money, but his desire to be a member of the legal establishment rather than a risible fringe player. Other lawyers inexplicably participated in economic frauds without any personal gain. Richard Shead (Chapter 11), once Winnipeg's most prominent tax lawyer, and Martin Wirick (Chapter 12), a Vancouver real estate practitioner, helped clients commit fraud and received only modest legal fees. Their professional lives, it seems, were ruined for nothing at all.

There are, of course, motives other than money. Lawyers are sometimes accused of using their status and power to extract sexual favours from vulnerable clients. This is said to be unprofessional behaviour—a breach of fiduciary duty—and, depending on the circumstances, to be criminal conduct as well. I tell at some length the stories of lawyers whose sexual appetite got them into trouble. But do the demands of libido plausibly explain how Agnew Johnston, a

Crown attorney and member of the Thunder Bay Establishment, became a suspect in the murder of an underage prostitute (Chapter 8)? Or explain the passage of Michael Bomek from prominent criminal defence lawyer to proprietor of a hot dog stand (Chapter 9)?

Stealing and sexual misconduct may be distractions from the grinding boredom that is a characteristic of even the best legal practice. Cameron Stracher, author of *Double Billing: A Young Lawyer's Tale of Greed, Sex, Lies, and the Pursuit of a Swivel Chair*,[8] has written in *The Wall Street Journal* that "[f]ew professions combine as much creative talent with so much mind-numbing work."[9] The risk-to-reward ratio of stealing and sexual misconduct is poor, but perhaps it's precisely the risk that is appealing. In *Seductions of Crime*,[10] Jack Katz writes about the "sensual dynamics" of crime, the "sneaky thrill" of the nonviolent property crime. Robert Hare, in his book *Without Conscience*,[11] observes that psychopaths "have an ongoing and excessive need for excitement—they long to live in the fast lane or 'on the edge,' where the action is." In *The Natural*,[12] his 2002 book about Bill Clinton (a lawyer, after all), Joe Klein reports the president's reply when, pre-Lewinsky, an aide asked him about his tendency to live dangerously. "Well," said Clinton tellingly, "they haven't caught me yet." (In April 2001, Clinton's Arkansas law licence was suspended for five years as part of an understanding with then Independent

Counsel Robert Ray to end the Monica Lewinsky investigation.) Perhaps the phenomenon has been best expressed by Theodore Dalrymple, a British doctor: "Untold numbers of my patients, with every opportunity to lead quiet, useful, and tolerably prosperous lives, chose instead the path of complication and, if not of violence and physical danger exactly, at least of drama and excitement, leading to sleepless nights and financial loss. They break up marriages, form disastrous liaisons, chase chimeras, and behave in ways that predictably will end in disaster. Like moths to the flame, they court catastrophe. As many have told me, they prefer disaster to boredom."[13]

Money, sex, a thrilling escape from a boring life and career—these are not always adequate explanations. Sometimes, it seems as if there is some kind of madness at work (I know of no other way to put this). Perhaps a lawyer who commits a seemingly inexplicable crime is one of Robert Hare's psychopaths, suffering from an antisocial personality disorder that makes him prone to irrational behaviour, deceit, and manipulation, and lack of regard for the rights of others. In *Without Conscience*, Hare describes psychopaths as "social predators who charm, manipulate, and ruthlessly plow their way through life … Completely lacking in conscience and in feelings for others, they selfishly take what they want and do as they please, violating social norms and expectations without the slightest sense of guilt or regret."[14] He writes that psychopaths "can be very effective in presenting themselves well and are often very likeable and charming."[15] More than one of the lawyers I write about in this book, likeable and charming, have been described (often by prosecuting Crown attorneys) as "psychopaths."

Contrary to what Jack Katz writes, sometimes it may not be the crime that is sensually appealing; it may be the criminal himself who is the attraction. A lawyer may become emotionally involved with a criminal client, becoming a confederate and abettor. Admiration, even love, explains what money, or other motives, cannot. The lawyer admires qualities in the client that he wishes he had himself, what the psychiatric literature calls "counter-transference." Richard Shead, with no discernible practical advantage for himself, destroyed his career to help a rogue. Shead was a shy and introverted tax lawyer with an unremarkable personal presence; his client was a flamboyant and charismatic con man. "Reaction formation" may also be present, the defence mechanism that converts an unconscious and unacceptable impulse or feeling into its opposite so it can become conscious and be expressed. In reaction formation, attitudes and behaviours are adopted that are the opposite of true inclinations. The latent criminal becomes a policeman. The law-breaker-in-waiting goes to law school.

It may be some other kind of psychological disability that leads a lawyer astray. Patrick Schiltz, lawyer and law professor, former editor of the

Harvard Law Review, former law clerk to Supreme Court Justice Antonin Scalia, wrote in the Autumn 1999 *Notre Dame Magazine*:[16] "Lawyers suffer from depression, anxiety, hostility, paranoia, social alienation and isolation, obsessive-compulsiveness, and interpersonal sensitivity at alarming rates." Schiltz refers to an oft-cited 1991 Johns Hopkins University study, which reported that lawyers suffer from major depressive disorder at a rate 3.6 times higher than non-lawyers who share their key socio-demographic traits. Shiltz thinks that lawyers are unhappy because they work too hard. To him, it's simple. Every hour a lawyer spends at his desk is an hour away from the things that give joy and meaning to life—playing with children, for example, or reading a book.

Martin Seligman, in *Authentic Happiness*,[17] offers another explanation for the misery of lawyers. They are naturally pessimistic, he says; they view bad events as pervasive, permanent, and uncontrollable, rather than local, temporary, and changeable. "And if you don't have this prudence to begin with," writes Seligman, "law school will seek to teach it to you. Unfortunately, though, a trait that makes you good at your profession does not always make you a happy human being."[18] Seligman argues that lawyers who can see clearly how badly things might turn out for their clients can also see clearly how badly things might turn out for themselves. He also blames competition, and the "classic win-loss" nature of legal practice, for the unhappiness of lawyers. Once the practice of law meant giving good counsel about justice and fairness, but now it is a big business in which billable hours, take-no-prisoners victories, and the bottom line are the principal ends. "Lawyers are trained to be aggressive, judgmental, intellectual, analytical and emotionally detached," he writes. "This produces predictable emotional consequences for the legal practitioner: he or she will be depressed, anxious, and angry a lot of the time."[19]

It all begins in law school, as Seligman suggests. There, students are not just taught to be pessimistic, aggressive, judgmental, intellectual, analytical, and emotionally detached. They also have part of their personal morality stripped away. They are instructed that a lawyer must represent all clients regardless of their moral character, and give advice devoid of moral content. When I was a law professor, I would tell my students that a lawyer was like a taxi driver. A taxi driver's job is not to tell his passenger who wants to go to the local whorehouse that the museum is a better destination, but to get the passenger safely to the whorehouse without attracting the attention of the police. Another law professor at the University of Western Ontario was famous for telling first-year students that the main job of a lawyer in practice was not to pass judgment on clients, but "to grab for himself some of the money that Mr. A was passing to Mr. B."

And then law students become lawyers and experience the "real world." They discover how clients are billed and lawyers are paid. Almost all law firms charge according to the hours spent on a file. The pay of a partner or associate depends in part, often in large part, on the number of billable hours he creates for himself (and others). The consequence is often "over docketing," the exaggeration by a lawyer of the number of billable hours he has worked. Over docketing is tolerated, if not encouraged, by firms that value profit above all else and set unrealistic billing goals for their partners and associates. Gripped by ambition, greed, fear, or panic, lawyers cheat. They cheat despite the fact that a law society may disbar a member found to have overbilled. In a 2002 Ontario disciplinary case about overbilling of the Ontario Legal Aid Plan by Toronto lawyer Angie Codina[20] (Chapter 15), the panel observed in its reasons that where "the lawyer has been dishonest in regard to the number of hours worked, the Law Society should impose a very serious disciplinary penalty.... The penalty for defrauding clients in a billing situation must be disbarment." Angie Codina's lover, lawyer Harry Kopyto, had already been disbarred for the same reason—overbilling Legal Aid. (In 2000, in unrelated proceedings, Codina was sent to prison in New York State for fraud, larceny, and practising law while not a member of the State bar.)

Out-and-out cheating about the number of hours worked is only the half of it. Billing by the hour, whether a lawyer is lying or not, creates bad incentives and encourages unprofessional behaviour. The longer it takes a lawyer to solve his client's problem, the greater his income. This system rewards the lead foot and the heavy hand. The contented lawyer is the one who in the morning has a pile of documents on the left-hand side of his desk that he can spend all day moving to the right-hand side. The worried lawyer is the one who creatively solves a client's big problem before it is time for morning coffee and wonders what he is going to do for the rest of the day. Efficiencies reducing time spent are unlikely to be adopted. This may be why the legal profession has been notoriously slow to embrace information technology. "Why be more efficient, why computerize, when you can bill by the hour?" a lawyer from Saskatchewan wrote to me.

It is, of course, absurd to value the work of an intelligent, well-educated person, and especially someone who is creative, according to how much time he or she spends doing that work. On that basis, sudden insight, however brilliant, has little or no value, while laboriously produced hackwork is worth a lot and is to be encouraged. This approach would value a painting by Picasso according to how long it had taken him to paint it.

Many lawyers exhibit a high degree of knowledge and competence, but there is vice in these apparently desirable attributes. Mastery of the rules of law, and the ability to manipulate them, encourages disdain for those rules. A lawyer may come to believe that his mastery of rules carries with it a personal exemption from their application. He may even come not to distinguish between legal rules and those of personal conduct and morality. He may come to believe that, in some sense, he is bigger than all rules, no matter what their content. As his ego swells, he may ignore or break rules as a form of self-assertion and a statement of personal power. Or, using his interpretive skill, he may give new and convenient content to rules of conduct.

Tax law practice often shows disdain for the ethical content of rules. No one likes paying tax, but many taxpayers consider that tax rules incorporate important principles of public policy, even of morality. As they sign their cheques payable to the taxation authorities, they may comfort themselves with the thought that redistribution of wealth through the tax system provides for the less fortunate, or that tax revenues allow the creation and maintenance of great public projects—universal medical care, for example. But the bread and butter of a tax lawyer or accountant is to facilitate the avoidance of tax. He is expected to manipulate the rules to minimize the tax payable by his clients. This can only distract attention from the rightful purpose of the tax system, and undermine its moral and public policy basis.

Since the 2001 Enron scandal, newspapers have been full of tales about the collapse of unbridled capitalism. For the most part, lawyers have watched safely from the wings as famous corporations file for bankruptcy, accounting firms disappear, boards of directors are sacked, and CEOs and other senior executives are indicted and jailed. Pundits have repeatedly asked, Where were the company's directors when all this was going on? Where were the auditors? Where were the regulators? Few have asked, Where were the lawyers?

It's peculiar that the legal profession has so far been largely untouched by this corporate crisis. The companies that got into trouble, and the people whose careers have been destroyed, all undoubtedly received expensive legal advice from top-drawer law firms. The average CEO, CFO, or director of a decent-sized company doesn't make a move without his lawyer by his side. Jonathan Glater observed in 2005, in *The New York Times*,[21] that, in the corporate world, nothing happens without the review and approval of a lawyer: "Lawyers have made themselves indispensable to public companies. Lawyers boast of their ability to learn the ins and outs of any problem and to know a client's interests better than the client does. But if lawyers are as wise as they profess, how is it that so many of their clients have been in the middle of devastating financial scandals over the last four years?"

Typically, a senior executive and his lawyer have a long-standing relationship. They go out together with their wives to expensive restaurants (the lawyer pays). They go on fly-fishing weekends (perhaps to a company-owned retreat). They play golf at the best courses. There's a good chance the lawyer sits on the company's board. Each gives to the other's favourite charity. They're friends (of a sort).

But the lawyer and the executive are also locked in a symbiotic relationship. The dictionary defines "symbiosis" as "an association of two different organisms living attached to one another: a relationship of mutual benefit or dependence." For the lawyer, status in his firm, and the income associated with that status, depends largely on control of one or more big clients. To lose a big client can be a personal economic disaster. A lawyer will do a lot to stop such a terrible thing from happening to him. For the corporate executive, the lawyer supplies a protective shield. When the going gets tough, the executive must be able to say, "My lawyer said it was okay!" Most times the lawyer will also have to put that in writing in a legal opinion.

This symbiotic relationship between client and lawyer can be perfectly respectable, particularly if the executive genuinely seeks, and is disposed to take, objective and candid legal advice. My favourite client when I practised law—the CEO of a large company in chronic difficulty—told me that my job was to argue with him. "Tell me what's wrong with what I want to say and why I shouldn't do what I want to do," he would say, waving his arms wildly. "Don't let me get away with anything!" I accepted this invitation with enthusiasm. My client and I had spirited arguments almost daily; sometimes I won, and sometimes he won. At the end of several years working together (the company eventually prospered and was taken over), we shook hands, declared a draw, and assured ourselves that the job had been well done by all concerned.

But not all CEOs are like my favourite client. Many a senior business executive, driven by the imperative of the bottom line and possessing an ego fuelled by his company's success (which he attributes to his own genius[22]), will brook little or no opposition. No arguments on fine points of legal interpretation for him! The job of his lawyer is not to give advice but to provide protection and get him where he wants to go, by hook or by crook. If the lawyer is in the way, then, "friendship" notwithstanding, golf games nonetheless, there is always another lawyer. After all, nothing personal, it's about money.

In these circumstances, the corporate lawyer fresh from that golf game or fly-fishing weekend often can easily be co-opted. "There's always a way, and it's up to me to find it," he tells himself. "After all," he rationalizes, "the corporate/securities/tax law is so complex and its meaning so uncertain. Almost anything is possible. And who can be certain what is right and what is wrong? My job is to be helpful, not judgmental."

It's unlikely that the lawyer will take a stand if he fears that he may lose the client by doing so. He knows that, if he loses the client, his partners, seeing the firm's billings shrink, will think his probity a trifle self-indulgent, and will punish him when it comes time to divvy up the profits of the partnership. So, in a Faustian bargain, to preserve a cozy relationship and protect his status and income, the lawyer does what his client tells him to do. Money is a harsh master.[23]

What is this? A sleazy abrogation of responsibility by the legal profession? The removal of a vital safeguard from the economic system? Bad conduct driven by greed? Or just an acceptable approach to a complex situation, with everyone doing just what he or she is supposed to do?

Enron is the poster boy for recent corporate scandal. The company filed for bankruptcy in December 2001, many of its executives have been under criminal investigation, and its auditor, Arthur Andersen, has been convicted for obstructing justice. But what about Vinson & Elkins, Enron's lead law firm? Julie Hilden asked in an article in *Slate*,[24] "How can the lawyers who approved the transactions be held blameless while the government takes down the company that merely trusted its lawyers' advice?" Jonathan Glater in his *New York Times* article offered the cynical answer of one lawyer: "A lawyer may brag of mastery of a deal in advance, but once prosecutors are interested, suddenly that lawyer's role consisted only of drafting a contract."

Hilden's own answer is that Vinson & Elkins may well have done nothing wrong. She writes, "It was to Enron, its shareholders, and the boundary constraints of the law, not the welfare of the public or abstract concepts of justice, that V & E owed its loyalties." Even if what was done were acts "taken on the very brink of legality," Hilden argues that Enron's law firm was ethically obligated to go to that brink. Accountants, she writes, have independence as their central virtue; lawyers, zealousness.

Formal canons of professional conduct typically dance around the issue of how "zealous" a lawyer should be in rendering his services. In Ontario, for example, one law society rule says, "When advising a client, a lawyer shall not knowingly assist in or encourage any dishonesty, fraud, crime, or illegal conduct." Another rule, given in the context of advocacy, requires that a lawyer represent the client "resolutely and honourably within the limits of the law." The official commentary on this bland rule of advocacy, however, puts forward an aggressive spin: "The lawyer has a duty to the client to raise fearlessly every issue, advance every argument, and ask every question, however distasteful, which the lawyer thinks will help the client's case." And so, the governing body of the legal profession, in a rather vague and offhand fashion, tells the lawyer to stay within the law, of course, but also, by the way, to advance every argument that may benefit his client. This is not exactly helpful.

What happens to a lawyer gone bad when his transgressions are discovered? In Canada, the legal profession is self-regulating and self-policing. Do law societies deal appropriately and expeditiously with serious complaints about their members? Do they merely suspend lawyers when they should be disbarred? Do they too easily readmit disbarred lawyers when their applications for readmission should be denied? Do they treat similar cases of misbehaving lawyers in a similar fashion, or is self-policing suffused by unpredictability and arbitrariness? Should the regulators have "zero tolerance" of lawyers having sex with clients, or would it be wiser to consider particular fiduciary responsibilities as they may arise in individual situations? And do the regulators move decisively to change legal practices vulnerable to abuse by practitioners?

In Britain—but not in Canada—a revolution is underway in the regulation of lawyers and the provision of legal services. The principal figure in this revolution is not some frightening left-wing ideologue, but the quintessential establishment man—Sir David Clementi. Sir David is the former deputy governor of the Bank of England and now runs Prudential PLC, the huge international insurance company. In 2003, the British Lord Chancellor, Lord Falconer, asked him to conduct a review of the regulation of the legal profession in England and Wales. The extraordinary Clementi report was published in December 2004.[25]

The Clementi report contains four main sets of recommendations. It proposes that the legal profession be overseen by a new legal services board with a lay majority chaired by a non-lawyer and accountable to Parliament. It advocates that the profession lose its powers to investigate complaints against lawyers, and that a new independent office be created for that purpose. It recommends that lawyers should be free to enter into partnerships with non-lawyers. And it proposes that companies or individuals outside the legal profession be allowed to own and manage a law practice. Said Sir David, summing up his work, "The current regulatory system is focused on those who provide legal services: the new framework will place the interests of consumers at its centre." The Lord Chancellor welcomed the recommendations of the Clementi report and said that the government would press ahead to implement them.[26] On May 24, 2006, the government published a draft Legal Services Bill incorporating the Clementi proposals. The final bill was published on November 24, 2006, and at the end of 2006 was under consideration by the British House of Lords.

Much of what Sir David Clementi proposed is not that novel. In most common law jurisdictions, for example, but not in Canada, disciplinary powers are exercised partly or completely by a body distinct from the law societies. In the United States, lawyers are regulated substantively and procedurally by state courts (although in some states the court, while retaining the ultimate disciplinary authority, has delegated the job of investigating complaints to the state bar association). The proposed British office for legal complaints is very similar to the highly successful Office of the Legal Services Commissioner in the Australian state of New South Wales.

THE LAWYERS whose stories are told in this book experienced spectacular falls from positions of high esteem. In some cases at least, the personal characteristics that led to their downfall, and the way they behaved as they made their transit, exemplify and explain general characteristics and behaviour of the legal profession. But, as I wrote at the beginning of this chapter, few lawyers fall dramatically and publicly, or at all. Most pass through their careers without attracting the attention of the investigative journalist or the law society disciplinarian, retiring with honour, praised by their peers, given testimonial dinners. What happens to the good lawyer, who behaves well, when his partner or employee turns out to be guilty of sharp practice, perhaps even to be a crook?

Once, law firm partners knew each other well and knew their firm's law practice intimately. Fifty years ago, Bay Street firms that now have hundreds of partners only had ten or fifteen. Until the early fifties, the general practice at these firms was for the partners to gather every morning and open the mail together, passing letters around the conference table for all to see. Until the eighties, an associate could be denied partnership simply because one or two existing partners were not comfortable with him or her. The comment "he makes me a little nervous" or "I don't really want her as a partner" would be enough to doom a candidacy.

But now, in huge firms with multiple offices, and even in smaller firms, one partner often knows little about the character and practice of another. He may not even recognize another partner when he passes him on the street. Questions of personal character, and the integrity of an individual law practice, are subsumed by efficiencies of scale, the reality of geographic spread, and the drive for profitability. The discovery of a rogue partner or associate is shocking. What can a law firm do to protect itself against the possibility of a partner or associate lawyer going bad? When it happens, what should the firm do? And how realistic is the current law and regulatory framework up against the realities of modern legal practice?

Many Canadian law firms have lately changed from general partnerships to limited liability partnerships, as legislation and professional rules have been amended to make such a change possible. When this transmogrification takes place (by simple amendment to the existing general partnership agreement), a discreet advertisement is placed in the local newspaper's business section and the firm quietly adds the letters *LLP* at the end of its name. (In many jurisdictions, such as Ontario, the formal requirement that clients be notified of the changed status is satisfied by advertising in a local newspaper.) Few clients, and certainly none but the most sophisticated, understand what has happened and that what has happened is to their disadvantage. And few law firm partners seem to realize that the world has significantly changed for them as well.

During the billing drive, some of Dan Cooper's accounts caught the credit committee's attention, and Chris Montague, together with McCarthy's business manager, started looking at them carefully. On Wednesday, November 7, the business manager went to see Arthur Scace, McCarthy Tétrault's managing partner.[7] He told Scace that expenses billed to several of Cooper's files, expenses paid by McCarthy's and then in turn charged to clients, had been billed by numbered companies owned by Cooper.[8] Over more than four years, these numbered companies had sent twenty-eight bills for false disbursements or fictitious services to clients and McCarthy Tétrault had paid them all, for a total of about $234,000 (the last phoney disbursement had been billed just days before, on November 2). After listening to the business manager, Scace started a file on Dan Cooper and made this entry: "It stinks. We have fraud." He called Cooper and asked him to come and see him the next morning, Thursday, November 8, 1990.

At the Thursday morning meeting, Scace confronted Cooper. Were the disbursements billed to McCarthy clients genuine, or were they fraudulent? What services, if any, had been provided by the numbered companies? At first Cooper denied the allegations. He had brought with him to Scace's office a "consultant," who claimed he had provided services for Cooper's clients through the numbered companies and had legitimately billed for the disbursements that were in issue. Scace told the consultant that he would have to supply an affidavit, and that if any part of the affidavit turned out to be wrong he would be in very serious trouble. The consultant, flustered, got up and left Scace's office, and was never seen or heard from again. Cooper seemed numb.

Later in the meeting Cooper broke down, admitted everything, asked for mercy, and offered his resignation from McCarthy Tétrault. Scace quickly accepted Cooper's resignation, and told him to clear out his office immediately and leave the building. Then Scace, mindful of the recent Lang Michener affair (just like Ted Donegan in the Bob Donaldson scandal),[9] telephoned the law society and gave an initial report of what had happened. Later in the day, Scace went to Cooper's office. Cooper, busy packing up his things, embraced Scace, cried, and said he had let Scace down. Cooper asked, "Will I go to jail?" "I hope not," replied Scace.

The following day Cooper asked Scace to speak to his father, Bernard Cooper, on the telephone, and Scace agreed to do so. Cooper's father was distraught. Dan was the golden boy of the family. Bernard Cooper, who by all accounts had made a lot of money in real estate, suggested that perhaps he could make restitution, if that would help. (Almost complete restitution was eventually made, but not by Cooper's father. In due course, McCarthy's simply applied Cooper's capital in the firm against the money he had stolen.) Bernard Cooper died on New

Year's Day, 1994. At his father's funeral, Dan delivered the eulogy. One account says that Dan talked of the high ethical standards his father had set and his own failure to live up to them.

Somebody picking up the newspaper on Tuesday, November 13, 1990, might have seen a Canadian Press wire story that began, "A partner in the Toronto-based law firm of McCarthy Tétrault has resigned after allegations that about $200,000 was diverted to a company he controlled. The partner, Daniel Cooper, a leading computer law expert, quit Thursday after 19 years at the firm, Canada's largest...." The story quoted Arthur Scace, who described Cooper as "a very successful lawyer." Scace said that McCarthy's had paid Cooper's company for fictitious consulting services. "It has come as a shock to us," Scace added.[10] In *The Globe and Mail*'s story the same day, Scace was quoted as saying, "It is a tragic situation for a man who had established an enviable reputation as one of Canada's leading computer law experts."[11] Some years later, in an interview, Scace offered a somewhat different point of view. "Cooper was cocky," he said. "He wasn't as smart as he thought he was."[12]

On November 16, 1990, Cooper made a voluntary assignment in bankruptcy listing approximately $600,000 in debts. He began working as claims manager for a car rental agency. He was quickly charged with one count of fraud over $1,000 under s. 380(1)(a) of the Criminal Code, and on April 24,

1991, pleaded guilty. The Crown prosecutor, Jim Atkinson, told the court that Cooper's fraud was driven by "greed to support a lifestyle far beyond his means." "The simple motivation," said Atkinson, "was greed." In a March 1991 letter, Arthur Scace wrote to the lawyer representing Cooper at his criminal proceedings: "His professional and personal life are in ruins. He has been disgraced publicly and privately."[13] Cooper was sent to the correctional centre in Mimico, Ontario, for twenty-one months. The sentence, said Justice Hugh Locke, was required to express the disgust of both the legal profession and the public at large. After less than two months in prison, Cooper was transferred to Bunton Lodge, a downtown Toronto halfway house, and he was granted full parole after serving a third of his sentence.

On April 25, 1991, at age forty-eight, he was disbarred.[14] The Law Society of Upper Canada discipline committee report said Cooper had "freely chosen the dishonest course that was his downfall and had appreciated that his behaviour was wrong. He had exploited the high degree of trust in which he was held to facilitate his fraudulent transactions." It pronounced "its condemnation of the Solicitor's conduct in the strongest possible terms." The committee agreed with the Crown prosecutor, who told the court that greed was at the bottom of the matter. It said Cooper and his wife "lived extremely well enjoying a comfortable home, expensive cars, furnishing and clothing. They entertained and dined out frequently. They spent $50,000 on a bat mitzvah. They traveled extensively and their children attended private schools." In an extraordinary passage, the committee noted the solicitor "ceased his wrongful activity for a period of 16 months at a time that coincided with an increase in his partnership earnings and a fulfilling extramarital relationship. When he recommenced the misappropriation, he was building up an art collection." One of the character references submitted to the law society discipline committee said, "I am convinced that he did not freely choose such a course. Rather, he has been taken there; perhaps by illness, or coercion or some other horrible tormenting thing."

Dr. Deborah Chesnie Cooper, Cooper's first wife and mother of his three children, now runs Toronto's Chesnie Cooper Educational Centre. She has developed what she calls the "childpathing system," designed to test the learning potential of very young children so that they can be appropriately placed in a school—a school for the gifted, or more likely, given the kind of practice she has developed, a school for children with severe learning difficulties. Debbie and Dan Cooper separated (for the second time) in 1989 and were divorced in October 1991.

"I'll never forget November 8, 1990," she told me.[15] "It was a Thursday. Dan and I were already separated. In the morning, I rang him at his office from my car to arrange to go to a parents-teacher meeting that night. His secretary said he wasn't at the office, he was at home, and so I called him there. He sounded odd. I asked, what's the matter. He wouldn't say. Finally, he said: 'I'm no longer at McCarthy's. I stole money. We've lost everything.' I pulled over, got out of the car and vomited. That evening we went to the parents-teacher meeting together and acted as if everything was okay." Debbie went on: "I was attracted to Daniel in the first place because he was a European, not just another Toronto Jewish man. He was twelve years old when he came to Canada from Israel in 1955. He was intelligent, cosmopolitan. He was different. Later I discovered what he really was. He was a kid who had never grown up."

Why did he steal? "He was addicted to money," Debbie said. Where did the money go? "Not to me, not to the family," she insisted in a declaration at odds with the Crown prosecutor's description of the expensive home, furniture, cars, clothes, dining out, travel, private schools for the children, and lavish bat mitzvah. "He was a poor provider. It went on women." Dan was a womanizer, she said. "That was why we separated the first time. He had an affair with a German woman, from Munich." Debbie said that after everything fell apart, she had to pay off bank loans that she had co-signed with Dan. And according to Debbie, Cooper never honoured the financial provisions of the divorce settlement, even though Cooper's father, who died in 1994, left him a "lot of money." "The lawyers told me I should go after him, but I didn't for the sake of the kids."

In 2002, Cooper applied to the law society for readmission to the bar, arguing that he had become a "fundamentally different person." The general principles for readmission are found in a hearing committee's report to Convocation, of January 27, 1997, dealing with the readmission application of George Weisman.[16] Weisman was disbarred in 1983 after misappropriations of client funds and other fraudulent acts over a period of eighteen months. The proceeds from his frauds went to support his family, and when the frauds were discovered Weisman and his wife mortgaged the matrimonial home and paid back all the money that had been taken.

In its report to Convocation, the *Weisman* committee set out a seven-part test for readmission to the bar:

- Readmission is the exception rather than the rule.
- Applicants must show by a long course of conduct that they are in every way fit to be lawyers.
- There must be evidence of trustworthy persons that an applicant's conduct is unimpeached and unimpeachable.
- A sufficient period of time must have elapsed before an application for readmission will be granted.
- Applicants must show that it is extremely unlikely that they will misconduct themselves in the future.

- Applicants must show that they have entirely purged their guilt.
- Applicants must show that they have remained, or can become, current in the law.

The committee held that Weisman failed to meet several of these tests, particularly the third ("evidence of trustworthy persons ..."), and his application for readmission was denied. The committee said, "With the exception of members of the profession who have had contact with him in a social and family context, the committee has received no evidence from anyone with whom the applicant has been associated since his disbarment." There was an "absence of evidence from persons who are able to attest to the applicant's good character in a business or professional context since his disbarment."

Cooper's readmission submission to the law society addressed the *Weisman* criteria. Cooper, said his written submission, "has demonstrated that he is a person to be trusted and that that [*sic*] he is, in every way fit to be a lawyer." The submission described praiseworthy conduct by Cooper since his crimes were committed. He had run a technology consulting business. He had been active in charitable enterprises. He lived a balanced life with involvement in business, the community, and the music world. He had remarried and enjoyed a loving and supportive family environment. He had demonstrated remorse. He had admitted his misdeeds. He had not been charged with any other criminal offence. He had worked diligently to rebuild his reputation. Cooper, argued his submission, was rehabilitated: "Changes in his life substantially and satisfactorily demonstrate that it is extremely unlikely that he will misconduct himself in the future. In the eleven-and-a-half years since his disbarment the applicant gained insight from his misconduct and he has become a fundamentally different person."

Cooper supplied twenty-six letters in support of his application for readmission. He was careful to avoid the mistake that George Weisman made, making sure that many of his letters were from people that he had worked with since his disbarment. The reinstatement letters are heavy with his praise. Phrases liberally used include "highest integrity," "intelligent," "extremely intelligent," "compassion," "courteous," "honesty and integrity" (almost every letter contains these words), "highest degree of honesty and integrity," "a nobility of grace and goodness" (this from David Cooper, his son), and "role model" (from his stepson).

Almost none of these letters question why Dan Cooper did what he did or explain why and how he had become a fundamentally different man (although some contain general comments such as "I see a very different person than the one who was disbarred"). One letter comments that Cooper took full responsibility for his fraud, but "never sought to explain away or justify what he did." One referred to a "sudden aberration from his normal behaviour" (the word "aberration" appears in several letters); another, to a "real deviation from his normal self." A doctor wrote that "a peculiar concatenation of circumstance had led to a unique and tragic moment." The most interesting comment came from a friend of Cooper's who had himself been sent to jail for fraud. This referee believed that Cooper, at the time he committed fraud, was suffering from "a kind of dysfunctional moral blindness or numbness." But, for the most part, Cooper's referees say his criminal conduct was an "aberration" (a much-used word in cases like these), throw up their hands at the mystery, and then stress what a fine person Cooper really is and always was. A psychiatric report revealed no mental disorder, other than depression, which was predictable under the circumstances.

During the 1991 discipline hearing that led to Cooper's disbarment, Cooper and his then counsel (John I. Laskin, now a judge of the Ontario Court of Appeal) supplied a collection of support letters. The adjectives used to describe Dan Cooper in the 1991 letters are much the same as those used in the 2002 letters. Said the discipline committee's 1991 report, "The letters of character reference from impressive authors are unanimous in their praise of Mr. Cooper. They resonate with words like 'integrity,' 'trust-worthy,' 'compassionate,' 'kind,' 'intelligent,' 'polite,' 'personable' and 'the best.'" Dan Cooper seemed as impressive to his referees in 1991, when he was disbarred, as he was in 2002, when he was readmitted. And yet in 2002, in the eyes of the law society, he was a fundamentally different man. Following a hearing on November 14, 2002, the hearing panel recommended Cooper's readmission, subject to minimal conditions.[17]

Cooper had told the 2002 disciplinary panel that he hoped to be employed "within a sizable law firm or as in-house counsel to a corporation in the technological field." Neither turned out to be the case. An advertisement in the July 25, 2003, *Ontario Reports* announced the opening, by Dan Cooper and Judy Kingston, of Cooper Kingston LLP, of a new law firm specializing in information technology and e-business. In 2006, the Canada Law List has him as a sole practitioner. Cooper's listing—which he would have supplied to the publisher—gives his year of call to the bar as 1971, not 2002 when he was readmitted more than ten years after being disbarred. Nothing hints at the lost decade.

FOUR

A Kid Who's Been Beat Up Bad

Ingrid Chen

Ingrid Chen is a person of high energy and great folly. She has enthusiastically made one mistake after another, destroying her career as a lawyer. Police, prosecutors, courts, and law society officials have seemed baffled by her conduct, responding in a slow, timorous, and confused way. Official institutions have creaked and groaned, offering further evidence (were any necessary) that it can be very difficult for officialdom to handle irrational attacks on its fabric.

LATE AT NIGHT, on January 11, 1999, Kris Swedlo, a twenty-seven-year-old Winnipeg car salesman, picked up Ferdinand "Dean" Gutierrez at his parents' house and drove him to a doughnut shop in Winnipeg's south end. Swedlo dropped Gutierrez off, and then kept on going, headed out of town, driving south.

At the doughnut shop, Gutierrez was met by Emilio Guevarra, a local realtor, and by a friend of Guevarra's, Glenn Gee. The three had coffee and then got into Guevarra's Lexus and, like Swedlo, drove south. They went fifty miles or so, down sleepy Highway 59, past the Fort Garry campus of the University of Manitoba, through the small Manitoba towns of La Rochelle, St. Malo, Rosa, and Tolstoi, to the Canada–United States border at Pembina. The immigration offices at Pembina were closed, as they always were at night in those peaceful days before September 11, 2001. Gutierrez and Gee got out of the Lexus and walked across the unpoliced border. Swedlo was waiting on the other side in his car. Swedlo drove Gutierrez to Fargo, North Dakota. From there, Gutierrez flew to Chicago. In Chicago, he changed planes and headed home, to California.

Dean Gutierrez was 32 when he made his covert nighttime crossing of the Canada–United States border. He and his family—parents and two siblings—had immigrated to Canada from the Philippines in 1991. Dean got a degree in computer science from the University of Manitoba and went to California, on a temporary work visa, to be a computer programmer. In 1998, he came back to Winnipeg to visit his family for Christmas. At

Winnipeg airport on January 6, 1999, there to catch a flight back to California, he told Patrick Rodgers, a U.S. immigration officer, that he was going to the United States to attend a cousin's wedding. "I didn't want to tell him about all my business activities down there," Gutierrez later said. "I was just trying to make a long story short." Rodgers was suspicious. Gutierrez had suitcases full of winter clothes. He had a California driver's licence. "I felt like he was lying about where he was going, and for what reason," Rodgers said later. He denied Gutierrez entry to the United States. Gutierrez left the airport, lugging his suitcases full of the wrong clothes back to his parents' house.

Gutierrez decided that he needed an immigration lawyer. He looked in the Winnipeg Yellow Pages. He saw the name Ingrid Chen. The next day, he went to her office. She suggested he apply for a green card, but Gutierrez explained that he had a job to get back to and couldn't go through a lengthy process. "Couldn't I just drive across the border and fly home from North Dakota?" he asked. Chen thought this was a good idea. She said she knew people who could get him across without running the risk of going through a checkpoint and being turned back. She said she had a 100 percent success rate in getting people across this way. The fee was $3,850, which Gutierrez handed over to Chen a few days later.

The people Ingrid Chen knew, who could get Gutierrez across the border, were Emilio Guevarra and Kris Swedlo. Guevarra was Chen's friend (he was also an acquaintance of Dean Gutierrez's father). Swedlo was her live-in lover. Perhaps thinking that the scheme was more than Guevarra and Swedlo could pull off by themselves, Chen promised Glen Gee $800 if he would help out. (Chen never paid Gee. An angry Gee later said he planned "on hiring someone to go after Chen." Chen says she only got Gee involved because she felt sorry for him.)

For Ingrid Chen, the timing of the plan to get Gutierrez across the border was unfortunate. On January 4, only three days before Gutierrez walked into her office, just before she lined up Emilio Guevarra to help with the illegal scheme, a judge gave the RCMP authorization to tap Guevarra's telephone as part of a major drug trafficking investigation called Project Devise. On March 4, Chen's own name was added to the list of people whose telephone could be tapped. Chen's conversations with Guevarra about Gutierrez were recorded by the police.

INGRID YIN-YU CHEN was born in Taiwan in 1968. She was an infant when she came to Canada with her parents. She had three siblings. In 2001 her brother, Dr. Justin Chi-Han Chen, died in his sleep at the age of twenty-nine. Justin Chen had both medical and law degrees, and was planning to study for a master's degree in business administration. Montreal's *Gazette*, in a July 20, 2001, article about Justin's death,[1] said the Chen parents told their four children the best way they could contribute to their new country was by studying. The father, Tieng-Min Chen, said, "When these kids were young in Winnipeg it was cold in the wintertime, so we would all go to the library to study."

Ingrid studied hard, as her father wanted. She went to the University of Manitoba and then won a Canadian Bar Association scholarship to attend the University of Alberta law school. She graduated with a bachelor of laws degree in 1995, and was admitted to the Manitoba bar in June 1996. Until February 1, 1999, she practised law with a variety of partners, and as a sole practitioner. Then Chen joined the well-known Winnipeg law firm of Walsh Micay as an associate lawyer. It seemed like an immigrant success story.

Chen's relationship with Walsh Micay didn't last long. On June 15, 1999, she gave notice that she would be leaving at the end of the month, and removed a number of files from the firm's offices. Walsh Micay insisted that the files be returned. Then, on June 29, Chen was arrested by the RCMP. Her home and the offices of Walsh Micay were searched. The wiretaps had given away the Gutierrez scheme. They had picked up possible evidence of a drug trafficking plan. Chen was charged with conspiracy to bring an alien into the United States, and conspiracy to buy a kilogram of cocaine. Swedlo and Guevarra were arrested and charged with drug and immigration offences.

The three of them were kept in prison overnight. The next morning, June 30, Guevarra and Swedlo were released on bail with the consent of the Crown, but bail for Chen was opposed. At a hearing before Judge Lismer of the Provincial Court, Chris Mainella for the Crown said, "It is a situation where there is a risk of flight with Ms. Chen and there is a risk of interference with the administration of justice if Ms. Chen is released from custody."[2] Mainella systematically reviewed the wiretaps on the telephones of Guevarra and Chen. He placed considerable emphasis on intercepted statements by Chen that she didn't like practising law and was going to give it up and move to Asia. Chen's counsel, Amanda Sansregret, replied, "God forbid I should ever be arrested because daily I talk about quitting the practice of law and moving to the Turks and Caicos and selling cocktails in a cabana."[3] Judge Lismer released Chen on $100,000 bail.

The Law Society of Manitoba, paying close attention, moved quickly. On July 6, the complaints investigation committee demanded that Chen meet with it on July 8. The committee's inquiry went beyond the drug and immigration charges. It had seen the extensive wiretap evidence put forward by the Crown at Chen's bail hearing. Reading the transcripts, the committee became particularly interested in what had happened to a retainer Chen had received from a client called Mei Ding, and in a recorded telephone conversation between Chen and someone called

Patrick Armstrong about "Dr. L.," another former client of Chen's.

The retainer issue seemed straightforward enough. Mei Ding had paid US$3,400 to Chen on June 14 or 15, 1999, in her last days at Walsh Micay. The money should have gone into a trust account, but didn't. It was alleged that Chen used it to pay her personal Visa bill and settle other debts. Chen maintains that the retainer issue was trumped up. "I still had the cash in an envelope when the RCMP raided my house on June 29," she says. "Later I asked my parents to return it to the client, and they did, and they got a receipt."[4]

The matter of Dr. L. was much more exciting. In 1995, Dr. L. and his wife were living in China and wanted to come to Canada. They hired Chen to help. Chen made representations on their behalf to Immigration Canada. Dr. and Mrs. L. ended up moving to Canada and living in Brandon, Manitoba. But there was trouble between Dr. L. and Chen over her fees, and Dr. L. complained to the law society. What happened then was described later by Justice Shulman of the Manitoba Court of Queen's Bench:[5]

In March and May 1999, Ms. Chen had telephone conversations with one Patrick Armstrong, a known associate of members of the Los Bravos motorcycle gang. Mr. Armstrong has a lengthy criminal record. In the March conversation, Ms. Chen told Mr. Armstrong about "a bunch of assholes stalking me". Mr. Armstrong told her that he had three to six Bravos and they knew how to handle it without getting anyone in trouble. Mr. Armstrong offered to break legs for $1,000.00. Ms. Chen stated that she had a list of about four people whom she was considering engaging Mr. Armstrong to deal with. Mr. Armstrong asked for a retainer of $100.00 prior to performing work. In the May conversation, Ms. Chen and Mr. Armstrong discussed a man in Brandon with whom Ms. Chen was having some difficulties. Ms. Chen called him "a fucking little weasel". She stated that this man owed her money for getting him into the country and that he was suing a client of hers for $1,000.00. Mr. Armstrong suggested that "they should kill him". Ms. Chen replied, "he has money". Mr. Armstrong replied, "he'll run to the cops right away so that's one we'll have to sit down and discuss". Ms. Chen stated, "no it has to be one shot and then gone". The evidence indicates that the person referred to in the conversation is likely Dr. L....[6]

Immediately after the July 8, 1999, hearing, the law society suspended Chen from legal practice "in the public interest." It charged her with nineteen counts of professional misconduct or conduct unbecoming a lawyer. A further appeal from the suspension was unsuccessful.[7] In the name of fairness, the law society settled in to wait for Chen's many trials to be over before considering whether she should be disbarred. The wait was to last almost seven years. In 2002, to pass the time, Chen wrote a self-published book, with left-wing freelance journalist Rod Graham, astonishingly called *Protect Yourself from Your Lawyer*.[8] The dust jacket describes Chen as a "successful entrepreneur." It describes Graham as a freelance journalist who "writes extensively about injustice, inequity and corruption."

In November 2003, Chen and Guevarra were in court, facing forgery and immigration offences, but it had nothing to do with the Dean Gutierrez affair. In a March 1999 conversation between Chen and Guevarra, one of many the RCMP recorded, Chen asked Guevarra to give one of her clients a job offer and told him, "I'll pay you money." "No problem," said Guevarra. The client was Manli Wong, a resident of Hong Kong who graduated from the University of Manitoba in 1999 and wanted to stay in Canada. Wong asked Chen for help, and paid her $5,000. Chen told Wong that the first thing for her to do was find a job in Canada. Wong followed Chen's advice and tried to get a job, but no one would hire her until she had a work permit. Mike McIntyre of the *Winnipeg Free Press*,[9] reporting on the trial, described the evidence of what happened next:[10]

Wong went back to Chen and told her the job search was fruitless. Chen then pulled out a stack of blank documents, asking her to sign and initial her name....

"She would just point out to me where I should sign," Wong said yesterday.

Weeks later, a work permit arrived in the mail from Canadian immigration officials.

The document indicated she had found a job at Green Hills Realty as a junior office manager. Her boss was Guevarra.

"When I saw it I was very surprised," Wong said yesterday.

In the courtroom, Wong studied Emilio Guevarra. She told Justice Albert Clearwater that she had never seen Guevarra before. She had never heard of Green Hills Realty. But, on cross-examination, Wong conceded that Chen might have said that she would find her a job. Chen's lawyer said the March 1999 conversations between Chen and Guevarra were just "chatter between two friends." The Crown attorney argued that they revealed a plot to create bogus legal documents. Justice Clearwater, although suspicious of Guevarra's job offer to Manli Wong, decided that the Crown had not proved Chen and Guevarra's guilt beyond a reasonable doubt. They were acquitted.

With the Manli Wong matter out of the way, Chen and Guevarra—joined this time by Swedlo—could now face the charges arising from the midnight border crossing of Dean Gutierrez, and of smuggling cocaine. This trial was in February 2004. Gutierrez, given immunity in exchange for his testimony, told his story by satellite link from California. Gutierrez's father testified that he didn't know how Dean got into the United States, although he admitted having some telephone conversations with Guevarra after his son had arrived back in California, conversations the RCMP recorded. The hapless and unreliable Glen Gee testified that he was "stiffed" by Chen and Guevarra (the police agreed not to press charges against Gee in exchange for his testimony). Gee spun a tale about a trip the four of them took to Vancouver to buy drugs for resale in Winnipeg.

On May 14, Chen and Guevarra were found not guilty of conspiring to traffic in cocaine. Justice Nathan Nurgitz found Gee's testimony about the trip to Vancouver to be unbelievable. But they were convicted of conspiring to break U.S. immigration laws, contrary to s. 465 of the Criminal Code. Chen was sentenced to house arrest for a year, and was allowed to leave her home only to work. Justice Nurgitz said that the fact Chen was a lawyer and profited from the crime were important factors in her sentence. Guevarra, who made nothing from the Gutierrez incident, was given a six-month conditional discharge. The *Winnipeg Free Press* described Chen as "visibly upset" when the sentence was imposed, reporting that she repeatedly berated her latest counsel during a courtroom recess.[11] (Chen has changed lawyers frequently.) When asked about the story that she publicly berated her lawyer, she says that she was shocked by her conviction and was very emotional. In 2004, the Manitoba Court of Appeal dismissed her appeal.[12] In June 2005, the Supreme Court of Canada refused leave to appeal. In August 2005, Chen, Guevarra, and Swedlo, who never give up, brought an action seeking damages for malicious prosecution from the Attorney General of Canada, Crown prosecutor Clyde Bond, and RCMP officer Margaret Gregory. The statement of claim accused the defendants of acting maliciously by allowing the press photo opportunities to embarrass the plaintiffs; exaggerating and sensationalizing the charges against them; communicating false, exaggerated, and sensationalized accounts to the Law Society of Manitoba to stop Ingrid Chen from earning a living; and furnishing confidential police and Crown reports to the law society before disclosure had been made to Chen.[13]

In February 2006, Chen was tried on extortion charges. The Crown alleged that Chen had paid Patrick Armstrong to visit two people and "slap them around." One was the husband of a client who had been in a dispute with Chen over her bill; the other was a client who had not repaid a loan. The judge found that Armstrong did not assault or threaten either of them, and never intended to do so; as a result, there had been no actual extortion. But, based

on wiretap evidence, the judge did find attempts at
extortion, saying that "Chen believed Armstrong to
be someone who would use force and threats to get
what he came for and that she hired him for that
reason."[14] In March 2007, Chen was sentenced to
eighteen months in jail for this crime. A fourth trial
is pending, on charges that Chen made a false statement in order to obtain a Canadian passport. In a
passport application, she gave as her "permanent
address" the address of a house that she and Swedlo
own, but rent out. Her lawyer points out that there
is no formal definition of "permanent address" for
passport purposes. For applying for a passport at all,
she has been accused of breaching the conditions of
her house arrest, which forbade such an application,
and yet another trial is possible.[15] Someone in the
passport office saw her application, remembered who
she was, and called the RCMP. Chen maintains that
the Crown gave her informal permission to apply for
a passport, and that she needed one as a qualification
for her immigration business.

Before going to prison, Ingrid Chen worked as an
internet-based immigration consultant. She conducted her business from an office in downtown
Winnipeg (the business, which still exists, is called
C & S Canadian Immigration Services Inc., but is
more generally known as webimmigration.com). Her
website offers immigration information and advice,
and free assessments of immigration eligibility, but
mostly solicits business from those who need help to

come to Canada. The site offers a page of testimonials. One reads, "Ms. Chen—I just wanted to write you a little thank you note. My family is now in Canada. We are very happy to be here. Thank you for all your help you did for us. You were so kind answering all my questions so quickly. I would recommend your services to anyone." Another says, "We sought the advise [*sic*] of a few lawyers, and they all said that they couldn't guarantee our immigration. We are so happy to get our immigrant visas in 6 months with your assistance. A person can't go wrong with your incredible service!!! Thank-you for helping us. We will be happy raising our children in Canada."

Articles in Winnipeg newspapers tell another story. On July 28, 2005, the *Winnipeg Free Press* reported "seventeen Pakistanis trying to emigrate to Canada claim they are out thousands of dollars following a contractual dispute between a Winnipeg Web-based immigration consulting firm and a private immigration agent from Pakistan."[16] The Pakistani agent, a retired Pakistan army colonel, said that he paid webimmigration.com $35,000 on behalf of his seventeen countrymen, but received no service. "People are after my blood," said the colonel. Chen claims, not surprisingly, that the Pakistani colonel is a con man who uses many aliases and is wanted by the Pakistani police. Later it was reported that, also on July 28, a lawsuit was filed claiming that webimmigration.com received $44,000 from nineteen clients

but didn't deliver services that were promised.[17] In
August 2005, the RCMP and Winnipeg police
confirmed that they were considering launching a
formal investigation into webimmigration.com.
Chen has described this as "jumping on the band
wagon," and says that there has not been any real
police investigation of her immigration business.

I wrote to Chen, asking if I could come and see
her. A lengthy reply arrived almost immediately. "I
think it is important that you do get my side of the
story," she wrote. "I have learned that stonewalling
only hurts my family, friends, and business interests.
I would rather you have my side of the store [*sic*],
which is the 'truth,' backed by 'evidence,' rather than
going on gossip and false statements."[18] In her email,
Chen attacked the Law Society of Manitoba and the
RCMP, accusing them of unethical and illegal behaviour, and of colluding against her. Two days later, I
received another message:[19]

> All of the newspaper stories were "black prop-
> aganda". The stories were published for the
> primary purpose of destroying my reputation,
> and instilling a belief in the community that I
> was the head of a smuggling drug and immi-
> gration ring. What the initial reports did was
> corrupt and twist the truth, and to amplify the
> falsehoods to the extend [*sic*] that they are
> believed without "evidence". And, it worked.
> The RCMP were hoping that these initial false

reports would destroy me. I was so young and naive, that I actually believed at the time that saying nothing was noble in character, but it worked to my detriment. How do you prove a negative??? You can't.

In November 2005, with Ingrid Chen's connection to Patrick Armstrong and the Los Bravos motorcycle gang much on my mind, I went to Winnipeg to see her. She asked that we meet at the offices of her lawyer, Gene Zazelenchuk, a sole practitioner. She wrote, "Please understand that we are meeting at my lawyers [sic] office so I can easily provide you with 'proof' or 'evidence,' not because I have anything to hide and need my lawyer to protect me."[20]

My appointment was for 9 a.m. on a cold and windy Thursday. I walked to Gene Zazelenchuk's office at the corner of Portage Avenue and Vaughan Street, just by Winnipeg's old Hudson's Bay store. Zazelenchuk's office is small, old-fashioned, and cluttered. His wife is secretary, receptionist, and office manager. Zazelenchuk, in his mid-fifties, is well dressed and articulate. He doesn't have fax or email. He says that he answers the telephone "sometimes."

Chen arrived late. She wore jeans, boots, and a colourful top. "I'm sorry I haven't talked to you on the telephone, and just used email," she said. "I don't like to talk to people on the phone anymore the way I used to, I've lost trust, there was the wiretaps, I've completely changed." We talked about the criminal actions that have been brought against her. Chen was excitable, forceful, and combative. Zazelenchuk worked hard to manage and restrain his client.

"Why are they picking on you?" I asked. "I don't fit the cookie mould," said Chen. "I'm Asian, female, young, an easy target. There are lots of racists in Winnipeg. I was born in Taiwan, and they hold that against me. They've always said, right from my bail hearing in 1999, that I'm a flight risk, that if I go to Taiwan I'll never come back. That's crazy, I have investments here, I have a lot of equity in my house, my parents are here, my nineteen-year-old son lives here. They thought I'd just fall over, but I'm a survivor, I'm not going to be a victim. My parents are behind me. My father says there are evil people in the world, and that's why I'm in trouble. But I have a lot of stress."

"She's just a kid who's been beat up bad," interrupted Zazelenchuk.

Who's beating her up? Chen told me that it was the RCMP, the law society, and the Crown, colluding to destroy her. "That is why we are suing for malicious prosecution," said Chen, referring to her action against RCMP officer Margaret Gregory, now with the Surrey B.C. detachment, and Clyde Bond, a Crown attorney. I asked why anyone would collude in this way. "I told you," said Chen. "They thought I was an easy target. And they were all after career advancement, this is how those people do it." Time was up, and I left Gene Zazelenchuk's office.

A few days after our meeting I received an email from Ingrid:[21]

Sunday I was speeding in my car, and arrested. There was an error on the police computer, and they couldn't get a copy of my court order until the next day. I was put into the remand center for two days, just to have the Crown consent to my release. But, at least this time I was psychologically prepared to accept the fact.

And then another, a few days after that:[22]

I am not a perfect person, but at least I can look anyone in the eye with pride.
    … What is the worst that they can do to me??? Jail??? I am not afraid of Jail. Been there, done it. Its not that bad. I can survive.
    The worst that they have done to me, is hurt my family, friends, and especially my boyfriend. The damage is already done, and that time lost, can not be repaired.

Why has Ingrid Chen got into so much trouble, so consistently, starting so early in her career? How is it that a young lawyer, in the first decade of her professional life, has faced four criminal trials, two criminal convictions, civil suits, suspension from the bar, likely disbarment, and numerous police investigations?

Some things are clear. Ingrid Chen has spectacularly bad judgment. She has the wrong friends. She talks in a foolish way. She leaps into situations that a lawyer should avoid at all costs. She lacks common sense. Some things are less clear. Does Ingrid also lack a sense of the values underpinning the Canadian legal system? Did law school fail to teach her these? It is hard to say. What is missing in Ingrid may be ineffable, unique to her.

IN MAY 2006, the Law Society of Manitoba finally held a hearing to consider Ingrid Chen's disbarment. The ponderous official machinery was still functioning. It was almost seven years from Ingrid's first arrest. The law society hearing lasted ten days. At the end of 2006, Ingrid Chen was still waiting to learn whether she will be disbarred.

WILD AND CRAZY GUYS

Simon Rosenfeld and Peter Shoniker

Crooks hire lawyers. Why shouldn't they? Crooks, like everyone else, buy and sell houses, get divorces, have contractual disputes, and so on; they need legal services and are entitled to them. But crooks, unlike most people, also commit crimes. Do lawyers sometimes use their special status to help them do so? Do lawyers use the principle of solicitor-client privilege to help launder the proceeds of crime? International organizations think they do. The Canadian government, the RCMP, the Auditor General, and close observers of the scene think they do. Well-known Toronto lawyers Simon Rosenfeld and Peter Shoniker did. How effective is the response of the law, and those who regulate the legal profession, when a lawyer works for the mob?

ON MARCH 11, 2002, Bill MacDonald, a Colombian drug cartel money man, was having dinner in Miami with Toronto lawyer Simon Rosenfeld. The fifty-five-year-old Rosenfeld had practised law since 1974. MacDonald pulled out a U.S. one-dollar bill. "If I give you this," MacDonald asked Rosenfeld, "do we have solicitor-client privilege?" "Yes," said Rosenfeld. "Okay," said MacDonald, and handed over the dollar. With that out of the way, the two men started talking about how Rosenfeld could help launder cocaine money for Colombian drug lords. Unfortunately for Rosenfeld, "Bill MacDonald" was really Bill Majcher, an undercover RCMP officer working on a joint RCMP/FBI sting called "Bermuda Short."[1] Majcher, a good-looking, middle-aged man who normally wears expensive suits, was once an investment banker, trading Euro-bonds in London.[2]

After the Miami meeting, the Rosenfeld sting moved to Toronto. On Friday, May 31, 2002, just before one o'clock in the afternoon, Majcher—wearing a purple checked shirt, black slacks, and a concealed recording device—parked his rented car in front of Rosenfeld's law office at 14 Prince Arthur Avenue in downtown Toronto. He went in and met Rosenfeld, and then the two men went down the street to have lunch at Opus, an expensive Italian restaurant. "The fresh cut flowers, artistic wine displays and soft lighting, combine to create a beautiful setting," says a website describing Opus. "The kitchen is noted for perfectly grilled meat, fish and

fowl, tantalizing pastas and risottos, adventurous vegetables, and inventive desserts."[3]

Over lunch, full of braggadocio, Rosenfeld told Majcher about trouble he was having with some ex–Russian Army explosives experts, a criminal group he referred to simply as "the Russians." The Russians, said Rosenfeld, had lost money in a deal with one of his "associates," and for a while thought that Rosenfeld himself might have been involved in ripping them off. His associate, said Rosenfeld, was going to be "taken out" by the Russians, who would probably blow up the associate's car or house with him in it.

The portly Rosenfeld, digging in to a dish of scaloppini, then explained that he was promoting the stock of a company that made a cream guaranteed to reduce stomach size if you rubbed it on the right places. He told Majcher that he could "load him up on company paper at $3 to $4," paper that could then be sold for $95. By the time Rosenfeld was eating his caramel crunch, the two men were deep in discussion about money that could be made from mortgages, bankruptcies, and receiverships.

Canada, said Rosenfeld enthusiastically over a latte, was "la-la land," a dream place for criminal activity, because the police had so few resources. "Sounds good to me," said Corporal Majcher. "I hope to take advantage of that." Then Rosenfeld invited Majcher to a private game at a golf club later that summer organized by a strip club owner. There would be two naked women at every hole, said Rosenfeld. "It's lots of fun!"

After lunch, the two men went back to 14 Prince Arthur. On Rosenfeld's desk were jars of cream and bottles of lotion for people with arthritis and wrinkles. Majcher told Rosenfeld that he had $250,000 Canadian of cocaine money that he wanted Rosenfeld to launder. If that went well, they would launder $2 million to $3 million a month. No problem, said Rosenfeld. It was agreed that Rosenfeld would send the laundered money to a Miami bank account three to five days after he got it, and that his fee would be 8 percent. As Majcher left, Rosenfeld gave him samples of the creams and lotions on his desk. With the bottles and jars, Majcher went to an RCMP safe house, briefed colleagues working on the sting, gave them his recording device, and wrote up his notes.

The following Tuesday morning, June 4, Majcher went to Rosenfeld's office carrying $250,000 in Canadian bills in a red and black tote bag. He gave the money to Rosenfeld, and they went to the Four Seasons Hotel in Yorkville for breakfast. At breakfast, Majcher told Rosenfeld to send the money to an account in the name of José Garcia at the North Miami branch of Wachovia Bank. Majcher also asked Rosenfeld if he could arrange "muscle." Yes, said Rosenfeld, he could do that, through the Hells Angels. That evening the two men had drinks and dinner. Rosenfeld bragged about his sexual exploits, his ability to get information on people, how he paid off cops, and the "$2 billion in business that he had available to place."

The laundering transaction did not go smoothly. First, there was a delay in transmission of funds to Miami. Rosenfeld told Majcher it was because the money was in Canadian dollars; his "system," said Rosenfeld, had been set up to launder U.S. dollars. Then, on Thursday, June 13, Rosenfeld said his "people" had found counterfeit bills in the $250,000. Majcher expressed suspicion and concern, and Rosenfeld quickly said it was okay, that $250,000 converted into U.S. dollars, with his fees deducted, would be sent to José Garcia's account anyway. Majcher expressed satisfaction and went to Miami to wait for the money.

It was a long wait. Nothing came on Monday. Nothing came on Tuesday. Nothing came on Wednesday. Majcher repeatedly telephoned Rosenfeld and asked, "Where's my money?" On Thursday, $71,000 in U.S. dollars arrived. Nothing more came. Majcher headed back to Toronto and checked into the Hyatt Hotel at the corner of Avenue Road and Bloor Street.

On Tuesday afternoon, June 25, Rosenfeld came to Majcher's room at the Hyatt. A second tranche had now arrived in the Miami account, Majcher told Rosenfeld, but it was only $30,000. Rosenfeld assured Majcher that the balance would arrive the next day. A long and rambling conversation ensued about money-laundering techniques in general; pump-and-dump stock schemes; "technicians" that Rosenfeld employed who would kill people if necessary; a recent visit to Rosenfeld from the Russians, who brought him strawberries and warned him that in the next couple of weeks they were going to "blow up" Rosenfeld's associate; Rosenfeld's house, and the waterfall his wife wanted put in the backyard; and the possibility of warehousing cocaine in eastern Canada. Then Rosenfeld and Majcher went for dinner, back to Opus on Prince Arthur. A day or two afterward, the rest of the money arrived in Miami, and all was well.

The following week, at the end of the afternoon on Thursday, July 4, Majcher visited Rosenfeld in his office to set up a second money-laundering transaction. As they discussed the details of the deal, Rosenfeld said that the situation between his associate and the Russians had become very serious. The Russians had just sprayed his associate's house with machine gun fire. Shortly, said Rosenfeld, they would be blowing up his associate's house or perhaps his car.

The next morning Rosenfeld came to Majcher's room at the Hyatt. A few minutes after he arrived, two undercover RCMP officers came in with a sports bag containing $200,000 in U.S. dollars and $800,000 in Canadian bills. By prearrangement, Majcher pretended to be angry when he saw the Canadian currency, screaming that the money was supposed to be in U.S. dollars. Rosenfeld told Majcher that the quality of Majcher's people was not very good, and that his own people were very good, so that he didn't encounter the type of problems Majcher was experiencing. Majcher and Rosenfeld started counting the U.S. dollars. The money-counting machine kept jamming. Rosenfeld said he "was no good with this as he had other people count all his cash." With the money finally counted, Rosenfeld left.

The proceeds of the second money-laundering transaction arrived slowly, in several tranches, in José Garcia's Miami account. At a July 17 meeting in his office, Rosenfeld made the by now familiar promise that Majcher would get the rest of the money "today or tomorrow." Majcher replied that "there are threads dangling" and that he didn't like it and didn't want to do business this way. The two men then discussed further money-laundering opportunities, importing cocaine into Canada, and Rosenfeld's associate's continuing difficulties with the Russians. Then Rosenfeld, not feeling well, went home. The following week, on July 24, Majcher, now in Miami, pressed Rosenfeld hard for $29,000 from the second transaction that he had still not received. It arrived later that day.

Rosenfeld and Majcher continued to talk frequently on the telephone. On Wednesday, July 31, they met at the Hyatt in Toronto to discuss possible schemes. Rosenfeld boasted about his prowess in making money and said that he had been making between $1 million and $3 million a year for many years. Majcher said he wanted to launder a million dollars in the next week or two. The two talked about the possibility of laundering as much as $10 million a month and how that might be done. Rosenfeld said that in a week or two he was flying to Switzerland to meet a Gibraltar banker who could be helpful.

Majcher went back to Miami. Rosenfeld never went to Switzerland. He and Rosenfeld talked several times in the first few days of August. They arranged to meet at Rosenfeld's office on the afternoon of August 14 so that Majcher could deliver more money for laundering. On the day, Rosenfeld was waiting for Majcher. Majcher didn't arrive at the appointed time. A police team did. Rosenfeld was arrested. That same day, in a coordinated effort across the country, fifty-eight other Bermuda Short sting targets were also arrested. Pursuant to a search warrant, fifteen boxes of documents were seized from Rosenfeld's office, and one box of documents from his home.[4] Rosenfeld was charged with money-laundering and possession of the proceeds of crime.

August 2002 was altogether not a good month for Rosenfeld. The day before he was arrested, an Ontario judge granted him a conditional discharge from bankruptcy, but on unusually onerous terms— actual payment to the bankruptcy trustee (as opposed to simply agreement to pay) of $250,000.[5] Rosenfeld's two principal creditors, the U.S. Securities and Exchange Commission (SEC) and his former partner, Michael Rinaldo, opposed discharge.

The SEC was a Rosenfeld creditor because of a 2001 US$2.8 million judgment against him for securities law violations (Rosenfeld did not defend the action).[6] A New York court found that Rosenfeld had orchestrated a "pump and dump" scheme in the early nineties involving the common stock of a company called Synpro Environmental Services. He released misleading information about Synpro's assets to "pump" up its value. Then he "dumped" millions of personally held unregistered shares on unsuspecting investors through a complex network of offshore corporations and brokerage accounts. He also made kickbacks to brokers and stock promoters. The SEC investigation disclosed that Rosenfeld maintained bank accounts in Switzerland, Italy, and the Caribbean.

Michael Rinaldo, Rosenfeld's law partner until 1990, was a Rosenfeld creditor because of Rosenfeld's breach of an agreement settling Rinaldo's suit against him for fraud and breach of fiduciary duty. The Rinaldo action, begun in 1991, was settled in 1997. The minutes of settlement required Rosenfeld to make a series of payments to Rinaldo. Rosenfeld defaulted on the first payment.

In Rosenfeld's discharge hearing, the bankruptcy judge noted that Rosenfeld claimed assets of $2,000 and liabilities of $4,629,731. And yet, said the judge, "he lives in a house owned by his wife which is valued at in excess of $1.3 million dollars and which contains personal property insured for in excess of $500,000.

During his bankruptcy, he has continued to enjoy a lifestyle replete with housekeeper, gardener, a peak season vacation in Barbados and private school fees." Rosenfeld had credit card debts of fifteen to sixteen times his disclosed assets. He claimed personal expenses as business expenses (including his wife's monthly cell phone bills of $400 to $500). The judge found Rosenfeld "evasive and ... not credible" and said "he was not honest with his creditors, the Trustee or this court. He was unwilling to make full disclosure of his financial affairs. He has not made any economic sacrifices during his bankruptcy or shown any remorse. His attitude is a slap in the faces of his creditors. I join the Trustee and his creditors in suspecting that he has undisclosed assets offshore."

Rosenfeld's three-week jury trial, on two charges of money laundering and one of attempting to possess the proceeds of crime, started at the beginning of February 2005. Bill Majcher gave extensive evidence. Excerpts from Majcher's tapes of his conversations with Rosenfeld were played, and the jury was shown a videotape of the money-counting meeting in the Hyatt Hotel. Glen Orr, Rosenfeld's lawyer, described his client as looking more like "a comptroller with a small company" than a drug kingpin. Addressing the jury, Orr argued that the Crown had not proved beyond a reasonable doubt that Rosenfeld believed the money to be drug proceeds because Rosenfeld was delusional and it was impossible to know what he believed. The prosecutor referred to a "serious problem in Canada" of shady lawyers hiding behind solicitor-client privilege. On February 22, the jury found Rosenfeld guilty.

At a March 18 sentencing hearing Majcher said that lawyers have become key players in money-laundering operations because they are not obliged by law to report suspicious financial transactions. "In almost every case we are doing," said Majcher, "lawyers are central." On March 30, a Toronto judge sentenced Rosenfeld to three years in prison and fined him $43,230 (the amount Rosenfeld was paid to launder the money). Adrian Humphreys reported in the *National Post* on March 31, 2005:[7]

It was an opportunity not missed by Rosenfeld.

Heavy set with thinning, greying hair and a heavy brow, Rosenfeld dressed like a successful lawyer to the end—choosing a dark suit with a silver and green tie and placing his dark-framed glasses on shortly before the judge entered the courtroom.

After his sentencing, he began his transformation from lawyer to convict.

He removed his tie—which is not allowed in prison over safety concerns—and passed it to his brother. He then pulled a more utilitarian coat, a red ski jacket, over his suit and placed his hands behind his back for a waiting officer's handcuffs.

Rosenfeld was taken to Toronto's Don Jail. Five days later he was released on bail of $1.95 million, with three of his relatives pledging money and property. He fired Glen Orr and hired another lawyer for an appeal. The Russians have yet to blow up his "associate." At the end of 2006, Rosenfeld's appeal had yet to be heard.

Bill Majcher says that he liked Rosenfeld and that Rosenfeld "almost had a crush on me." Rosenfeld was "in some ways a sort of Falstaff," says Majcher, referring to the buffoon and braggart created by Shakespeare, but he adds, "Make no mistake, there was much truth to many of his claims about criminal activity. He did all those things he said he did." After his spectacular Bermuda Short success, Majcher, a twenty-year veteran of the RCMP, was given the rank of inspector and assigned to run the RCMP's Integrated Markets Enforcement Team (IMET), based in Vancouver, which investigates serious capital markets fraud. But Majcher himself was set for a fall. On June 29, 2005, he was removed as head of IMET and the next day was suspended with pay pending the outcome of an internal investigation. This followed a May 21 column by David Baines in *The Vancouver Sun*, which pointed out that Majcher, while on active RCMP duty, had sought a federal Conservative nomination (unsuccessfully), and that Majcher and Kevin Garner, a convicted felon, were considering a deal for a movie based on the Bermuda Short sting.[8] Majcher is now a director of a Hong Kong–based investment bank. In another strange twist, Kevin Garner, who served fifteen months in a U.S. prison for money laundering as a result of Bermuda Short, invented a board game called "Dirty Money: The Money Laundering Game." On September 29, 2005, Betsy Powell reported in the *Toronto Star* that Garner spoke about money laundering and his board game in Toronto to more than a hundred branch managers with ScotiaMcLeod, a major Canadian brokerage house, and received a standing ovation.[9]

PETER SHONIKER is another Toronto lawyer who enjoyed dining at Opus on Prince Arthur Avenue (*Toronto Star* reporter Betsy Powell has referred to Shoniker as a "permanent fixture at Opus."[10]) He is the son of the late Eddie Shoniker, a respected Conservative Party insider who served as chairman of the Ontario Transport Board in the seventies. Peter Shoniker, a graduate of the University of Ottawa law school, came to serious public attention in 1986, when he was a thirty-one-year-old assistant Crown attorney driving a car with the vanity licence plate "JAIL4U." Wearing a bulletproof vest and accompanied by two bodyguards, Shoniker told a Quebec conference that Canadian terrorists trained in Libya, South Yemen, and Lebanon were getting ready to kidnap and assassinate Canadian politicians. Shoniker said that studying terrorism was his hobby, and that he had taken courses on terrorism from experts in the CIA, FBI, U.S. Navy Intelligence, and New York

Police Department. A variety of academics who attended the conference roundly condemned what he said, severely questioning both his facts and his bona fides, and Shoniker was suspended for a month from his job as an assistant Crown attorney and disciplined for speaking out in a way inappropriate to his office.

Despite this early and very public false step, Shoniker went on to considerable legal and political eminence. After three years as a Crown prosecutor, he took up private practice as a defence lawyer, acquiring high-profile clients. In 1993, he defended Raymond Twinney, a former Newmarket mayor who ended up pleading guilty to corruption. In 1998, Shoniker represented Bryan Cousineau, former York Region police chief who pleaded guilty to two counts of breach of trust. Shoniker also represented the Niagara Board of Police Commissioners at a royal commission inquiry into allegations of wrongdoing in the Niagara police force; Major-General Lewis MacKenzie at the 1995 Somalia inquiry; and four Christian brothers charged with physical and sexual abuse of students at the school where they taught. Shoniker—some say trading initially on his father's reputation—became closely associated with provincial Conservative Party members. His friends included former Toronto chairman Paul Godfrey, former Toronto mayor Mel Lastman, former Ontario premier Ernie Eves, and Roy McMurtry, who became Chief Justice of Ontario. Shoniker was widely credited with helping secure the job of Toronto police chief for Julian Fantino in 2000.

During this period, Shoniker also established close links with the Cayman Islands. In 1989, he bought a condominium there, and in 1991 he and Renée Vinett—now a lawyer in Toronto—were married on Grand Cayman (they are estranged). He also, for a time, acted as coordinator of the Cayman Islands National Drug Council. An October 18, 2002, Cayman Islands government press release announced that the governor had given Sir Peter Shoniker an award for his pro bono work in raising the international profile of the National Drug Council. (Inexplicably, Shoniker had taken to using the title "Sir" from time to time.)

It was a considerable shock to the Ontario establishment, and presumably to Shoniker's eminent friends, when, on June 14, 2004, he was arrested on money-laundering and related charges. Shoniker was arrested near his home as he returned from a business trip to Europe. He was accused of laundering about $750,000 supplied by RCMP undercover agent Corporal Al Lewis as part of an elaborate fifteen-month sting operation called Project OJUST. An undercover police officer told Shoniker that the money had been skimmed from the pension account of the United Steelworkers of America's Hamilton branch. The money, laundered from Canada via several other countries, ended up in a New York City Citibank account. Shoniker claimed a fee of about

10 percent and took another $50,000 for fictitious bribes paid to police and customs officers. In a recorded telephone conversation with Corporal Lewis, Shoniker said that Lewis could tell him anything because of solicitor-client privilege, and that they needn't worry about wiretaps. "There isn't a fucking judge in the city who would grant an authorization on my line," he said. In another taped conversation, Shoniker described himself as "untouchable."

"Today's arrests demonstrate that no aspect of our society is immune to criminal activity," said RCMP Inspector Don Panchuk, head of the Toronto Integrated Proceeds of Crime Section. "Investigations into alleged criminal activity involving a lawyer are uniquely difficult and complex," said Chief Superintendent Ben Soave, head of the Combined Forces Special Enforcement Unit, on the day of Shoniker's arrest. Soave continued, "Investigative tools that police could normally employ are extremely restricted when the subject of an investigation is a lawyer. The unfortunate consequence of these restrictions is that the legal profession can be exploited to cloak criminal activity." After spending the weekend in a holding cell, Shoniker was released on $75,000 bail, posted by his wife Renée.

The legal process creaked along. It was not until August 18, 2006, that Shoniker pleaded guilty to one charge of money laundering and one charge of theft. In court to show support was former Toronto police chief Julian Fantino (who embraced Shoniker), former deputy police chief Steve Reesor, former Canadian Armed Forces major-general Lewis MacKenzie, and former judge David Humphrey Sr. Glowing testimonials were read to the judge. MacKenzie described Shoniker as having been a "lawyer of integrity, honesty, professionalism, devotion and ability." Others (including Paul Godfrey) wrote in a similar vein. There were sixteen letters of praise. His adopted daughter said Shoniker helped her fight an eye disease that could lead to blindness; while that letter was being read, Shoniker burst into tears. Friends attributed his downfall to a combination of too much work, alcohol dependence, a sleep disorder, and abuse of prescription drugs. Major-General MacKenzie made an extraordinary and fatuous statement: "As they say in the military, 'You don't die for the Queen. You don't die for God. You don't die for your country. You die for your buddies.'" It was left to John Barber, writing about Shoniker a few days later in *The Globe and Mail*, to put common sense and good judgment on the record:[11]

The scary thing is that so many still love him. Even after seeing the truth laid bare in a scathing indictment detailing the man's greed and criminality—an open-and-shut, irrefutable case—they hug him tight and make ludicrous excuses. The reason Mr. Shoniker engaged in sophisticated schemes to launder stolen money, they say, is because he had trouble sleeping at night.

But beneath all the special pleading and tear-jerking flummery, there is one message that all Mr. Shoniker's supporters share. It doesn't matter what he did, he was one of us: untouchable. What is most striking about their interventions is not love, certainly not sorrow, but indignation. It's creepy.

Christie Blatchford wrote a profile of Peter Shoniker in the June 26, 2004, *Globe and Mail*:[12]

When almost two weeks ago, Peter Shoniker was arrested by the Royal Canadian Mounted Police and charged with a sheaf of money-laundering offences, it is fair to say that some of the most powerful people in Toronto shud- dered in apprehension.... He is improbably well-connected to police officers both of high and low rank, police organizations ..., a smat- tering of Ontario judges, and political movers and shakers mostly but not exclusively within the Ontario Conservative Party.

One of Shoniker's business cards, Blatchford wrote, identified him as Sir Peter A.E. Shoniker, Order of the British Empire, and Counsellor/Special Envoy to the United Nations. But, Blatchford reported, there was no record of his ever having received a British award, and the United Nations had never heard of him. On September 6, 2006, Shoniker, fifty-two, was sentenced to fifteen months in jail. As sentence was handed down, Shoniker collapsed back into his chair. He was wearing cowboy boots.

DRUG USERS don't use credit cards to score cocaine.[13] Mobsters don't write cheques to buy automatic weapons. In the world of crime, cash is king. This creates a problem for a criminal. He can't use wads of dollar bills carried in a briefcase to buy a fancy automobile, a penthouse in Hawaii, or a gold watch studded with diamonds. Even were such transactions possible, they would attract too much dangerous attention. To enjoy the fruits of his labours, the crook has to inject his criminal cash into the legitimate financial system. Al Capone, so legend says, did it by pretending that his money came from a chain of laundromats that he happened to own. This effective approach to the problem gave rise, according to legend, to the term "money laundering."

The scale and complexity of crime have changed since Al Capone ran his brutal empire from a huge and luxurious suite in Chicago's Lexington Hotel. The International Monetary Fund estimates that today the annual amount laundered worldwide is between 2 and 5 percent of the world's gross domestic product (GDP), between $1 and $5 trillion

U.S. dollars. (Canada's annual GDP is about $1 trillion U.S. dollars.) The few laundromats that remain are not up to the job. They have largely been replaced by sophisticated financial intermediaries— including lawyers.

Lawyers have a particular advantage as money launderers. The rule of solicitor-client privilege prevents forced disclosure of what a client tells his lawyer.[14] The international financial community and the Canadian government, including the RCMP, think that solicitor-client privilege can be used by a lawyer to hide money laundering by organized crime. This, they believe, is vaulting the legal profession into the forefront of money laundering.

At its 1989 meeting in Paris, the G-7 established the Financial Action Task Force (FATF) to develop an international response to money laundering. Thirty-one countries—including Canada—and two regional organizations now belong to the FATF. By 1990, the organization had developed "40 Recommendations" (most recently revised in 2003), setting out what national governments should do to implement effective anti-money-laundering programs. Canada made money laundering a crime in 1989. Two years later, the Proceeds of Crime (Money Laundering) Act introduced a wide range of record-keeping requirements for transactions that involved more than $10,000 cash. But several times in the nineties Canada ran up against the FATF. Canada was criticized for not complying fully with the 40 Recommendations, particularly when it came to the key requirement that suspicious transactions be reported to a central authority.

It was to meet these embarrassing criticisms that Parliament, in 2000, replaced the 1991 statute with a new Proceeds of Crime (Money Laundering) Act. The new act established the Financial Transactions and Reports Analysis Centre of Canada (FINTRAC). Financial industry participants must collect certain transaction data and send it to FINTRAC, which analyzes the data for evidence of money laundering and may disclose "designated" information to national, foreign, or international law enforcement agencies. In 2001, FINTRAC was additionally authorized by amendments to the act, which became the Proceeds of Crime (Money Laundering) and Terrorist Financing Act, to look for financial transactions that constitute threats to the security of Canada and to disclose this information to the Canadian Security Intelligence Service and other law enforcement agencies.

Regulations under the 2000 act required lawyers (along with other professionals, financial institutions, brokers, casinos, etc.) to report a client's suspicious financial transactions to FINTRAC. The client's identity had to be disclosed, but it was illegal to tell the client that a report had been made. A suspicious financial transaction was defined as one where "there are reasonable grounds to suspect that the transaction is related to the commission of a money laundering offence." The regulations provided that legal counsel was not required to disclose "any communication that is subject to solicitor-client privilege," but the scope of solicitor-client privilege was not defined.

The legal profession was outraged by these provisions, perceiving them as a dramatic attack on the traditional relationship between lawyer and client. Several provincial law societies quickly went to court, arguing that the constitution protects communications between a lawyer and a client, even communications not covered by solicitor-client privilege. The new regulations, it was argued, forced lawyers to act inconsistently with their duty of loyalty and confidentiality to clients.

The courts were highly sympathetic to these arguments, and across the country granted law societies temporary exemptions from the reporting requirement pending full determination of the constitutional challenge. In a January 2002 Ontario decision, for example, Justice Maurice Cullity said, "In imposing a duty on legal practitioners to give secret reports of their clients' transactions to a government agency, the legislation clearly impinges on, and alters, the traditional relationship between solicitors, or counsel, and their clients.... It strikes at the lawyer's duty of loyalty and the client's privilege against self-incrimination as well as the principle that lawyers should be independent of government."[15] The various judgments across the country indicated that the exclusion of privileged communication from the reporting requirement did not sufficiently address the potential for constitutional breach.

Faced with these successful court challenges, in March 2003 the federal government repealed the regulations making lawyers subject to the reporting requirement. "This is a testament to the resolve of Canada's law societies," said a spokesman for the Federation of Law Societies of Canada. The government pushed back and said, "It is important that Canada's anti-money laundering and anti-terrorist financing regime covers all entities that act as financial intermediaries, including legal counsel and legal firms.... The government therefore intends, following consultations, to put in place a new regime for legal counsel."

Presumably to head off further unpalatable government action, the law societies moved to deal with the acknowledged problem through internal codes of conduct. Adopting a model rule developed by the Federation of Law Societies of Canada, all provincial law societies have now prohibited lawyers from accepting cash in the amount of $7,500 or greater, subject to limited exceptions, and to adopt more stringent record keeping of cash receipts. The Ontario rules came into force at the end of January 2005.[16] The pending constitutional challenge has been adjourned indefinitely, but may be revived if the government again tries to bring lawyers within the reporting system.

The issue remains hot. In June 2003, just months after the Canadian government exempted lawyers from the reporting requirement, the FATF revised the 40 Recommendations to include a provision that "lawyers, notaries, other independent legal professionals and accountants should be required to report suspicious transactions when, on behalf of or for a client, they engage in a financial transaction." The 2004 Report of the Auditor General of Canada, referring to the 2003 revision of the 40 Recommendations, commented that the new exemption for lawyers "is widely regarded as a serious gap in the coverage of the anti-money-laundering legislation. It means that individuals can now do banking through a lawyer without having their identity revealed, bypassing a key component of the anti-money-laundering system." The report went on: "The removal of lawyers from the reporting requirements of the legislation in Canada means that our anti-money-laundering system does not fully meet international standards."

A 2004 study by criminologist Dr. Stephen Schneider of York University reported that of 149 major money-laundering and proceeds-of-crime cases the RCMP solved between 1993 and 1998, lawyers played a role in half of them.[17] In most cases, the lawyers were unaware of the criminal source of funds. But, writes Schneider,

some lawyers appeared to offer services that were tailored expressly to satisfy the objectives of money laundering. This included converting substantial amounts of cash into less suspicious assets, concealing the criminal ownership of assets, incorporating numerous companies that carried out no commercial activities, fabricating or falsifying financial or legal documents, and transferring funds between bank accounts or between multiple trust account files established on behalf of client and/or companies beneficially controlled by the client for no apparent commercial reason or financial gain.

A 2005 RCMP report, *Lawyers and Complicity in Criminal Conduct—Exploitation of Solicitor-Client Privilege*, suggested that by insisting on an exemption from money-laundering regulations, lawyers are left "bearing the brunt of increasingly desperate criminals with vast sums of dirty drug cash needing conversion into something that can be spent without arousing suspicion." At the beginning of October 2006, the Senate banking, trade, and commerce committee recommended that the federal government should monitor lawyers, among others, for suspicious transactions.[18] On October 5, 2006, the Minister of Finance introduced a bill designed to strengthen the Proceeds of Crime (Money Laundering) and Terrorist Financing Act and bring Canada in line with the latest FATF standards, but the proposed amendments did not seriously address the problem with lawyers; indeed, the bill removed the formal requirement that lawyers report suspicious transactions.[19]

There remain two strongly opposed views. The international community and the Canadian government, including the RCMP and the Auditor General, remain convinced that lawyers should be brought within the official reporting system, as a critical part of the fight against organized crime and for the good of lawyers themselves. The legal profession is overwhelmingly opposed, believing that the reporting of suspicious transactions is unconstitutional and a horrible violation of the traditional and valuable rules governing the lawyer-client relationship.

Who is right? Is it really unconstitutional to require lawyers to report a financial transaction to government if there are reasonable grounds to believe that the transaction is connected to money laundering by organized crime? Would such a reporting requirement seriously erode general principles behind the average lawyer-client relationship? Is involvement by lawyers in suspicious transactions, ones that may promote and protect organized crime, best treated as an internal law society disciplinary matter? Or should we be calling the police?

I'd make that call.

SIX

A SMALL ARMY

David Cay Johnston is a Pulitzer Prize–winning journalist who covers the tax beat for *The New York Times*. In his 2003 book, *Perfectly Legal*,[1] Johnston writes that "most tax cheats rely on the accounting and legal firms to craft … complex, hard to find and even harder to understand tax shelters … Like guerrilla soldiers, a small army that moves stealthily in darkness can disrupt and perhaps even destroy a society that operates in the open." The army described by Johnston knows no borders; it operates in Canada, and other countries, as it does in the United States. As it moves stealthily in darkness, it deprives the public purse of tax revenue and raises fundamental questions about the responsibilities of lawyers and accountants to the society in which they live, work, and prosper.

In the United States, improbably, there is drama in the tax shelter world. In 2003, a Manhattan grand jury began investigating KPMG for its work on shelters sold from 1996 to 2002, complex transactions creating paper losses and bearing endearing and confidence-inspiring names like Blips, Flip, Opis, and SOS. (KPMG is one of the so-called Big Four accounting firms, and is one of the largest professional services firms in the world.) Investigators said these tax shelters created $11 billion in fake losses that cost the U.S. government $2.5 billion in tax revenue. In June 2005, KPMG issued a press release admitting that former KPMG partners had broken the law. In August 2005, the firm came to a deal with prosecutors to avoid a criminal indictment, once more acknowledging wrongdoing, and agreeing to pay almost half a billion dollars and accept an outside monitor of its operations. In a statement issued that August, KPMG acknowledged that "some KPMG tax partners and tax leaders routinely attempted to cloak in the attorney-client privilege communications that revealed the true nature of their conduct ... by routinely copying an associate general counsel on e-mail communications and memoranda in an effort to conceal information contained in those communications and memoranda from the I.R.S. and others." Days later federal prosecutors charged seventeen former employees of KPMG (including an associate general counsel), an outside investment banker, and R.J. Ruble, a former lawyer at Sidley Austin Brown & Wood (one of the world's largest law firms, with almost two thousand lawyers and multiple offices), with conspiracy to devise and sell fraudulent tax shelters. In September 2005, addressing some of the civil claims against them arising out of legal opinions or representations given to investors, KPMG and Sidley Austin agreed to pay $195 million to about 280 investors who bought questionable shelters. (Negotiations leading to the settlement were led by class action specialist Milberg Weiss Bershad & Schulman, who were paid $30 million for their work. Milberg Weiss itself was indicted on May 18, 2006, on unrelated charges of making secret illegal payments to individuals who served as class action plaintiffs.)

KPMG and its lawyers have not been alone in all this difficulty. In 2003, Ernst & Young, another Big Four accounting firm, paid $15 million to the U.S. Internal Revenue Service to settle claims concerning tax shelters it had marketed. Several prominent law firms have been sucked into the Ernst & Young mess. Jenkens & Gilchrist, which emailed legal opinions on these Ernst & Young tax shelters to potential investors, is in arbitration with investors who paid interest and penalties because the shelters failed. *The New York Times* reported in January 2006 that "federal prosecutors are investigating three lawyers at a prominent Dallas law firm, Jenkens & Gilchrist, in a widening of an investigation into questionable shelters …"[2] Scheef & Stone, a Dallas law firm, is a defendant in a civil action brought by investors who claim that it introduced Ernst & Young to Jenkens & Gilchrist when the accounting firm wanted legal opinions, earning fees that were not disclosed. In

1999, the Texas law firm of Locke Liddell supplied a legal opinion to Ernst & Young, for $3.5 million, to support a tax shelter known as CDS (Contingent Deferred Swap). In 2005, a U.S. Senate subcommittee said the only purpose of CDS was "the avoidance or evasion of federal, state or local tax in a manner not intended by law." (At the time Locke Liddell supplied the opinion, Harriet Miers was the co-managing partner. In 2005, Miers was nominated by President Bush for a U.S. Supreme Court seat, but the politically unpopular nomination was later withdrawn.)

These tax shelter scandals, and particularly the conduct of accountants and lawyers, have attracted serious attention from the U.S. Senate. In February 2005, the Permanent Subcommittee on Investigations of the U.S. Senate Committee on Homeland Security and Governmental Affairs released a report titled *The Role of Professional Firms in the U.S. Tax Shelter Industry*.[3] Senator Norm Coleman, chairman of the subcommittee, said in a press release, "This Report details how accountants, lawyers, bankers, and investment advisors developed, implemented, and mass-marketed cookie-cutter tax shelters used to rip off the Treasury of billions of dollars in taxes." The subcommittee found that the law firm of Sidley Austin "provided legal services that facilitated the development and sale of potentially abusive or illegal tax shelters, including by providing design assistance, collaboration on allegedly 'independent' tax opinion letters, and hundreds of boilerplate tax opinion letters to clients ..." The report noted that Sidley Austin partner R.J. Ruble had spent about 2,500 hours preparing legal opinions for which he was paid $23 million in fees—an average hourly rate of more than $9,000 per billable hour.

On August 1, 2006, the subcommittee issued another report, this one describing a range of sophisticated schemes being used to enable U.S citizens to shift assets offshore and dodge taxes. In a press release, Senator Carl Levin, ranking Democrat on the subcommittee, said, "I'm particularly troubled by an industry of tax professionals, lawyers, trust specialists, bankers, and brokers, that permit, facilitate, promote, and exploit loopholes in the tax code. We need our professional community to be pillars of commerce rather than pillars of circumvention. We need to close these loopholes."[4] Senator Levin was quoted in *The New York Times* as saying, "We need to significantly strengthen the aiding and abetting statutes to get at the lawyers and accountants and other advisors who enable this cheating."[5]

Canada has not enjoyed dramatic investigations of tax shelters, expressions of outrage by prominent politicians at their use and effect (using colourful phrases like "rip off"), and confessions of wrongdoing and contrition by lawyers and accountants. No one seems very interested in this complex subject or sufficiently industrious to tackle it. But one recent high-profile case, *Monarch Entertainment v. Strother*, has given us a look at the Canadian tax shelter industry and in the process raised fundamental questions about the conduct and principles of the legal profession. Are lawyers pillars of commerce, or pillars of circumvention? How aggressive should lawyers be in helping clients avoid paying tax? What is the extent of a lawyer's duty to his client, and how long does that duty last? Is it based on contract, or loyalty? How much responsibility does a law firm have for a breach of the duty by one of its members?

At the end of 2006, there has yet to be a final decision in the *Strother* case answering these questions. The Supreme Court of Canada heard the case in October 2006; we await its judgment.

IMAGINE AN ELEGANT BOARDROOM, on a high floor in a downtown Vancouver office building, on a late autumn afternoon in 1996.[6] Soft leather chairs surrounded a granite conference table. Several middle-aged men sat around this table. Some were dressed in expensive casual clothes—colourful silk shirts, designer pants and jackets, Italian shoes worn without socks. These men seemed relaxed. They looked out of the windows. They chatted quietly. The weather was good; perhaps the meeting would end soon and they could go sailing. The other men at this meeting were dressed in suits and ties (although, if you had looked under the table, you would have noticed that one was wearing cowboy boots). Each of the men in suits studied a large red book—an annotated version of the Canadian Income Tax Act. Suddenly the one wearing cowboy boots looked up. "Gentlemen," he said dolefully. He paused, and then continued, "There is a turd in the punch bowl. There is no technical fix that avoids the new rules. The tax shelter business is over."

The men in casual clothes liked to describe themselves as being in the movie business, but really they were brokers who sold tax shelters to wealthy Canadians, shelters derived from production services agreements entered into with Hollywood studios that wanted to produce films in Canada. These men made millions of dollars a year, in commissions and fees, selling these shelters. The men in suits were their tax lawyers; they were the ones who structured the enormously complicated transactions that made their clients rich, bobbing and weaving around arcane tax rules that the federal government kept changing in an attempt to close down shelters seen as abusive. The lawyer in cowboy boots was Robert Collingwood Strother, senior partner in the venerable Vancouver law firm of Davis & Company,[7] and one of the cleverest and most imaginative tax lawyers in Canada. Strother was normally at least one jump ahead of federal tax officials, to the enormous financial benefit of his clients. But, on this particular day, there was a big problem. Maybe, just maybe, the government had finally found a way to close down film-financing tax shelters.

Davis & Company was founded in 1892. Its main office is in Vancouver, but it has smaller offices across Canada, and one in Tokyo. Today the firm has about a hundred partners. Davis has the reputation of being a solid, if somewhat dull, law firm—reliable, but not very exciting or innovative. Robert Strother's reputation is the opposite: He is regarded as brilliant and flamboyant, but—in the eyes of some, at least—as too clever by half. A native of Calgary, son of a medical doctor, Strother graduated from Dalhousie law school in 1974 (winning the gold medal), and obtained a master's degree in law from Harvard the following year. Before arriving at Davis, Strother moved around more than most lawyers. He practised in England and Texas between 1975 and 1977 (as an employee of Vinson & Elkins, a major Texas-based law firm that later acted as counsel to Enron Corporation); articled with Jones, Black and Company in Calgary in 1977/78; practised with Parlee Irving in Calgary from 1978 to 1980; practised in Vancouver with Lawrence and Shaw from 1980 to 1985; was a partner of Ladner Downs from 1985 to 1990; and then joined Davis & Company. Those who know Strother say that he regards himself as a member of the Canadian establishment and wants others to think of him that way.

In 1993, Strother acquired a client called Monarch Entertainment Corporation (now called 3464920 Canada Inc.). Created in 1992, Monarch's business was the creation and sale of tax-assisted production services financing, known by the abbreviation TAPSF, which offered tax shelter to people with big incomes. "Investors" bought units in a limited partnership that theoretically was charged with producing a film. Accounting principles produced a loss to the partnership because of a carefully designed mismatch between the large expenses incurred in producing the film, mostly incurred early on, and the small fee the partnership received at the outset of the investment's life. This loss could then be deducted by investors from other income.[8] Between 1993 and 1997, Monarch closed TAPSF transactions totalling almost $460 million and had operating profits of more than $13 million. Davis was paid fees of close to $10 million, which made Monarch the firm's second-biggest client. Largely on the strength of the Monarch billings, Strother became an important and highly paid partner of Davis & Company.

Monarch Entertainment was owned and run by Harry Knutson and Steve Cheikes, who had been introduced to each other by Strother. Knutson is a long-time West Coast investment banker, who normally acts through Nova Bancorp Group, a private investment company he founded in 1982. People consider Knutson to be smart and tough. Before creating Nova Bancorp, Knutson worked for Peter Pocklington, the controversial entrepreneur and one-time owner of the Edmonton Oilers. In a lengthy 1986 newspaper article by well-known business writers

Patricia Best and Ann Shortell, describing Pocklington's unsavoury business dealings of the 1970s, Knutson was referred to as Pocklington's "corporate lieutenant and backgammon partner." Best and Shortell describe him as "the balding, bearding Knutson, who favored fast cars, European tailoring and $40 bottles of wine ... described variously as the brains behind Pocklington and a hotshot ..."[9] Cheikes, a 1974 graduate of Cornell law school and originally a Los Angeles entertainment lawyer, moved to Vancouver in 1987 and began creating and operating film industry tax shelters, originally as a principal in the Beacon Group of Companies.

For some years, the Government of Canada was intent on shutting TAPSF down. It regarded the shelter as contrived, unfairly benefiting the rich and depriving the government of legitimate tax revenue. It was not swayed by the argument that TAPSF created employment in Canada by luring U.S. film production to the country (Hollywood studios took a share of the tax benefit achieved by the deferral enjoyed by individual investors), believing that other less objectionable policies could accomplish the same effect. In 1995, David Anderson, then federal Minister of National Revenue, described tax shelters like TAPSF as "abusive."[10] On November 18, 1996, as part of the government's move against shelters, the so-called matchable expenditures rules were announced, to come into effect some months later by amendment to the Income Tax Act (the rules finally

came into force on October 31, 1997). These rules
were intended to defeat the mismatch of expenditures and revenue by requiring the prorating of
expenditures over the life of the right to receive
income. This requirement apparently destroyed the
technique at the heart of TAPSF.

Strother told Monarch that he had no technical fix
for the new matchable expenditure rules, and that
the "tax shelter business was over." There was what
Justice Lowry of the British Columbia Supreme
Court later called "a bitter-sweet boardroom cham-
pagne toast to both past success and the unhappy end
of the business." Monarch closed up its tax shelter
business at the end of October 1997. An exclusive
written retainer agreement signed on October 8,
1996, which prevented Davis from acting for
anybody else in TAPSF transactions, lapsed at the
end of December 1997.

Early in 1998, Strother concluded that perhaps
there was a fix to the new matchable expenditures
rules after all, and started working on a "new idea"
for tax shelters. He worked on this new idea, not
with Monarch, but with a former employee of
Monarch, Paul Darc, a chartered accountant. Crucial
evidence in the subsequent litigation suggested that
Darc had thought up the new idea, and counsel
opposing Monarch's claim consistently referred to it
as "Darc's idea." On January 30, 1998, using his
personal letterhead, Strother signed an agreement
with Darc to provide him with legal services in

connection with the idea, an agreement that gave Strother a substantial personal participation in any profits of the new business. In March, Strother and Darc formed Sentinel Hill Entertainment Corporation, apparently named after the Vancouver neighbourhood where Strother then lived, and Sentinel Hill became a Davis client. Then, also in March, Strother applied for an advance tax ruling for a tax-assisted production financing of a U.S. film, an application based on an exception to the matchable expenditures rule that said that the rule would not apply where more than 80 percent of the right to receive income was realized before the end of the year in which the expenditure was made. (Davis had opened a file for the tax ruling on January 19, and Strother had a draft prepared by January 26. The request was submitted to Revenue Canada on March 3.) Strother prepared the ruling request without a fee. Darc agreed that, if the request was successful, Strother personally, through a Sentinel share option he was granted, would participate approximately equally in any profit. Expenses were to be borne equally by the two men.

Strother said nothing about any of this to Knutson or Cheikes, although he and other lawyers at Davis continued to do a limited amount of other legal work for Monarch. The B.C. Court of Appeal later said that, during 1998, Strother "took pains to ensure that no one at Davis let slip to Monarch the fact that the firm was acting for Sentinel Hill in connection with a new ... tax ruling."[11] (It was argued later that it would have been a breach of confidentiality if Strother and Davis had told Monarch anything about the business of another client.) Nor did Strother tell his partners at Davis & Company about his personal agreement with Sentinel Hill until many months after it had been entered into, and even then, as the trial judge in the subsequent litigation noted, "not with complete accuracy." (Strother and Monarch both dispute this and say many Davis partners, including the managing partner, were aware of Strother's involvement with Darc early on.) When he finally sent a memorandum about the agreement to Davis's managing partner, Doug Buchanan, on August 4, Buchanan wrote back that Strother was not to "personally have any kind of ownership interest in Sentinel Hill." Mr. Strother signed Buchanan's memorandum under the words, "This is correct." Despite this exchange, nothing seems to have been done formally to set aside Strother's January agreement with Darc giving him an ownership interest in Sentinel, although Strother and Darc have consistently maintained that the agreement terminated when Davis approval was denied, and that thereafter, until he left Davis, Strother acted only as Sentinel Hill's lawyer.

In October 1998, Strother obtained a favourable advance tax ruling for the new tax shelter scheme.[12] Only then did he prepare a retainer agreement between Sentinel and Davis & Company, which Darc quickly signed. It was similar to the agreement the firm had with Monarch, except it was more than twice as remunerative. There was celebration in the halls of the law firm. A new and big fish had been landed. By the end of 1998, Sentinel Hill had closed transactions worth $260 million in studio production. In March 1999, Strother resigned as a partner of Davis to devote himself full-time to the lucrative business of Sentinel Hill.

After Strother left Davis, he received 50 percent of the common shares of Sentinel Hill Entertainment Corporation for a nominal amount. By the time the government tried once more to terminate tax shelters, through amendments to the Income Tax Act introduced in September 2001, Sentinel Hill had closed transactions exceeding $4 billion in studio production, with profits said to have approached $130 million. Darc and Strother had together, personally, realized in excess of $60 million. Davis had been paid fees by Sentinel that exceeded $9 million.

One day in the spring of 1999, Harry Knutson of Monarch Entertainment saw a Sentinel Hill offering memorandum for the new tax shelter. "I couldn't believe it," he says now. "I went and saw my then friend Doug Buchanan, who was the managing partner at Davis & Company. I asked him, what the hell is going on. He wouldn't talk about it. He said he couldn't—client confidentiality." In March 1999, Monarch Entertainment began a legal action against

Strother and Davis, arguing that Strother had deliberately concealed tax shelter knowledge from it to
usurp a business opportunity for his personal
benefit.[13] Monarch alleged breaches of fiduciary obligations by Strother and Davis & Company, obligations created by the lawyer-client relationship that
were separate from, and went beyond, any contractual obligations that existed. Knutson says that
before the trial Davis & Company offered Monarch
a $10-million settlement. He regarded the offer,
given the stakes, as "not serious."

The complex trial before Justice Lowry of the
B.C. Supreme Court (now a judge of the B.C. Court
of Appeal) took nine weeks. It was not without its
lighter moments. Consider the cross-examination of
Strother by R.D. Holmes, one of Monarch's lawyers:

Holmes: Was it your view that you were to
prefer Monarch's interests to your own?

Strother: Again, it depends on the context in
which you're asking me that question.

Holmes: What do you mean by that?

Strother: Well, if we were ordering lunch and
the Monarch principals preferred pizza, and I
preferred turkey sandwiches I would feel myself
free to order turkey sandwiches.

Holmes: If you could focus on financial
matters, sir.

In the end, Justice Lowry agreed with the arguments put forward by the lawyers for Strother and Davis & Company. He agreed that Strother's fiduciary obligations were tied to the contractual obligations created by the retainer agreement between Monarch and Davis that expired at the end of 1997: When the retainer agreement came to an end, Strother's fiduciary obligations came to an end as well. Strother was free to take the new idea about tax shelters and turn it into a business for himself. Justice Lowry said that Strother "employed only the skill and knowledge [he was] entitled to employ...."

In January 2005, the B.C. Court of Appeal unanimously reversed Justice Lowry. In lengthy and erudite reasons given by Justice Newbury, the court found Strother in breach of his fiduciary duties, and instructed him to account to Monarch for over $30 million personally gained from breach of those duties. It didn't matter to the court that the Monarch retainer had expired when Strother embarked on his Sentinel business venture; the judges were clear that he had fiduciary duties that went far beyond those that were strictly contractual.

Strother, said the Court of Appeal, had created an undisclosed dual conflict—a conflict between Monarch and Sentinel, and, because of his financial interest in Sentinel, a conflict between Monarch and himself. Even after the retainer agreement expired, Strother and Davis still had obligations to Monarch. Justice Newbury said, "One must not ... equate the scope of a lawyer's contractual duty to advise his client ... with his fiduciary duties, including the duty not to place himself in a position of conflict and the duty to disclose any personal interest he may have that might affect his loyalty and dedication to the client's cause. The latter duties are implied by law and are unlikely to be validly excluded or diminished by contract."

The court rejected the argument that Strother, once his Monarch retainer expired, had no obligation to continue giving Monarch advice on tax shelter matters, and rejected as well the further argument that Monarch was no longer entitled to such advice. Said Justice Newbury, of the Monarch representatives, "They were not legally knowledgeable, and whether they '*expected*' to be told that there was a possible solution to their predicament, they were *entitled* to candid and complete advice from a lawyer who was not in a position of conflict." [original emphasis]

What about Davis & Company? The court called for further arguments, within two months or so, on a variety of points dealing with the law firm's possible liability. Those arguments were heard in May 2005. On July 25, the court gave its unanimous judgment.[14]

The Court of Appeal first considered whether Davis should be held directly liable with Strother for all the profits and benefits Strother received from the Sentinel Hill enterprise. That, said the court,

depended on whether Davis gave "knowing assistance" to Strother in breaching his duty toward
Monarch, or was reckless or wilfully blind to his
misconduct. The court decided that neither was the
case. Davis had no direct liability to Monarch for
Strother's gains at Monarch's expense.

But should Davis & Company be held vicariously
liable for the money made by Strother? Applying the
usual test, the court asked whether Strother was
acting in "the ordinary course" of the firm's business
when enmeshed in his conflicts of interest. It noted
that "the fact that an agent has contravened the principal's instructions (and, by analogy, the fact a
partner has contravened his firm's partnership agreement or policies) does not necessarily mean that he
or she was acting outside the ordinary course of business." The question was "whether the practice of law
as carried out by Davis materially increased the risk of
Mr. Strother's taking of a personal interest, or
whether there were only 'incidental' connections
such as time and place, with the law practice." The
court decided that there were only incidental
connections. What Strother did was not in the ordinary course of the firm's business. Davis & Company
did not have vicarious liability for the money Strother
put in his own pocket.

So far so good, the partners of Davis & Company
must have thought, as they eagerly leafed through
the judgment. But then the court turned to a new
issue—Monarch's claim for "disgorgement" by Davis

of the profits Davis itself earned in the form of legal fees paid by Sentinel Hill.

The purpose of an order for disgorgement, said Justice Newbury, is to maintain the integrity of fiduciary relationships by ensuring that persons who are subject to fiduciary duties cannot profit from them. She said:

> Although it does not appear that the partners of the firm were aware of the advice Mr. Strother was giving, either directly or by his silence to Monarch, in 1998 that there was "nothing to be done", Davis's *vicarious* liability for that breach seems to me clear: the firm acted for both Monarch and Sentinel Hill in the ordinary course of its business and with the authorization of its partners; Mr. Strother's advising them on tax-related matters was what he was retained by both to do; the firm earned substantial profits (the ultimate amount of which has yet to be determined in the court below) under its contingent arrangements with Sentinel Hill; and ... logically [*sic*] requires that the firm not be permitted to retain them, even if the partners (other than Mr. Strother) were personally innocent.

Davis was ordered to "account for and disgorge the profits it earned from acting for Sentinel Hill in breach of its duty to Monarch."

Some questions remained: What were those "profits"? Must Davis disgorge the gross amount of fees Sentinel Hill paid? Or can it deduct some amount for costs and overheads and, if so, how much? This issue was sent back to the trial division for determination. Justice Newbury then gave a final twist of the knife and ordered Davis to return all fees Monarch paid subsequent to the date when the conflicts of interest arose, judged to be January 1, 1998. The gross amount of fees Sentinel paid to Davis is thought to be about $9 million, and the fees Monarch paid (that must be returned) to be another $1 million or so.[15] Based on the decision of the Court of Appeal, the partners of Davis & Company had a big bill to split.

On December 15, 2005, the Supreme Court of Canada gave leave to appeal to the parties in the Strother litigation.[16] Strother, of course, had appealed against the order that he disgorge $30 million or so. He argued that the Court of Appeal improperly "departed from the findings of the trial judge in a number of substantial respects, and in others made findings of fact not supportable by the evidence";[17] that the court acted in error when it said that Davis's acceptance of a retainer from Sentinel Hill in 1998 created a conflict of interest with Monarch; and that the court's use of the accounting principle as a remedy was incorrect.[18] Davis & Company argued, for a variety of reasons, that it should not be required to give up the substantial profit it made from Strother's activities. Said Davis of the Court of Appeal, "The Court's view is, apparently, that once a solicitor has given an opinion to a client ... he or she may not, without disloyalty, later accept instructions from another client to assert an opinion contrary to that first opinion. Davis submits that this surprising result constitutes an unnecessary expansion of the duty of loyalty which is not warranted by precedent or policy."[19]

Monarch, the company that had been Strother's principal client and believed that it should have had the benefit of the new tax idea, argued that it should recover a much greater amount than awarded by the Court of Appeal—possibly as much as $140 million, representing the total of Sentinel Hill profits—and that all defendants, including Paul Darc, should be held jointly and severally liable.[20] The Canadian Bar Association was given intervenor status, saying that it "wishes to provide the Court with the benefit of its expertise and perspective concerning the nature and extent of a lawyer's duty of loyalty."[21]

Harry Knutson of Monarch was optimistic about his prospects before the Supreme Court. First, he believed that Paul Darc was vulnerable. "Why shouldn't an accountant be held to the same standard of fiduciary duty as a lawyer?" he asked.[22] But his real interest was in what happened to Davis & Company. "My lawyers tell me that our arguments on the joint and several liability of Davis are very strong," he said. "I expect to be sending them a very big bill, and it'll be up to them to collect what they can from Strother." He added, "Davis partners needn't worry. I'll work out a payment plan for them."

Strother seemed sanguine about his fate. A December 15, 2005, press release put out by his public relations firm, Sullivan Media, said this: "Robert Strother … is pleased and grateful that the Supreme Court of Canada decided today to hear the case. 'This case has occupied my life for almost half a decade, and it is my hope that the Supreme Court will restore the Trial Judge's findings and conclusions,' said Mr. Strother in Vancouver today. '… Obviously the court has seen the important elements of the case and has moved to address them.'" The press release referred to the B.C. Court of Appeal decision as "surprising and controversial." A December 17, 2005, article by David Baines in *The Vancouver Sun* described Strother as striking "a philosophical pose" when asked about the Court of Appeal ruling, and saying—of the forthcoming Supreme Court decision—"whatever the decision I will live with it." Commented Baines, "It is a brave front, but not terribly convincing…. He cringes when he reflects on the impact on his family, particularly his 13-year-old daughter, who could never be expected to understand the nuances of the case."[23]

Arguments before the Supreme Court took place in early October 2006.[24] At the end of 2006, no judgment had been delivered. The Supreme Court will address these questions: What is the duty of a lawyer to his client? What is the duty of a lawyer to his law firm? And what is the duty of a law firm to the client of an individual law firm member?

ROBERT STROTHER and Paul Darc are still in the tax shelter business, most recently selling units in a limited partnership mining scheme called Red Mile Resources Fund Limited Partnership, which Harry Knutson described as having a "financial and tax profile like TAPSF." Strother has lavish houses in Vancouver and Phoenix, Arizona, and Darc has built a $7-million house in West Vancouver. Meanwhile, by all accounts, the investors in Sentinel Hill financings are being subjected to aggressive audits by the income tax authorities.

SEVEN

SLEEPING WITH A CLIENT

A lawyer sleeps with a client.[1] What happens if, later on, things go sour, and the client complains to the law society? Canadian discipline cases suggest the lawyer might (i) be reprimanded or (ii) be suspended from the bar for anywhere from thirty days to eighteen months or (iii) be disbarred. What's he or she done wrong? Having sex with a client is generally thought to be a conflict of interest. What determines the severity of the penalty? Any number of unknowable factors, including whatever is blowing in the political and cultural wind at the time.

ON JULY 17, 1991, in New Liskeard, Ontario, fifty-five-year-old Mrs. A. went to see her lawyer, fifty-four-year-old Peter Ramsey. She wanted to add a codicil to her will.

Mrs. A. asked the Solicitor the cost of the codicil and when she was advised that the fee would be $75.00, she pointed out that he had previously indicated that the fee would be approximately $50.00. The Solicitor responded by indicating that there would be no charge if Mrs. A. would come to his office without a brassiere and provide him a viewing of her breasts.[2]

Mrs. A. complained about Peter Ramsey to the Law Society of Upper Canada. A discipline committee said it was "not prepared to regard the Solicitor's comments as an ill-advised attempt at humour." In November 1992, Ramsey was reprimanded, the lightest possible penalty. The Ramsey case, with its simple and compelling facts, has become part of legal legend, and to this day is often the subject of ribald commentary by lawyers as they drink at the local bar at the end of the day.

In 1995, in Dartmouth, Nova Scotia, forty-nine-year-old lawyer Norman Rose tried to seduce a seventeen-year-old single mother who was his client (she had been arrested for forging a cheque). The suave Rose plied the girl with liquor, flowers, and Kentucky Fried Chicken. He brought vodka, candles, and a pink rose to her apartment, and suggested a "dating relationship" in exchange for legal services. She refused and complained to the Nova Scotia Barristers' Society. A discipline committee found that Rose, contrary to ethical rules, had requested a dating relationship as a fee, and that he had used inappropriate pressure tactics to try to obtain a personal advantage. In December 1996, Rose was suspended from the bar for thirty days.[3]

The unfortunate Paul Adams from Edmonton is still the only Canadian lawyer (as of the end of 2006) to have been disbarred for sexual misconduct with a client. On September 10, 1996, police burst into a room in Edmonton's Kingsway Hotel and found thirty-four-year-old Adams with a sixteen-year-old prostitute. His pants were down around his ankles. The prostitute was wearing a police recording device (she had earlier been picked up by the police and had told them about her impending date). She was a client of Adams. He pleaded guilty to one charge of sexual exploitation under s. 153(1)(b) of the Criminal Code, which makes it an indictable offence for someone in a position of trust or authority to invite a young person to touch his body, and received a fifteen-month conditional sentence that allowed him to serve his time at home rather than in prison. (The evidence established that he and the girl had not had sexual intercourse.) In October 1997, an Alberta Law Society hearing committee, as it disbarred Adams, said the following: "A professional must be above taking advantage of the client's feelings and vulnerability and must suppress his own desires ... It breaches the trust that underlays a solicitor-client relationship and cannot be tolerated if the profession is to continue to enjoy the respect of the public."[4] The committee thought it irrelevant that the client was a prostitute. Another law society committee,[5] and then the Alberta Court of Appeal,[6] dismissed appeals from this decision, and the short career of Paul Adams as a lawyer was over. At age thirty-five, the feckless Adams had been a member of the bar for less than two years.

The story of Paul Adams has a curious footnote. Finished as a lawyer, he went on to a new career as a paralegal, running a business called Affordable Paralegal Services and charging up to $100 an hour for his services. He joined the Edmonton branch of the Equitable Child Maintenance and Access Society (ECMAS), an Alberta volunteer non-custodial parents' lobby group. At meetings of the group, Adams often handed out business cards showing that he had a law degree. After a while, a quarter of his paralegal clients came from ECMAS. Another member of the Edmonton branch of ECMAS was Ferrel Christensen, an emeritus professor of philosophy at the University of Alberta. In 1990, Christensen published a controversial book called *Pornography: The Other Side*,[7] which he described to the *Calgary Herald* as a defence of pornography.[8] One section of the book is titled "Sex and Young People." The journalist Donna Laframboise, in a *National Post* feature article, quoted Christensen as saying that "the idea that sex is bad for young people is at best another self-fulfilling prophesy.... In cultures where they are not prevented from doing so, children begin sexuality, sometimes even coitus

itself, at a very early age."[9] Laframboise described
Christensen as a dominant personality in the
Edmonton branch of ECMAS, and a strong supporter
of Paul Adams. Several people she interviewed claimed
that Christensen frequently suggested to ECMAS
members, persistently and in very strong terms, that
they get legal advice from Adams. On March 12,
2001, Adams was elected vice-president of the
Edmonton branch of ECMAS. Days later, after a
storm of protest about the election to office of a
convicted sex offender, he was forced to resign from
his new position. He had never concealed his conviction from the group. "Am I forever a pariah?" asked
Adams.[10]

After the sudden and severe penalty imposed in the
1997 Adams case, disciplinary committees for some
years seemed to revert to the gentler and more
tolerant days of Ramsey and Rose. Consider the case
of Halifax lawyer Andrew Pavey. In July 1997
(according to December 2000 findings of a Nova
Scotia Barristers' Society discipline subcommittee[11]),
Pavey and his client, Lisa Nicholson, together bought
crack cocaine (Pavey paid). They spent the next day
using the cocaine and having repeated oral sex and
sexual intercourse. Pavey, a cocaine user for some time,
with a history of psychiatric illness, had become
Nicholson's lawyer in November 1996, and was trying
to regain custody of her three children from the
Department of Community Services. Lisa Nicholson
later told several people what had happened between

her and Pavey, and word got around. She was called by a reporter from *Frank*, a satirical and gossip magazine, but refused to say anything. Eventually, in August 1999, she complained to the barristers' society. A discipline subcommittee, in a rambling and repetitious judgment, found that Pavey had taken advantage of his client's vulnerability, and in January 2001 suspended him for eighteen months. In imposing the penalty, the committee referred to the "mitigating factor" of Pavey's dissociative identity disorder, sometimes termed a "multiple personality disorder," and described evidence given by Pavey's psychiatrist, Dr. John Curtis:

> There are five main areas or dissociative orders relating to a dissociative identity disorder. They are amnesia, depersonalization, derealization, identity confusion, and identity alteration. Dr. Curtis testified all five were manifested in Mr. Pavey....
>
> Amnesia is the forgetting for "punched-out" periods of time, what one has done. Depersonalization is what is referred to as "an out-of-body experience".... Derealization is where the person separates from their environment and in a sense distances themselves from that which is stressful. Identity confusion is where the person has many independent states and they are not sure who they are. And identity alteration, is where the person actually changes

states, which is what happens when the person
has the amnestic episodes.

When he gave his evidence, Pavey testified that
when he was under stress he would "split":

Under extreme pressure I would disassociate
and become someone else. At the very extreme
points of this disorder, my experience was highly
compartmentalized, so that what was happening
in one area of existence was completely separated from another area of experience. That
person who was going out using drugs didn't
give a shit about anything—didn't care. The
other part had to pick up the pieces and did.

To this day, Pavey denies Lisa Nicholson's cocaine
and sex allegations.[12] After he was suspended from the
Nova Scotia bar, with his livelihood lost at least
temporarily, he moved to Vancouver to live with his
mother. "She gave me food and shelter," he says. He
started a mediation practice, married again, and had a
daughter (Pavey has grown-up children by a previous
marriage). He believes that the Nova Scotia
Barristers' Society, when it dealt with his case, was
neither intelligent nor reasonable. "Members of these
panels have no real adjudicative experience," he says.

They don't know how to interpret the evidence
properly. The panel hearing my case showed

me no respect at all, either in the way the proceedings were handled, or in the reasons that were eventually given.... The panel's reasons were a mess. Lack of respect was inherent in the process. I felt dehumanized and depersonalized.

Pavey feels that he doesn't really fit into the legal profession, and that lawyers find him easy to dismiss. He says that's because he processes information differently than most lawyers; he is not particularly analytical, but rather is intuitive and interested in the big picture. Pavey was reinstated by the Nova Scotia Barristers' Society in December 2003, but continues to live and work in Vancouver.

Some might say that Toronto lawyer Mark Joseph got off easy. Called to the bar in 1982, Joseph was retained by "Mary Doe" in December 1994. Doe had been sexually assaulted by another tenant in her apartment building and wanted to sue the landlord. She had a troubled history, suffered from depression, and was receiving a disability pension under the Ontario Family Benefits Act. In March 1995, Joseph and Doe began a personal relationship, having sex about once a week. Two weeks after they started sleeping together, Joseph insisted that Doe find another lawyer (she didn't want to do this, believing that Joseph was the only lawyer who could properly handle her case). The two continued to have sex, although less and less frequently, until the fall of 1996.

In June 1997, Doe made a written complaint about Joseph to the Law Society of Upper Canada. In an agreed statement of facts, Joseph formally agreed with the discipline committee on several points: that his sexual relationship with Doe violated the trust that was fundamental to the fiduciary nature of the solicitor-client relationship, particularly in light of the client's vulnerability; that it was not the client's responsibility to understand the dynamics of the solicitor-client relationship and set the boundaries on the sexual or financial interaction between the lawyer and the client; and that he had created a conflict of interest between his responsibility to act in the best interests of his client and his personal interest in having a sexual relationship with her. In November 2003, Joseph was suspended for three months.[13] The hearing panel carefully noted that "Our decision ... leaves open the broader questions as to whether all solicitor and client relationships are necessarily rooted in inequality and whether all sexual relationships between a solicitor and client constitute a breach of fiduciary duty and a conflict of interest." The chastened and disingenuous Mark Joseph said that he wished there had been a specific rule governing sex with clients because he had not been aware of the problems that could arise from such a relationship.

Then there is the case of Toronto lawyer Gary Neinstein. Born in 1942, he became a lawyer in 1970. In November 2003, after hearings that had

stretched over fifteen months, a law society disciplinary panel found as facts that he had sex on several
occasions in 1990 with a client known as CT, and
that he had also behaved inappropriately with CT at
other times.[14] (The last "inappropriate incident" was
said to have taken place ten years before, in 1993. CT
waited until 1997 to complain to the law society.)
The panel accepted CT's evidence that she was
unable to stop Neinstein's behaviour because he was
her lawyer, she had come from a dysfunctional family,
and she was raised to believe that lawyers were
persons in authority who were there to provide
protection. "She could do nothing," said the panel,
"and thus felt she was vulnerable, humiliated and
ashamed." The panel also found that, in the early
nineties, Neinstein had sexually harassed a secretary
at his firm (touching, leering, and making sexually
suggestive comments and gestures).

A further hearing was scheduled to consider what
sanction should be imposed on Neinstein. It was held
in January 2004. That same month, the law society's
professional regulation committee recommended to
Convocation, the society's governing body, that
there be an absolute prohibition on sexual relationships between lawyers and clients, with a limited and
insignificant exception for relationships that predate
the lawyer and client relationship. The committee's
report argued that "the essence and justification for
the proposed new rules is the inherent conflict of
interest that a sexual relationship presents to a lawyer

and client relationship."[15] Perhaps it was not surprising that, in June 2004, following the sweeping recommendations made by the professional regulation committee, the Neinstein sanction panel decided that he should be disbarred. Neinstein immediately appealed, and his disbarment was stayed pending his appeal (the law society opposed the stay). Brian Greenspan, Neinstein's lawyer, was quoted in the press as saying that the original findings were "inexplicable," the process of arriving at a penalty was "fundamentally flawed," and Neinstein's treatment was "outrageous" and "improper."[16]

And then, just as abruptly, the climate changed yet again. In August 2004, delegates to the Canadian Bar Association's annual meeting were asked to adopt a complete sex-with-clients ban. The proposed ban was overwhelmingly rejected, following what one newspaper described as "a spirited, and oftentimes jocular" debate. Delegates described the proposal as "paternalistic," "absolutist," and "stereotypical." One delegate, echoing a famous comment by Pierre Trudeau, said, "The Canadian Bar Association and the law societies of this country have no place in the bedrooms of its lawyers." Another asked, "Who are we to impose a prohibition on falling in love?" Another said, "Wake up, we're in 2004. Sex is not always bad.... It is possible to have a love affair that's good."[17]

In October 2004, the Law Society of Upper Canada, no doubt chastened by the profession's backlash at the recent Canadian Bar Association annual meeting, and following a new and much watered down report by the professional regulation committee, decided that, after all, it would be a mistake to have an outright ban on lawyers having sex with clients. Instead, in a modest move, it adjusted the official commentary on professional conduct rule 2.04 dealing with conflicts of interest.[18] In making these cautious changes, Ontario followed the general approach already taken by Nova Scotia and British Columbia, the only other Canadian jurisdictions that explicitly address the sex-with-clients issue. Nova Scotia rule 7(a), in the society's *Legal Ethics and Professional Conduct Handbook*, says that "a lawyer has a duty not to act for a client when the interests of the client and the personal interests of the lawyer ... are in conflict." Commentary on the rule says that it is intended to prohibit, inter alia, sexual exploitation by a lawyer in the course of a professional representation. The *Professional Conduct Handbook of the Law Society of British Columbia*, in a footnote to the general integrity rule, says, "A lawyer must not exploit the relationship between solicitor and client to the lawyer's own advantage. An intimate relationship between a lawyer and a client, such as a sexual one, may constitute exploitation."

The Neinstein case now surfaced again, in a different and more laissez-faire environment. A five-person appeal panel heard arguments in December 2004, giving its decision on February 10, 2005.[19] It

found that the original hearing panel did not properly instruct itself as to the way in which a witness's
credibility should be assessed,[20] and that it failed to
give adequate reasons for its decision.[21] In particular,
the appeal panel found that the hearing panel had
imposed an unreasonable penalty:

> The range of activity constituting sexual harass-
> ment can be vast: from an unwelcome dinner
> invitation made by a lawyer to a client or
> employee, to sexual assault.
>
> ... Sexual harassment is contextual: actions
> or words may be sexual harassment in one
> instance, but not in another. What makes
> behaviour "unwelcome" or "unwanted" in
> most circumstances, turns on the context in
> which it occurs and whether, in that context,
> there was consent to the behaviour.

The reasons continued:

> The Society, in argument, was asked whether
> two declined dinner invitations, made by a
> lawyer to a client ... would constitute profes-
> sional misconduct in which disbarment would
> be presumed. The Society confirmed that this
> accurately reflected their position. Given the
> nature of human interaction, one can certainly
> envision circumstances when it could be difficult
> for the lawyer issuing the invitation to discern

whether it was "unwelcome" or "unwanted". In such circumstances, it would be unreasonable to presume disbarment if the unwelcome nature of the invitation was ultimately proven.

The appeal panel ordered a new hearing in the Neinstein case. The law society appealed this decision to the divisional court, which, in March 2007, ruled that Neinstein was indeed guilty of professional misconduct, but agreed that disbarment was an unreasonable penalty. It would be more appropriate, said the court, to suspend Neinstein for twelve months. Neinstein is appealing his twelve-month suspension.[22]

The chairman of the original law society panel hearing the Neinstein case (which decided in June 2004 that Neinstein should be disbarred for sexually harassing a client) was George Hunter, senior partner of the blue-chip firm Borden Ladner Gervais. In June 2005, Hunter was elected treasurer of the Law Society of Upper Canada, and, shortly thereafter, president of the Federation of Law Societies, thus becoming the most powerful representative and regulator of Canadian lawyers. In December 2005, Hunter suddenly resigned both positions, and went on medical leave from his law firm, citing vague family and personal reasons (Hunter is married and has two children). Many rumours circulated, but it was not until September 2006 that journalist Cristin Schmitz broke the story in the *Ottawa Citizen*: "A

respected senior partner of a national law firm ... is
under investigation by Ontario's law society after his
intimate relationship with a divorced client turned
sour."[23] The relationship between Hunter and JH,
whom Hunter was representing in a bitter divorce,
had lasted at least two and a half years, starting well
before Hunter chaired the Neinstein panel. In a later
story, Schmitz described a document that Hunter
drafted and asked JH to sign in November 2005
without giving her the opportunity to seek independent legal advice (once JH signed, Hunter
unwisely confessed to her a number of simultaneous
affairs). In this document, JH "acknowledged" that
her personal relationship with Hunter had no effect
on their professional relationship.[24] Kirk Makin,
justice reporter for *The Globe and Mail*, gave details
of a notice filed in September 2006 by the law society
that led to a disciplinary hearing into allegations that
Hunter engaged in professional misconduct:[25]

> It alleges that Mr. Hunter went so far as to show
> up at JH's home to try to persuade her to tell his
> law partners that he had behaved properly—an
> unexpected visit that caused JH "concern and
> emotional distress," the notice says. Mr. Hunter
> then launched a phone and e-mail campaign to
> get her to agree to his request, the notice says.
>   It also alleges that during the course of their
> relationship, Mr. Hunter did not provide JH
> with competent advice on issues involving

access to her daughter and supervision for the child during visits with her ex-husband.

"You failed to take appropriate action to protect the interests of JH's daughter after you were notified by JH, on or about June 5, 2005, that her daughter had been injured while in the care of JH's ex-husband." The allegations note that throughout their 2-year relationship, JH was "emotionally vulnerable," yet Mr. Hunter failed to recommend that she obtain independent legal advice.

On February 2, 2007, Hunter admitted misconduct to a law society disciplinary panel and was suspended from the practice of law for sixty days.

NANCY MOORE of Boston University School of Law, a leading U.S. commentator on legal ethics, has written that "there can be no dispute that sex with clients is a serious problem for the legal profession."[26] Moore recognizes that there are strong arguments against an outright ban. Opponents argue that the problem can be addressed through existing rules, such as those governing conflicts of interest; that a ban may violate the right to privacy of clients and lawyers; and, what may be the most powerful argument of all, that sex with clients is "perfectly okay" in some situations.

But Moore replies that there are important advantages to what she calls a "bright-line black letter" rule prohibiting sex with clients. Such a rule, she believes, provides necessary protection for the majority of clients who are significantly at risk and whose lawyers are likely to mistakenly conclude that their relationship is one of the "good ones." It protects well-intentioned lawyers by alerting them to the dangers of sexual relationships with clients and the serious possibility of discipline if the relationship goes sour and the client complains. And it puts clients on notice that such conduct by their lawyer is unethical. Jim Hodgson, a senior Canadian litigator and former president of the Advocates' Society, who has represented lawyers accused of sexual impropriety, puts it succinctly: "Forget all that argument about what's personal life and what's professional life. No sex with clients is the best rule. It is very clear. It's a rule that, in the end, will save everybody an awful lot of trouble."[27] Mark Joseph, we may remember, wished there had been such a rule.[28]

Few subjects are more fraught than love and sex. Few circumstances are more complicated than those involving romantic and sexual relationships. And, accordingly, few issues confronting the legal profession are more difficult that the issue of lawyer-client sex. Does this difficulty argue for the simple solution, a sweeping ban on lawyer-client relationships designed to remove the issue from the agenda? Or is a case-by-case approach preferable, one that applies the accepted test of conflict of interest to particular facts, finding some relationships acceptable and others not, and attempting to standardize penalties for the unacceptable as it goes along? Many lawyers support a vague approach, arguing that, in the tradition of the common law, individual facts are what count. A general prohibition fails to distinguish between wildly different situations, for example, between the client who is a vulnerable and poorly educated juvenile, and one who is a sophisticated and well-educated vice-president of a large corporation expecting to be wined and dined.

The Canadian legal profession has no clear rule about how to deal with lawyers who have sex with clients. The few disciplinary cases of the last decade or so have focused on conflict of interest in a muddled sort of way, and have imposed widely differing penalties on lawyers found lubricious. Only three provinces address the issue in their rules of conduct, and then only in passing. The Ontario bar flexed its muscles and proposed a sex ban, but changed its mind. A ban put before the Canadian Bar Association was treated with derision by its members. More generally, there seems to be growing resistance to the ever-expanding concept of "professional misconduct," and to the idea that law societies should be policemen of lawyers' lives, supplementing if not supplanting everything from the teachings of the church to the strictures of the criminal law.

EIGHT

AN ORDINARY MAN

Agnew Johnston

John Andrew Agnew Johnston, known as "Agnew," was born to an Establishment family in a small city where he grew up, practised law, married, and had a child. For a while, he enjoyed middle-class success and the happiness of an ordinary man. Then, as a result of unexceptional weaknesses in his character, unhappy circumstances, and a series of bad judgments, his happy and successful life came to an end, and was replaced by crisis and catastrophe. Beset by marital problems, drinking too much, unable to think straight, he started using young prostitutes, and became a suspect in the murder of one of them. The Establishment, drawing together to protect itself from lurid accusations, abandoned Agnew and sent him on his way.

AGNEW JOHNSTON was born in Fort William, Ontario, on October 15, 1952.[1] In those days, the cities of Fort William and Port Arthur, separated by just a few miles and with a combined population of about eighty thousand, were uneasy rivals. The rivalry ended in 1970 when the provincial government forced them to amalgamate into a single city, Thunder Bay. When Agnew was a small boy, his father, the Reverend Dr. Agnew Herbert Johnston, would sometimes, for an outing, take him by ferry from Port Arthur to Fort William, and then back to Port Arthur by streetcar.

Agnew's father graduated from Osgoode Hall Law School in Toronto and articled with a trust company, but quickly gave up the law to become a Presbyterian minister. He was minister of St. Andrew's Church in Thunder Bay for fifty-three years. In 1973, he was elected the ninety-ninth moderator of the General Assembly of the Presbyterian Church in Canada. He served for a time as chairman of the board of education in Fort William (a school in Thunder Bay is named after him). The Reverend Johnston never completely lost interest in legal matters, and once was chairman of the discipline committee of Ontario's Board of Funeral Services, which regulates the practices of the province's funeral directors. Agnew's father was named after Agnew's great-uncle, William Agnew Johnston, who was Chief Justice of Kansas from 1903 until 1935, a fact that Agnew still refers to with pride.

In 1975, Agnew graduated with a bachelor of arts degree from Thunder Bay's Lakehead University. He majored in history, a lifelong interest. "I should have been a historian," he says. Knowing that being a historian was not a job, but that he could make a living as a lawyer, he went to Osgoode Hall Law School, where he was an average student. He graduated in 1978 and went home to Thunder Bay, where he articled for Alfred Petrone, a Thunder Bay criminal defence lawyer. He worked in Petrone's law office for ten years. In 1979, he married Amy Evelyn Gertz, and in 1982 their daughter, Anne, was born. Things seemed to be going well for Johnston. He was a rising professional, settled in his personal life and respected in the community. He started doing part-time Crown attorney work, which he liked. In 1990, he left Alfred Petrone's office to become a full-time assistant Crown attorney.

But there was growing trouble. In 1985, Johnston's wife, Amy, left him, taking their daughter, Anne, with her. Johnston's attempts to gain custody of his daughter were unsuccessful. In October 1987, Johnston's much-loved father died, at the age of eighty. In 1988, Johnston struck up a relationship with Sheilagh Warren. Eventually they bought a house together, on Selkirk Street in the old Fort William part of Thunder Bay, but by 1992 the relationship had collapsed. Johnston became depressed and started drinking a lot. And then, one morning during the winter of 1992/93 (he does not remember exactly when), at the provincial court-house where he was appearing as a Crown attorney, Johnston met Stephanie Edwards, an eighteen-year-old prostitute whom he later described as beautiful and charismatic. Stephanie was in court that morning as a "support person" for an accused, bumped into Johnston, asked him for advice and reassurance, and later, as a gesture of gratitude, bought him a coffee.

Johnston says that Stephanie came on to him, and he thought, "Why not?" They started having sex. It is not clear whether Johnston realized at the beginning that Stephanie was a prostitute, but it was not long before she started asking for money. In the summer of 1993, Stephanie Edwards's brother broke into Johnston's house (why he did so is not apparent) and was arrested. Stephanie called Johnston and told him that if he didn't get her brother out of jail, she was going to tell everyone that he used underage hookers. Johnston denies that he helped Stephanie's brother in any way.

The rumours, whether started by Stephanie or by someone else, began in 1993. It was said that Johnston was a regular customer of prostitutes under the age of eighteen, picking girls up on Simpson Street, the notorious Fort William "track." (The Criminal Code makes it a crime to pay for sex with someone younger than eighteen.) The rumours said that Stephanie was blackmailing Johnston. The police, half-heartedly, began an investigation, but it went nowhere. Meanwhile, despite the gossip,

Johnston's life seemed to be settling down. In September 1993, he married Michelle. "Michelle was beautiful," he said many years later. "She was the only woman I ever really loved."

And then Stephanie Edwards, the prostitute whom Johnston also thought beautiful, was murdered. In January 1994, her frozen body, torn apart by wolves, was found in a snowbank. "There were more people at her funeral than there were at my father's," Johnston said. Years later he admitted that when he heard about Stephanie's murder, his first feeling was one of relief. But the relief was temporary. Because of the rumours, particularly those of blackmail, he quickly became a prime suspect. Perhaps, the Thunder Bay police conjectured, Johnston killed Stephanie to ensure her silence.

On February 10, 1994, the police interviewed Johnston. A few days later, Thunder Bay street people, who believed he'd killed Stephanie, marched up and down outside the courthouse carrying a coffin with his name on it. But it was quickly apparent to the police that Johnston was innocent. For one thing, he was at his stepdaughter's birthday party at the time Stephanie was probably murdered. In March, the police arrested Robert Wayne Valey Jr. for the crime, and in 1995 Valey was convicted. But rumours about Johnston persisted. A prostitute friend of Stephanie's, who was visiting Toronto around the time of the arrest, went to *The Globe and*

Mail with a story of murder, cover-up, and the use of underage hookers by prominent citizens of Thunder Bay. On March 30, *The Globe* sent Henry Hess, the paper's national police reporter, to Thunder Bay to investigate. Hess tracked Johnston to a motel in Kenora, where he was prosecuting an Anglican priest charged with indecently assaulting Aboriginal youths, but Johnston refused to say anything. Johnston waited with trepidation for *The Globe*'s story to appear. Two months went by and nothing happened. Johnston heaved another sigh of relief. Perhaps the nightmare was over. Life with Michelle was good.

In June 1994, Johnston went to Ottawa to attend his daughter Anne's dance recital. (That was the last time he ever saw Anne.) A few days later, he went on a business trip to the small community of Armstrong, 240 kilometres north of Thunder Bay. When he arrived back at Thunder Bay airport, a colleague met him, holding the latest edition of the *Thunder Bay Post*, a weekly tabloid. The *Post* reported that an unnamed Crown attorney was under police investigation for sex crimes. Now *The Globe and Mail*, which for unknown reasons had not yet published the story, went ahead and did so, perhaps feeling that its hand had been forced by the little weekly newspaper. On June 21, a story by Hess, buried on page 8 of the news section, began, "He holds a position of the utmost public trust.... Four teen-aged girls say he paid them for sexual services while they were minors...."[2] (It wasn't long before the stories about Agnew Johnston moved to *The Globe*'s front page.)

Now under considerable pressure, the Thunder Bay police reopened the investigation into Johnston that they had abandoned the year before. In the Ontario legislature, questions about what was going on were asked of Marion Boyd, the Attorney General. Johnston was put on paid leave from his job. On August 15, he was arrested and charged with five counts of obtaining, and one of attempting to obtain, the sexual services for consideration of a person under the age of eighteen, contrary to s. 212(4) of the Criminal Code. He was released on bail subject to normal conditions, including a curfew, a requirement that he not consume or possess alcohol, and that he report to the Balmoral Street Police Station every Wednesday. Of the requirement that he report to the Balmoral Street Police Station, Johnston later commented, "What goes around comes around. When I was a Crown, I always asked for that bail condition. It's tough to get to Balmoral Street. There's no public transport there. If you don't have a car, you have to walk for blocks, and that's miserable in the winter, trudging through the snow and wind. They—we—could have named a police station that's easier to get to."

Enveloped by rumour and speculation, waiting for his trial, suspended from his job, his reputation already ruined, Johnston entered a deep depression and began to drink heavily again, breaching one of his bail conditions. He said later that he was "afraid to go out, afraid to look people in the eye. The only time I went out was to go to the liquor store. I stayed home. I watched Jerry Springer on TV. My mind was addled." In January 1995, Johnston's lawyer, Robert Topp, negotiated a deal with the Crown: If Johnston pleaded guilty to one charge, the Crown would be satisfied with a conditional discharge. But Johnston, not thinking straight (as he later admitted), and not wanting to admit anything while his ailing mother, Christine Johnston, was still alive, refused the offer and fired Topp. Ian Scott, the Crown attorney charged with prosecuting Johnston (not to be confused with his namesake who was once Ontario's Attorney General), was amazed.[3] Johnston later agreed that he had made a terrible mistake not accepting the Crown's offer.

Months went by. Early in September 1995, Johnston received three letters with bad news: His suspension from his job as a Crown attorney was now without pay (he was finally fired on October 28, 1996, following his conviction); his bank refused to renew the mortgage on his house (the mortgage was renewed when Johnston found a guarantor); and the Law Society of Upper Canada was preparing to take disciplinary action against him (for breaching the condition of his bail that he not consume or possess alcohol). A few days later, Johnston tried to kill himself with an overdose of medication and alcohol. There was a suicide note, and a loaded gun was found in his house. A few days later, drunk, Johnston tried again. Michelle called the police, and they found Johnston dishevelled and bleeding, with the house in disarray.

Intense media interest in the story continued. On October 7, 1995, *The Globe and Mail* published a front-page story by Estanislao Oziewicz about "unusual circumstances" besetting the Johnston case "as it winds its way through the court system."[4] The newspaper suggested that the media had been "stonewalled" in various ways—for example, a hearing was moved from one courtroom to another without the media being told. The article continued:

> People who live here sometimes describe Thunder Bay as a city that still acts like a town. Some say that includes occasionally winking at the peccadilloes of the privileged or powerful.
>
> "Old Thunder Bay covers up for each other," commented one woman who has been here for the past decade.
>
> Various court-related officials in Thunder Bay are known to be sympathetic to what they consider to be Mr Johnston's plight....
>
> This week, one official described Mr Johnston as a cultured, intelligent man, interested in military artifacts and antiques who was beset by tragedy brought on by allegations made by prostitutes.

Right from the start, Johnston argued that he was being treated unfairly. Why had he been singled out? Why hadn't the police charged other prominent citizens of Thunder Bay who, as the police and many other people knew, patronized underage prostitutes? In March 1996, Johnston's new defence counsel, Peter Ross (Ross was the fourth, but not the last, lawyer Johnston engaged), sought a stay of proceedings. Charging only Johnston, he argued, constituted selective prosecution, which is an abuse of process that violates the Charter of Rights. Most unusually, during some of the pretrial proceedings dealing with the selective prosecution argument, lawyers representing unnamed third parties were present; these "third parties" were apparently prominent citizens of Thunder Bay, anxious to keep their names out of the record. One of these lawyers, from Toronto, later said that, once he sized the situation up, he got out of town quickly. "Hell," he said, "just by being there I was attracting attention, which was exactly the opposite of what my client wanted!" Ian Scott, the Crown attorney prosecuting Johnston, later said, "The whole town was freaking out. Who was going to be named? The case was creating havoc in Thunder Bay. It was a cancer." Justice Then, a former Toronto Crown attorney who was to preside over Johnston's trial, rejected the application for a stay:[5]

It is troubling that the police have not appeared, on the evidence, to be vigorous in

enforcing 212(4). However, it does not follow
that even if the police have turned a blind eye
to this offence in the past, and even if such
conduct can amount to neglect of duty, that
such police conduct can vitiate the present
charges unless it can be shown that the present
charges have been laid in bad faith or for
improper motives. This, in my opinion, the
applicant has not shown, nor has an improper
or discriminating exercise of discretion been
demonstrated by the mere fact that other
prominent citizens, who have been implicated,
have as yet not been charged.

In late June, Ross tried once more to get a stay
based on selective prosecution, this time relying on
an affidavit sworn on June 21 by a Thunder Bay
police officer called André Lichtenfeld. Lichtenfeld
had telephoned Ross and had offered to help in
Johnston's case. In his affidavit, Lichtenfeld said, "I
have personally seen prominent individuals in the
community, including members of the judiciary and
other prominent citizens on Simpson Street." He
said, "It was in fact general knowledge throughout
members of the uniformed branch of the Thunder
Bay Police Department that members of the judiciary
were seen on Simpson Street apparently making use
of the services of the prostitutes, as well as other
prominent citizens." The Lichtenfeld affidavit
continued:

If you were well known, you wouldn't get charged and if you were just an average citizen you might well get charged. It seems to me it is a question of "who knows who" and the situation "You don't charge *him*".... In my view, it is grossly unfair for Agnew Johnston to be prosecuted where others in the same and similar position are not being prosecuted under similar circumstances.

Johnston later said of Lichtenfeld that he "breached the 'blue wall' to try and help me, and ... has been pilloried and pursued by his superiors ... ever since."[6]

On June 24, Frank Sargent, a provincial court judge in Thunder Bay, was listening to a local news broadcast on the radio and heard about the Lichtenfeld affidavit. He quickly got a copy. On June 25 or 26, Peter Ross, Johnston's lawyer, was appearing before Judge Sargent in another case. Judge Sargent took Ross aside and spoke to him. It is not certain what passed between them, but in one version, which the Ontario Court of Appeal later accepted, Sargent told Ross that, since the Lichtenfeld affidavit did not name particular members of the judiciary, in effect all judges in the region were being accused of frequenting underage prostitutes. Ross, said Sargent, could not appear before him until the Johnston stay motion had been dealt with.

Ross was severely shaken by the meeting with Judge Sargent. When the new hearing for a stay in the

Johnston case started, in the middle of the afternoon of June 26, 1996, he sought an adjournment.[7] An impatient Justice Then, saying that there had already been too many delays, refused an adjournment and, after Lichtenfeld appeared as a witness, dismissed the motion for a stay, holding that the new evidence did not support an allegation of selective prosecution.

And so, at the beginning of July 1996, Johnston's trial, before Justice Then, finally began. John Ibbitson wrote in *The Vancouver Sun*:[8]

> As a big old Lincoln prowls past in the night, a prostitute dressed neck to thigh in flaming-red imitation patent leather curses the city that brought Agnew Johnston to trial.
>
> "It's crazy!" she screams. "Why are they picking on Agnew? What's he ever done wrong?"
>
> … The Agnew Johnston affair is about far more than a local lawyer who may or may not have strayed. In a pre-trial hearing, a Thunder Bay constable testified to having seen a number of prominent citizens—including local politicians, judges, business leaders and teachers—with women down on Simpson Street in the city's red-light district.
>
> Now people in this city of 114,000, which has long thought of its large red-light district as the price of being a port, are wondering just how much a part of their culture prostitution has become.

The family of the murdered prostitute Stephanie Edwards sat through the entire trial.

The first witness for the prosecution was Candus Chopp, a twenty-year-old butcher, who in the summer of 1992 had been a seventeen-year-old prostitute working Simpson Street. Candus described two incidents with Johnston. Once she gave him oral sex in his Jeep Cherokee and was paid $50. Two weeks later Johnston picked her and Kim Gavin up in the Jeep, and drove them to his mother's cottage on Lake Superior. (Kim, another underage prostitute, was Candus's roommate.) At the cottage, for $700, Kim performed oral sex on Johnston, while Candus, topless, watched. Kim, who was the second prosecution witness, corroborated Candus's account, and testified that she had sex with Johnston for money at his house on about ten occasions, sometimes with other underage prostitutes present.

The third witness, Shannon Kuchiak, gave evidence that she first met Johnston when he prosecuted a rape trial in which she was the complainant:

Kuchiak: I met him at the courthouse. He was acting as my lawyer trying to put this guy in jail. But he didn't.

Ian Scott, Counsel for the Crown: Alright. And how old were you at the time you met him at the courthouse?

Kuchiak: I believe I was 15.

Shannon testified that later Johnston paid her $400 to spend the night at his house, but her boyfriend (later killed in a traffic accident) suddenly arrived and took her home.

Scott: Were any words exchanged between your boyfriend and Mr. Johnston?

Kuchiak: I think my boyfriend had a few choice words. Like I remember him being very mad. But Agnew didn't say a word.

The fourth witness was Linda Vlassoff, who although a prostitute at the relevant times, was not underage. Linda gave evidence about two occasions when she and Kim Gavin had sex with Johnston at his house. Finally, Tanya Belmore testified about going to Johnston's house for sex, with Stephanie Edwards, in 1993 when she was fifteen years old.

Next, sergeants Roger Dobson and Milan Vilcek of the Thunder Bay police testified about the statement Johnston gave as part of the Stephanie Edwards murder investigation. After protests by defence lawyer Ross, the statement was admitted into evidence. In it, Johnston admitted that he had sex with underage prostitutes, including Stephanie.

Dobson: Agnew as you'll appreciate we've talked to most of the street people Stephanie's associations some of them also implicated you

as being involved in a sexual activity with them
Can you comment on that [*sic*]

Johnston: I was at that time Stephanie often
would bring someone else over with her and ah
I don't know their names and I haven't seen
them before but that was about three months
in my life when that was going on.... [*sic*]

Finally, Johnston took the stand. At the end of the
relatively brief examination by his lawyer, Peter Ross,
the following exchange occurred:

Ross: Mr. Johnston, you know that there are
five counts before the Court?

Johnston: Yes.

Ross: Each one of them alleging either that you
did obtain sexual services for consideration
from persons under the age of 18 or you
attempted to do so?

Johnston: Yes.

Ross: Are you guilty of any of those?

Johnston: No, I am not.

In his cross-examination, Ian Scott made much of
Johnston's admission, in his statement to the police
about Stephanie Edwards, that he had had sex with
underage prostitutes. Johnston replied to Scott that

he had lied in his statement. He said that he had been afraid of being considered a murder suspect. He had wanted the police to think that, as a customer of a number of underage prostitutes, he had no particular reason to single out and kill one of them.

Scott: Well, like what's in it for you to mislead the police about this?

Johnston: Because I think, and I've certainly given this a lot of thought, my feeling is, I was trying to convey that Stephanie Edwards was just one of a number, and so why should she have any particular hold over me. Because I was scared about being a leading candidate in her murder.

Scott: I see. So, you thought it would defuse the prospect of you as a suspect in the murder by suggesting that there might have been a bunch of other prostitutes over at your house?

Johnston: I suppose.

Scott: Well, you tell me. I mean, you were there. I wasn't there.

Johnston: I don't know, Mr. Scott, I don't know. I've had to live with this statement for two years, too. And I know what's there. I've read it and re-read it. It's like that hanging curve ball if you want to have back.

Scott: Oh, I'm sure you'd like to have it back. Because I'm going to suggest to you that the answer you gave to the police was absolutely dead true.

Johnston: It was not dead true. It wasn't then and it isn't now....

Scott: Just help me with why telling the police, lying to the police that you had hookers in your house helps you in terms of your alibi with respect to a crime that you didn't commit. Just help me with this.

Johnston: My feeling is, looking back at it, that I was trying to convey that she was one of a number of hookers and that I would have no particular reason to kill her.

Ian Scott later said that Johnston presented well as a witness; he was, said Scott, "mellifluous," and a "superb liar."

On September 20, Justice Then gave his verdict. Johnston was acquitted on one count because his accuser, although subpoenaed, did not appear. The missing witness was the hooker who had originally gone to *The Globe and Mail* with the Agnew Johnston story; the Crown did not chase after her because she was caring for a child who was ill with leukemia (and later died). He was acquitted on the counts involving Candus Chopp and Tanya Belmore

because Justice Then found Chopp and Belmore to
be persons of "unsavoury character" and their
evidence not credible. But he was convicted on the
counts relating to Kim Gavin (obtaining the services
of an underage prostitute) and Shannon Kuchiak
(attempting to obtain the services of an underage
prostitute). On the issue of Johnston's statement to
the police investigating the murder of Stephanie
Edwards, Then said, "I have no confidence whatever
in Mr. Johnston's explanation of the assertions made
in his statement to the police. These explanations, in
my opinion, are an affront to reason and common
sense." The judge rejected the defence submission
that Johnston was the victim of a conspiracy by a
close-knit group of prostitutes to accuse him of sex
with underage prostitutes because they blamed him
in some way for Stephanie Edwards's death. As
Justice Then gave his verdict, Johnston's wife,
Michelle, shouted at him, "You are not God" and
"Fuck you!" Police escorted her from the courtroom.

A sentencing hearing was held on November 19.
Two witnesses were heard, Edward Burton, a former
regional Crown attorney for the District of Thunder
Bay, and Alfred Petrone, the long-time Thunder Bay
lawyer who had employed Johnston before he
became a Crown attorney.[9] Burton testified to
Johnston's "exemplary character," his excellent reputation, and his "warm, caring" nature. He talked
about Johnston's alcohol problem:

He was, unquestionably, an alcoholic, and that is the only explanation I can offer for what he did. I know that he was at low-end in his life because of personal problems, family problems, and that this weighed on him. Being a decent caring sort of a person, I think the family problems got the better of him more so than they would most people. On top of that, being an alcoholic, it affected him, and he went out and did some pretty stupid things. It was an aberration in his life. It's not the Agnew Johnston that I know, not the Agnew Johnston that 125,000 other people in this area know.

Burton continued:

There was a cabal of people in the area who had an agenda. They wanted to bring disrepute down upon the administration of justice, and they've largely succeeded, I can tell you. They enlisted the aid of the press, the local daily newspaper and the local tabloid weekly, and the *Globe & Mail* in Toronto even got a hand on the act [*sic*], and they have tried to bring a lot of pressure to bear on the administration of justice to have Mr Johnston charged with a variety of offences, including the murder of a young prostitute. And they're apparently disappointed that he was never charged with that, but someone else was charged and convicted of that.

Then Petrone testified:

Today I still find him to be an honourable,
decent, caring individual as of this very
moment as I speak. He is the first to acknowledge that for a period of time those occur-
rences which he indulged in was morally
reprehensible. He's the first one to acknowledge that. That is not his true character. It is as
a Dr. Jekyll and Hyde situation. If his father
had not died at that point in time, if it was not
a breakup of a relationship, and the combination of alcohol, at least that set of circumstances triggered alcohol. And that was the
temporary demise of a superb honourable
human being. Once that sickness is cured, once
the abuse of alcohol evaporates, or if it has
evaporated, we're back to a very noble,
honourable and decent friend. That's his reputation that he enjoys in this community.

Affidavit evidence was given by Dr. J. O'Doherty,
chief of psychiatry at Mackellar General Hospital in
Thunder Bay, who had treated Johnston in 1995 and
had prepared a physician's statement in 1996 in
support of Johnston's application for long-term
disability payments. Dr. O'Doherty's evidence was
that Johnston suffered from a major depressive
disorder with mild alcohol dependence; the depression, said Dr. O'Doherty, was recurrent and chronic,

and would likely require treatment for the rest of Johnston's life.

On November 20, Justice Then sentenced Johnston to five months in jail—three months for the count involving Kim Gavin, and two months for the count relating to Shannon Kuchiak. His bail was continued pending an appeal. Johnston later said that at this point he made yet another mistake: "I should have served my time right away," he said. "I should have done what Martha Stewart did, get it over with. I could have appealed anyway."

In June 1997, Johnston, on bail and waiting for his appeal to be heard, pleaded guilty to assaulting a woman and breaching a bail condition forbidding him to use alcohol (his third breach of that condition), and was sentenced to eighty-nine days in jail to be served on weekends. The woman told police that Johnston came to her house drunk, had more drinks, and then threw her to the floor, put her in a head-lock, and sat on her chest. Johnston says that the woman was a prostitute who lured him to her house on the pretence that she had information that would help him, and then turned violent when he refused to give her any money. Michelle left Johnston in 2000. "She just couldn't take it any more," he said. Peter Ross, Johnston's defence counsel at trial, died in March 1998.

On September 6, 2000, the Ontario Court of Appeal dismissed Johnston's appeal.[10] The same day he reported to the Thunder Bay District Jail. The

first two days he was in "the hole"—segregated from
the general prison population, with the lights left on
twenty-four hours a day. Then he was moved out of
the hole and put to work in the laundry. He was
treated all right by guards and inmates, he says. Jail
was a tolerable experience. Johnston served ninety
days.

He was disbarred in January 2001, following a
hearing that he did not attend, for conduct unbecoming a barrister and solicitor.[11] The Law Society of
Upper Canada panel said this: "Clients need to be
able to trust their lawyers, both as individuals and as
members of the legal profession, and young persons
need to be able to trust adults and those in positions
of trust. The actions and misconduct of this lawyer
strike so strongly to the quick of the essence of the
legal profession that no other penalty is appropriate
or available." Johnston appealed his disbarment to a
law society appeal panel on the grounds that at the
original hearing his counsel did not plead his case
adequately; the appeal panel dismissed the appeal,
saying that his complaint about counsel didn't really
matter since disbarment was the only suitable punish-
ment given the "abhorrent nature of the member's
misconduct."[12]

When I went to see him in the winter of 2005,
Johnston was surviving on payments he received
from the Ontario Disability Support Program, a
government scheme for people who have substantial
physical or mental impairment and have very little

money. Since 1998, he had lived in what was once Alf
Petrone's law office, in the old Lyceum Theatre on
Cumberland Street in downtown Port Arthur, across
the street from the Prince Arthur Hotel and near the
old railway station and Lake Superior. In the window
of his room, facing out toward the street, was a
poster for Johnston's favourite football team, the
Green Bay Packers.

Johnston was pudgy. He had a bushy beard, wore
jeans, and sported a Green Bay Packers baseball cap.
He drove an old Jeep Cherokee (not the one
mentioned in his trial). He was edgy and emotional,
and, if he was upset, sometimes (he told me)
wouldn't eat for several days. "My mother called it
the MacKay stomach," he said (MacKay was his
mother's maiden name). He said he read a lot, particularly history, and "watched much too much television." He tried not to think about what happened to
him. When I saw him, he had a girlfriend, Debby, but
they didn't live together. Debby is four years older
than he is. He had some friends that stick by him, like
Alf Petrone and Ed Burton. He had a dog.
Occasionally he helped out at a law office down the
street, answering the telephone. He hoped to do
some paralegal work.

Johnston still has ambitions. He asked me, "Do
you think I could get readmitted to the bar? I'm
thinking I'd like to move further north and do legal
aid for Natives." Perhaps he could get readmitted.
He said that he doesn't drink much anymore. He

lives quietly. He has a stable relationship with Debby. He has friends in Thunder Bay's legal community who will support him. The crisis he created for the Thunder Bay elite is forgotten. Northern Aboriginal people could use his help.

The law society described Johnston's conduct as abhorrent. Alf Petrone, who has seen it all in many years of practising criminal law in Thunder Bay, described Johnston as an "honourable, decent, caring individual." Who is right? Perhaps both are right, in this tawdry tale of an ordinary man.

NINE

A LONELY TIME

Michael Bomek

Lawyer Michael Bomek was sued by his parents over a mortgage swindle, went to prison for sexually assaulting men who were his clients, ran a hot dog stand when he got out of jail, sold marijuana as well as frankfurters, pleaded guilty to drug charges, and then was convicted of fresh sex crimes, including ones involving children. But, once upon a time, he was an admired defence lawyer who upset the RCMP by his vigorous advocacy on behalf of the Cree of northern Saskatchewan, and who competed aggressively with lawyers in the small northern Manitoba town of Flin Flon, where he practised law after leaving Winnipeg. Some see Bomek, charming and articulate, as the classic psychopath, others, as a vulnerable and misunderstood man persecuted by homophobes, by cops angry at having their racist behaviour attacked, and by small-town lawyers whose comfortable lives were disturbed by a flamboyant outsider.

ON TUESDAY, SEPTEMBER 17, 2002, Michael Bomek, dressed in lawyer's robes, was leaving the courtroom in the northern Saskatchewan town of Pelican Narrows, where he had just appeared on behalf of a client. Suddenly, the RCMP appeared, arrested him, put him in handcuffs and took him away.[1]

Two days later he appeared in provincial court in Prince Albert, flown there from Pelican Narrows in an RCMP plane. He was charged with seven counts of sexual assault, two of obstructing justice, three of communicating for the purposes of prostitution or obtaining sexual services, and five of attempting to procure illicit sexual intercourse. The complainants were clients or former clients of Bomek: all were men, all were Aboriginal, and all but one were between the ages of eighteen and twenty-two (the one exception was older). Most lived in Pelican Narrows, although some were from other northern Cree communities, such as Sandy Bay and Deschambault Lake.

Sexual assault is an offence under s. 271 of the Criminal Code. For sex to be an assault, the complainant must not have consented to what occurred. There is no consent, says the Criminal Code, if it can be proven that the accused induced the complainant to have sex by abusing a position of

trust, power, or authority. And that, said the prosecutor, is what lawyer Bomek did when he had sex
with his clients.

When Bomek was arrested, the RCMP found a
one-way ticket from Minneapolis to Amsterdam in
his house. Considered a flight risk as a result, he was
denied bail. (Bomek says he was just planning a long
visit to friends in Europe.) He was sent to Prince
Albert's Community Training Residence, a halfway
house for provincial inmates. Further charges were
laid, bringing the total to forty-seven, involving
twenty people. On July 14, 2003, he pleaded guilty
to six counts of sexual assault, one count of communicating for the purpose of obtaining sexual services,
and one count of obstructing justice, and was
sentenced to three and a half years in prison (with
credit against that sentence for the nearly ten months
already spent in custody). In court the Crown prosecutor, Dennis Cann, described what led to the
various charges. Count number five, as described by
Cann, was typical of the rest:

> [X] was before the court in police custody. The
> accused had represented him on criminal
> matters before the court. The accused took
> him to—they used the washroom I guess on
> that particular location as an interview room,
> to discuss matters. The accused told the victim
> that if the accused, if he got the victim out of
> custody he could go home with him and he

also told the victim that he didn't have to pay the accused's legal bill, he could go home with him and "experiment" and party with the two of them.

The remaining thirty-nine counts were stayed as part of an agreement between Bomek and the Crown. Cann wanted to involve as few of the Aboriginal complainants as possible. "They were horribly embarrassed," he said, "and many had never even been south before and were frightened to come."[2] Bomek told me, "Do you think anyone who had sex with me really would want to admit it in front of a crowd of people? It would have been long and arduous and I would no doubt have prevailed with some success but I chose not to hurt some of the people I cared about."[3] Cornelius Ballantyne, a spokesman for the Peter Ballantyne Cree Nation (a Cree band of about six thousand, approximately half of whom live in Pelican Narrows), has a different point of view. He has said that staying the charges denied closure to the victims and is another example of the justice system failing Aboriginal people.

Maggie Siggins, in *Bitter Embrace: White Society's Assault on the Woodland Cree*,[4] describes the Michael Bomek story in almost apocalyptic terms. She sees it as a case study of white-Cree relations and part of a historical pattern. In her prologue, she writes about the impact of Bomek on the people of Pelican Narrows: "Once again a white authority figure had

infiltrated their community, full of promises, bloated
with best intentions, only to despoil and debauch. I
began to see reflected in the Bomek case the entire
sad history of white-Indian relations."[5]

I WENT TO SEE Michael Bomek in the spring of 2004,
a few days after he was let out of prison on parole. He
was living in Prince Albert, Saskatchewan, in the
windowless basement of an electronics store owned
by a friend. The store is in a low-rise red brick
building constructed as law offices in 1911. Next
door is a Metis drop-in centre, and on the next block
is a down-at-the-heels hotel favoured by Aboriginal
people. As I drove up to the building, Bomek,
wearing shorts and a sweatshirt, was picking up trash
from the sidewalk in front. He was fifty-five years old,
of medium height, a little paunchy, clean-shaven with
short hair, an earring in his left ear.

Bomek invited me into the store for coffee. He
showed me an office he had set up for himself in a
spare room. It looked like a lawyer's office. Shelves
along one wall were lined with law books. Framed
certificates and citations filled another. There were
pictures of his two daughters by his first wife (he has
been married twice). One daughter is a doctor, the
other, a physiotherapist. A computer sat on a modern
desk.

"I knew Lord Denning," he said suddenly, for no
apparent reason. (Lord Denning, now dead, headed
England's Court of Appeal and was a cult figure,

particularly among law students, in the seventies and eighties. He was famous for his eccentric and path-breaking judgments, and for homespun wisdom.) "I have four of Denning's books, autographed, and he sent me a twelve-page letter," Bomek told me.

I asked him what he was doing these days. "Not much," he said. "It's hard to get a job when you're gay, bankrupt, and just got out of jail. See that?" He pointed to a bicycle propped against the wall. "That's how I get around. I have a motorcycle in the shop, but I can't get it out because I don't have $390 to pay the repair bill."

How did an educated professional end up like this? That day and the next, we talked about his life. Bomek was born in Shoal Lake, a small town in northwestern Manitoba, and grew up in Brandon. Before becoming a lawyer, he owned a pizza business. He graduated from the University of Manitoba law school in 1985, articled in Winnipeg, but soon moved to Flin Flon where he built up a strong practice, mostly among the Cree of northern Manitoba and Saskatchewan. Bomek told me that criminal law was his passion. Why? "Because it was easy. And I loved dealing with people."

Bomek quickly achieved a high profile in northern Manitoba and Saskatchewan, particularly by acting as defence counsel in dramatic criminal cases. In 2000, for example, he represented Gerald Carter, an Aboriginal man described by the Saskatoon *StarPhoenix* as a "violent sexual predator" who had been on "a 15-year crime spree."[6] The Crown sought a dangerous offender designation for Carter, permitting an indefinite sentence. Saskatchewan Chief Justice Frank Gerein, presiding over Carter's trial, found that he was a dangerous offender, but sentenced him to ten years rather than giving him an indefinite sentence. It was Chief Justice Gerein who, three years after the Carter trial, accepted Bomek's own plea of guilty and sentenced him.

Many people in Flin Flon held Bomek in high regard, both as a lawyer and a person. Lois Burke runs the Greenstone Community Futures Development Corporation. Greenstone provides self-employment training and assistance for small businesses, administers loan funds, and assists the region in economic strategic planning. Bomek was Greenstone's lawyer for several years, and Burke says his legal work was outstanding. "Michael had an excellent reputation as a lawyer, and he gave a lot of time to the community. He was a very good fundraiser, for example, for the Crisis Centre. He presented himself well, and was very likeable."[7]

Arnold Goodman, a lawyer who now practises in Watrous, Saskatchewan, worked for five years in Bomek's Flin Flon office. Goodman said he liked Bomek:

He was a very good lawyer. People liked and trusted him; he had a lot of friends. He was a regular guy who went astray. It was stress-related. Stress pushed him over the edge, working too hard, financial pressures. But he never showed the stress. He was an upbeat guy—his point of view was that everything is okay, we're moving ahead. He listened to inspirational tapes while he was driving around.[8]

Bomek first became interested in the law when he was sued by his parents in 1981. His father had a grade three education, could barely read, and worked as a labourer in Brandon. His mother had a grade nine education. Their modest home was their only significant asset. In 1977, Bomek's pizza business was in financial difficulty, and the Dauphin Plains Credit Union was pressuring him to reduce his overdraft. With the connivance of the credit union, he arranged for his parents to mortgage their house with the proceeds being used to reduce the loan. Bomek took the mortgage papers to his parents who signed without reading them. He promised that he would make the mortgage payments, but didn't honour his promise.

The courts found the Bomek mortgage unconscionable and set it aside.[9] As Bomek puts it, "That's when I decided I wanted to be the guy who sues rather than the guy who gets sued. That's when I decided to become a lawyer." The case, he says now, "did not in any way affect the relationship with my parents." In an ironic twist, Bomek's lawyer in this litigation, Lawrence Greenberg, in a 1998 disciplinary hearing of the Law Society of Manitoba, pleaded guilty to thirty-seven counts of professional misconduct and was indefinitely suspended from the practice of law.[10]

By his own admission, Bomek was a very poor manager of money. On September 6, 2002, just days before he was arrested, he was declared bankrupt. His principal creditor was the Government of Canada, for unpaid income taxes of about $250,000. Where did the money go? "Well," Bomek says, "I was building a house and I couldn't afford to build the house and pay taxes at the same time." When I asked him if he missed the status he used to have— once a prominent lawyer, now an ex-convict—he said, "I'll tell you what I miss. Before, I'd go into a jewellery store, look at a watch, and say I'll take that one, the one with the titanium bracelet. It didn't matter how much it was. I wouldn't even ask the price. I miss that."

But Arnold Goodman says that Bomek wasn't a high liver. "He drove a Ford Tempo. Sometimes when he was travelling he'd sleep in the car, at a campground. Mind you, in my view he was over-housed. He built this $400,000 house; it was for his wife Beatrice, we called her Queen Bea. And he ran a Cadillac office, the best photocopying machine, and all that."

Bomek says he had had sex with both men and women beginning when he was about eighteen. He started sleeping with male Aboriginal clients after his

second marriage collapsed in 1997. Bomek says that
his second wife, Beatrice, ran off with her high school
sweetheart without warning. He came home late at
night from a business trip to Brandon to find her
gone. Sex with clients began when Peter (not his real
name), a young Aboriginal man appealing his
sentence after being convicted of spousal assault and
represented by Bomek, suddenly kissed him passionately in an interview room at the Pelican Narrows
community hall that functioned as a courthouse
when the judge was in town. "You're gay, I can tell,"
Peter told Bomek. Peter was twenty-five years old,
had a grade ten education, was the father of five children, and lived on welfare.

Peter went to prison for nine months, but as soon
as he got out he came to Bomek's luxurious house on
Lake Athapapuskow, and a sexual relationship began
that lasted more than two years. "That relationship
meant a lot to me," said Bomek, "a lot more than
either of my marriages." Shortly after Bomek was
arrested, Peter attempted suicide.

Meanwhile, said Bomek, the RCMP was gun-
ning for him because he stood up for Aboriginal
people. "I complained about conditions in the cells
in Pelican Narrows. The food was bad, there
weren't any blankets, they wouldn't let the Indians
shower and clean up before court appearances. The
cops called me 'Indian lover.'"[11] Back in the cells,
after the kissing incident, Peter had told whoever
would listen that he thought his lawyer was gay.

"Because of that," said Bomek when addressing the judge at his sentencing, "the RCMP asked all of my clients, male clients, if I ever traded sexual favours for legal services." Aboriginal men started showing up at Bomek's house. "They were all gay," said Bomek. "They slept with me willingly. It was my private life. What was wrong with it? Where does my professional life end and my personal life begin?"

At his sentencing, Bomek's lawyer said:

It doesn't matter that in some cases, the victims themselves, at one time or another, made sexual advances to Mr Bomek. The fact of the matter is that Mr Bomek ought not to have had this kind of a relationship with his clients and that is what makes the whole thing wrong. Mr Bomek understands that now and admits that it is wrong.

Bomek himself, at the sentencing, described how "a number of people ... would call me and say, look, I'm gay and I understand you might be; could we get together." And then:

I forgot that just because it's 9:30 at night and the doorbell rings and someone comes to my door, that he's a client, that even though my lifestyle continues that my duty as a solicitor must continue as well.... I was so interested

and so happy that someone rang my bell, it was
a lonely time for me.

Friends and former colleagues of Bomek all say that
he was devastated when Beatrice left him, and that he
fell into a deep depression.

The story of Bomek's troubled legal career goes
beyond sexual transgression. In March 2004, he was
disbarred by the Law Society of Manitoba in proceedings that, formally at least, had nothing to do with his
criminal convictions. It was the conclusion of a long
disciplinary history that, in the words of Kristen
Dangerfield, senior general counsel of the law society,
was "integrity related and not competency related."[12]
Dangerfield described Bomek's conduct over a seven-
year period, involving dishonesty and failure to
discharge his duties, as "disgraceful and dishonourable in every respect." The chairman of the disciplinary panel commented, "Bomek should never have
been a practising lawyer." (He was disbarred in
Saskatchewan in October 2003 following his criminal
conviction.)

Bomek's disciplinary problems in Manitoba
began with a law society reprimand in 1988; he had
admitted to swearing a false statutory declaration in
connection with a compromise between himself and
a creditor. In 1994, Bomek was disciplined three
times: He was cautioned for failing to disclose to a
client a potential conflict of interest; he was fined for
failing to disclose to the vendor of a business (when

acting for the prospective purchasers) that his client's cheque for the balance due at closing was subject to conditions that probably could not be met; and he was fined again for placing himself in another conflict of interest position.[13] In early 2002, Bomek was fined yet again for eight counts of professional misconduct involving five separate estate matters: The principal complaints were that he withdrew money from his trust account for payment of fees and disbursements prior to performing legal services, and charged fees in excess of the prevailing law society tariff.[14] Later in 2002, the law society served Bomek with four new citations containing a total of twenty-six counts of professional misconduct. These new citations covered a wide range of disciplinary offences: Some were connected with Bomek's borrowing money from three of his clients, and others had to do with various other transactions involving clients.

Shortly before his arrest on September 17, 2002, Bomek struck a deal with the Law Society of Manitoba. He agreed to turn over his practice to Lore Mirwaldt and Scott Gray, partners in a respected legal practice at The Pas, Manitoba (and married to each other); to take a year away from the practice of law; and on his return to practise only criminal law, subject to the supervision of Mirwaldt and Gray. But his arrest overtook this arrangement, and disbarment, ostensibly for reasons unconnected with the arrest, followed.

Gavin Wood represented Bomek at his Manitoba disbarment proceedings. Wood is a senior and well-respected Winnipeg litigator and former bencher of the Law Society of Manitoba. He has had a relationship with Michael Bomek for many years, as co-counsel on Bomek files from time to time, and as a friend. Wood has a generous view of Bomek's history. "I believe Michael was genuinely interested in giving service in the north," he told me.[15] Wood continued:

> It's not fair to describe him as manipulative, as some people have done. Complex, multi-dimensional, but not manipulative. In the legal community, there are two very different views of Michael. Not everyone thinks he is a bad man. And by the way, he was a very hard worker. Sometimes on the way from one small town to another, he would sleep at night in his car, by the side of some lonely road....
>
> I think Michael was fighting demons. I've often thought about it, but I don't know exactly what the demons were. Maybe, for a time at least, he felt guilty about his homosexuality. I knew him for years, and he never told me he was gay.

Wood paused. "Michael's a strange guy. He sent me a birthday card from jail."

Lore Mirwaldt and Scott Gray, who were supposed to take over Bomek's practice, are sympathetic to him. (They represented Bomek in his divorce from Beatrice, his second wife.) Mirwaldt told me this:

It's true that Michael was a bit of a wheeler-dealer, and had a tendency to get into strange predicaments. But he went to the mat for his clients. And he was capable of great acts of kindness. Michael would give his last $20 to a man begging in the street.[16]

I told Mirwaldt and Gray that Bomek attributed a lot of his disciplinary problems to political infighting in the Flin Flon legal community, and particularly to his rivalry with the other criminal lawyer in town. Gray thought there was a lot of truth to this: "Flin Flon is a boiling pot. It's a hard mining town, it's abandoned. We would never open up an office there."

Arnold Goodman told much the same story. He said that Bomek and the other lawyer arranged for complaints about each other to be made to the law society. "It was tit for tat," said Goodman. "Also, Bomek was regarded as an interloper."

I asked Mirwaldt and Gray about Bomek's relationship with the RCMP. Gray replied:

In a criminal practice you're bound to butt heads with the cops. You can't give them even a toehold to question your integrity. And this is not the big city: you can't hide up here. But, that said, at the time, I questioned the validity of the charges against him.

Mirwaldt added:

The number one thing that bugs me is the way they arrested Michael. They should have rung his office and said, we have a warrant for your arrest and want to make arrangements for you to turn yourself in. But they arrested him as he walked out of the courtroom and then they put him on the same RCMP plane as some of the people he had just been representing. They gave him no dignity.

In his sentencing submissions, Dennis Cann suggested that a probation order prohibit Bomek from going to northern Saskatchewan for his own good: "Mr. Bomek, to put it lightly, would not be welcome back in that area ... as I've expressed to his counsel and the police have advised me, should he attend to that area his personal safety would in all likelihood be in danger." The judge declined to restrict Bomek in this way. Bomek's defence lawyer said, "He knows that it would be unhealthy for him to be wandering about certain communities in northern Saskatchewan." I asked Mirwaldt and Gray what the Aboriginal people thought of Michael.

They said that they didn't hate him at all. "Michael used to take groceries to families on the reserve," Mirwaldt told me.

> Other lawyers would fly in and out on the court plane. Not Michael. I think he could work for the Aboriginals again. Being gay is difficult. There is a sizeable homosexual Aboriginal community—but it's underground. By the way, we never knew he was gay. I was stunned when the story came out.

Goodman was also amazed: "I had no idea he was gay. Even after Beatrice left him, he dated women."

After a final meeting with Bomek over breakfast at Tim Hortons, I left Prince Albert and drove west along the Yellowhead Highway to North Battleford, to see Dennis Cann, the Crown attorney who handled his case. Cann is in his early fifties and has been a prosecutor for most of his professional life. He is calm, measured, and purposeful. A plaque on his office wall announces a recent hole-in-one on the golf course. "Bomek is a psychopath," Cann said.

> Bomek is out for Bomek. He is only interested in self-gratification. He uses people. He has no moral sense. He abused his authority and privilege. All that matters to him is not getting caught. He just doesn't get it. There's no more to be said.

After talking with Cann, I headed for Pelican Narrows, 550 kilometres by highway from North Battleford, northeast across the plains of Saskatchewan, a place written about so dramatically by Maggie Siggins in *Bitter Embrace*. As you drive beyond Prince Albert, there are few towns and little traffic. The last 45 kilometres of the trip is on a bleak and depressing gravel side road. The occasional truck heading in the opposite direction throws up blinding dust and you must stop the car until the dust settles.

At the entrance to Pelican Narrows is Mista Nosayew Outfitters (*mista nosayew* means "big fish" in Cree). Arthur Bear runs the place. It includes a tiny restaurant where you can get coffee and have a chat. Someone asks me, "Are there trees in Toronto like here?" I ask Arthur Bear if business is good, and he says, "No. I need to publicize my business, but I don't know how to do that and I have no money." The town, population about one thousand, is the centre of the Peter Ballantyne Cree Nation. (Peter Ballantyne was the first chief of the band, elected in 1900.) The town's Cree name is Wapowikoscikan, which means "Narrows of Fear." The nearest places to buy supplies are the mining towns of Creighton and Flin Flon, both about 120 kilometres away.

Government underfunding and poor money management by the Native band has created a housing crisis in Pelican Narrows. Living conditions have been compared to those in Afghanistan. Litter is everywhere. There are few private facilities—a general store, a taxi service, a church—and little sign of commercial or community life. Visual bleakness signals poverty, depression, and inability to deal effectively with the outside world. Only large buildings provided by government—schools, the health centre, and a community arena—are modern and well maintained, gleaming like giant spaceships that have arrived from another world. The RCMP detachment is the best-looking building of all, clean and neat, with a well-tended lawn in front and the Canadian flag snapping in the breeze.

WHEN HE GOT OUT OF JAIL, Michael Bomek was for a time the proprietor of a hot dog stand on the banks of the North Saskatchewan River. Then, on September 28, 2005, the Prince Albert Police Service issued a press release:

On the 27 September 2005 at approx. 11:30 a.m. the Joint Forces Unit comprised of members of the Prince Albert City Police and RCMP entered into a Drug Investigation which resulted in the arrest of a 56 year old male from Prince Albert. He is charged with Possession for the Purpose of Trafficking (Marihuana) under the Controlled Drugs and Substances Act and Breach of Probation.

A further search was conducted at a residence in the 1000 Blk 1st Ave. W. Police seized approximately 171 marihuana cigarettes and approximately 33 grams of loose marihuana worth an approximate street value of $1360.00.

In addition, police also seized an undisclosed amount of cash as proceeds of crime and a hotdog vending cart as offence related property to the drug trafficking.

Charged with Possession for the Purpose of Trafficking in a controlled substance is James Michael Bomek Dob: 11 February 1949. Bomek has been held in custody and will be appearing in Provincial Court this morning.

The police had seized Michael Bomek's hot dog stand.

Some weeks later, the story took another and ominous twist. CBC Radio aired this report on November 9, 2005:

A former lawyer from Flin Flon, Man. accused of possessing child pornography, sexual touching of a minor and drug dealing has been denied bail and remains behind bars in Prince Albert. James Michael Bomek, who is in is mid-50s, faces a total of 18 charges. Many of the charges are alleged to have occurred while Bomek was on parole or probation.[17]

Jonathon Naylor reported on November 21 in *The Reminder*, Flin Flon's daily newspaper, that the charges stemmed from incidents that allegedly occurred in and around Prince Albert between August 2004 and September 2005.[18] The new alleged offences included one charge of sexual touching of a minor under the age of fourteen; two charges of inviting, counselling or inciting a person under fourteen to engage in sexual touching; one charge of sexually touching a minor under eighteen; and one charge of obtaining for consideration the sexual services of a person under eighteen. There were also two charges each of possessing child pornography and making child pornography, and two charges of sexually assaulting a male.

Naylor has covered the Bomek story from the beginning. In several conversations with him, I had expressed sympathy for Bomek and an expectation that his life would now improve. After the new charges were laid, Naylor sent me an email and asked, "Do you feel Bomek suckered you with an act?"[19] Perhaps he did sucker me. Naylor says that these days it is hard to find anybody in Flin Flon with a good word for Michael Bomek. Early in April 2006 he pleaded guilty in Prince Albert provincial court to trafficking in marijuana, possession for the purpose of trafficking, and breach of probation; in May he was sentenced to a year in jail. His trial on the sex charges took place in December 2006, in Prince Albert. Bomek pleaded not guilty. On January 10, 2007, he was found guilty of six offences, including sexual assault and making and possessing child pornography. On January 19, Justice Grant Currie sentenced him to three and a half years in prison. Bomek's own lawyer described the sentence as "fair."

TEN

COAL MINER'S SON AND ROCK SOLID GUY

Reeves Matheson

A coal miner's son from Cape Breton married his high school sweetheart, became a lawyer, and was elected to the provincial legislature. He gave a maiden speech of unusual eloquence and power. Four days before he gave that speech, he had been disbarred. Later he was convicted of theft and fraud. It all happened he told the judge, because he suffered from attention deficit hyperactivity disorder (ADHD).

REEVES MATHESON WAS BORN in 1952, in the hardscrabble coal mining town of Glace Bay, on the beautiful Nova Scotia island of Cape Breton, where "the wild road clambers along the brink of the coast."[1] He was a miner's son, the fifteenth of seventeen children.

His father, Murdoch Matheson, had to buy a second house on Sixth Street, next door to the original home, to accommodate his huge family. Murdoch, who died of lung cancer in 1979, was a prominent figure in Glace Bay left-wing politics.

After high school, Reeves Matheson went to study in Halifax, first at Saint Mary's University, and then at Dalhousie law school where he graduated in 1976. When his studies in the city were finished, Matheson, a true Cape Bretoner, returned home. Michael Greenberg, the New York author who spends his summers in Cape Breton, has written that "those who never forsake Cape Breton enjoy a special reverence. They are ... uncorrupted."[2] Or, as a very senior Nova Scotia politician put it to me when we started chatting about Matheson, "once you cross the Canso Causeway into Cape Breton, you're in a different world." (Perhaps my politician acquaintance had a somewhat different point in mind than Michael Greenberg.)

Matheson became a respected lawyer in Glace Bay, and was town solicitor for ten years. He coached junior hockey and taught religion in the Catholic parish church of St. Anne's. He married his high school sweetheart, Valerie Turnbull, and had four children. He bought a house on South Street, where the "mucky mucks" lived, paying $100,000, a lot of money in Glace Bay. He lived in the fancy part of town, but, like his father, Reeves Matheson was a hard-working member of the New Democratic Party.

He was regarded as a "rock solid guy" with ideal working-class credentials. Matheson reached the apex of his career on March 24, 1998, when, representing the NDP, he was elected to the Nova Scotia legislature by the voters of Cape Breton East.

In the dramatic general election of 1998, the NDP won nineteen seats, the same number as the governing Liberals led by Premier Russell MacLellan, another lawyer from Cape Breton. Every seat was vital, and so it was startling when, only six weeks after being elected, Reeves Matheson, the rock solid guy, resigned from the NDP caucus and announced that he would sit as an independent. It had suddenly become public knowledge that he was being investigated by the Nova Scotia Barristers' Society for stealing money from a client's trust fund. The investigation had started the previous November, long before the election, and his licence to practise law had been suspended a few weeks after that. The Cape Breton regional police were interested in the matter, looking into possible theft and fraud. Matheson was the only NDP candidate who had not filed a party form that asked nominees to declare any criminal or professional investigations that might prove embarrassing. It is not clear how much the NDP knew about his trouble when Matheson was running for the legislature.

On June 1, 1998, Matheson was disbarred.[3] In an agreed statement of facts, he admitted that, between November 1995 and April 1998, he had deposited cheques into his personal account that were payable only to his lawyer's trust account. He admitted that he had misappropriated other client funds. Similar problems in his earlier legal career in Glace Bay now came to light. In 1981, he had been "severely reprimanded" by the barristers' society. (Also in 1981, his then law partner, Martin Kennedy, had been disbarred and was sent to prison for two years for misappropriation of trust funds.) In 1991, the barristers' society had fined him $5,000 plus costs for professional misconduct. That was because Matheson hadn't paid money owed to Mickey Ludlow, a client. Mickey, who couldn't read or write, wasn't just a client; he was also one of Matheson's oldest friends. Halifax's *Daily News* reported that "the young Matheson played cowboys and Indians with Mickey Ludlow, who lived down the street; they would stop playing at about 4 p.m., when Matheson's parents called him inside to say the rosary."[4]

On June 5, Reeves Matheson rose in the Nova Scotia legislature to give his maiden speech. His wife, Valerie, looked on from the visitors' gallery. The circumstances were extraordinary. He had resigned from his party; his political career was over. Four days earlier, he had been disbarred; his career as a lawyer was finished. He faced the possibility of jail. But Matheson gave an eloquent and lengthy speech of considerable substance:

Glace Bay is a proud mining community. There are no mines there now but I can assure you that growing up and coming home from school I can remember bare-faced miners, their faces blackened, coming from No. 26 Colliery and from No. 20 Colliery and walking down the roads of New Aberdeen to their houses, with their children coming from school. I can remember a time when despite tough, economic conditions, there was a spirit of pride, a spirit of hope and a real promise of a future for my community. Those men, those miners, were the symbol of that hope and the hopes and aspirations of all of the people in the community in which I lived.

Things have never been easy in Glace Bay, at least not in my experience. We have and the community has always existed and functioned under the spectre of systemic unemployment that seemed to defy every reasonable attempt to come up with some solution to make it go away. We have had unemployment rates of 25 per cent, 30 per cent, 40 per cent and indeed, Mr. Speaker, if you can believe it, at times quoted to be as high as 50 per cent in a community of approximately 20,000 people.

As a result, we have had to watch year after year, month after month, every day, our young people leave because there is no work, to go away because there is no reasonable prospect for them to raise a family and to live out their lives in the town with some degree of economic certainty and some degree of reasonable expectation for the families that I am sure they all wished and wanted to raise in Glace Bay.

He went on at great length to attack government policy with respect to Cape Breton, particularly federal government policy. Then, at the end of his speech, Matheson turned to personal matters:

Mr. Speaker, I want to conclude by just briefly addressing those circumstances that you are, I am sure, all aware of in relation to my personal affairs. I want to assure this House that in due course, I will do the honourable thing but I also want to assure this House that the in honour [*sic*]—and its very definition—covers a broad range of responsibilities. You can do one thing and be dishonourable and do something else and be honourable. I know and I feel in my heart that I was elected by the people of Glace Bay to bring a message to this House on their behalf and there are significant questions in the next few weeks that this House will have to address that very much embody the type of message that they asked me to send. So I intend to stay here long enough to ensure that the voice of my constituents, at least, on those issues is heard and I intend to stay, as hobbled as I am by my personal situation, to vote in the interests of and on behalf of the people who sent me here to deliver that message.

Mr. Speaker, I will in due course do the honourable thing and until that time I intend to lend my voice to the people who elected me to stay and speak on their behalf and to make sure that they are heard on those issues they sent me here to speak on. It may not be a long time, it may be a short time, but they have the right, they deserve to be heard and it is my intention to stay and vote on their behalf on those issues as they are presented over the next couple of weeks in this House.[5]

The Halifax *Daily News* was not impressed. A June 8 editorial commented, "So far, the new MLA has represented constituents mostly in silence, sitting at a distance from the embarrassed NDP members, who wish he could be much further away—at least as far as Glace Bay."[6] His former NDP riding association demanded that he resign his seat. "I don't have a response to that right now," Matheson replied. There was speculation that he was hanging on because, deprived of his income as a lawyer, he desperately needed the $42,000 salary that went with his seat in the legislature. On June 17, Alexa McDonough, then national leader of the NDP, added her voice to those demanding his resignation. On June 21, *The Daily News* reported yet more reaction.[7] Jeremy Ackerman, a former Cape Breton East MLA, said that Matheson "must have been driven to this by extreme circumstances." Mary Hamood, who ran a store where Matheson used to "hang around" when he was a boy, and said she regarded him as a son, claimed she was overcharged by Matheson when he acted for her in a property transaction. Hamood said, 'I'm very hurt he did turn out that way.... He came from a coal-mining family, and a very big family; he was probably trying to break the barrier." *The Daily News* reported that Hamood wanted to encourage Matheson "to step down gracefully, and come home to his people." People also came forward who, as it turned out, never had much time for Matheson. Russell MacKinnon, a surveyor from Sydney who was Nova Scotia's Minister of Labour, said that he had had bad business dealings with Matheson early on, and that Matheson showed "greed, and the feeling that he was above the law, above reproach." Other locals claimed that Matheson didn't pay his bills.

On June 29, Matheson gave an unusual response to those asking that he step down. He introduced a private member's bill allowing for the recall of members of the legislative assembly. The bill gave voters the power to get rid of an MLA before the next election if he broke the law or failed to live up to promises. If 40 percent of voters in an MLA's district signed a recall petition, a by-election would be called. The following day, the Halifax *Daily News* reported on the initiative: "Disgraced lawyer Reeves Matheson wants to make it easier to get rid of MLAs who are, well, like him.…'If there's anything that is patently clear as the result of the debate with respect to my personal circumstances, it's that there is not a very clear mechanism for an electorate to assess the conduct of an MLA,' Matheson said with no trace of irony." *The Daily News* described reporters covering this event as "dumbfounded."[8]

When the legislature resumed sitting in October, Matheson was still there. The pressure for him to resign increased. Reported *The Daily News* on October 16, "Matheson was under pressure to quit his seat throughout the spring session, and promised to consult his constituents during the summer. He said five or six constituents dropped by his office daily and not a single one wanted him to resign."[9]

In May 1999, Premier MacLellan's government was defeated on a budget vote. On June 18, a general election was called for July 27. In Cape Breton East, Matheson's childhood friend, Cecil Saccary, a worker at the Modern Co-op, was picked to replace him as the NDP candidate. The Liberal candidate was Dave Wilson, known as "Talk Back" because he once ran a phone-in show on the local radio station. Tera Camus wrote in Halifax's *Chronicle-Herald* on July 10, "Home to traditional but dying industries such as coal mining and fishing, this blue-collar political hotbed is ripe for the picking."[10] On July 27, John Hamm's Conservatives won a majority. Cecil Saccary got five votes more than Talk Back Wilson, but a judicial recount on August 17 reversed the result, giving Talk Back five votes more than Cecil. Cecil then petitioned the courts under the Nova Scotia Controverted Elections Act. In January 2001, Justice Merlin Nunn, finding voting irregularities but rejecting any suggestion of corrupt practices, threw out the election and ordered a by-election.[11] In the new election, Talk Back won by several hundred votes. Just another Nova Scotia election, said some. Reeves Matheson was no longer a political figure.

Meanwhile, on December 16, 1998, Matheson had been charged by the Cape Breton Regional Police with four counts of theft, four counts of fraud, three counts of uttering forged documents, and one count of breach of trust.[12] He refused to comment to reporters on these charges. The wheels of justice turned at their usual glacial speed. Two years went by. On November 7, 2000, he pleaded guilty to five charges involving breach of trust, theft, and forgery (the remaining charges were dropped). Perhaps the most egregious charge (Matheson pleaded guilty to it) was Count Three, criminal breach of trust; he was charged with misappropriating $55,000 of a $100,000 settlement he negotiated on behalf of a child whose mother was killed in an automobile accident. On April 12, 2001, sentence was imposed. The judge described a pre-sentence report as "extremely supportive and reflects a range of support from the offender from his family, his friends and his former co-workers." The judge went on:[13]

> Other friends spoke favourably of Mr. Matheson, including his inability to say no when asked to assist persons, suggesting in some cases these persons had taken advantage of him....
>
> A former colleague in the Town of Glace Bay, at a time when Mr. Matheson was the town solicitor, stated he continued to trust Mr. Matheson and described him as a great guy who was very well liked and well respected throughout the community....
>
> Mr. Clarke, the former mayor of Glace Bay, with whom Mr. Matheson would have worked as Town Solicitor, described him as a man who was always upright, courteous, obliging and professional, noting he was not a "high living man" and his focus was on family and community.
>
> Mr. Matheson was also active in his church, including teaching Catholic Confirmation classes. The coordinator of the program described him as a good person and an excellent family man.

After he was charged, in an inspired moment, Matheson had himself tested for ADHD. The test was positive (two of his four children also tested positive). His family physician gave testimony to the court:

When I first saw Reeves he had combined type of symptoms of marked inattention, very concrete thinking, inability to recognize events as they would pertain, spur of the moment decisions, impulsive decisions.... They are not able to process and put their thoughts together and hence they are unable to express them. They need a lot more time. For example children in school need time to write exams, extra time, they need extra time for homework, they need extra time for projects. The same thing applies in the adult life, they are scattered all over. Their thoughts are scattered. And their thoughts have to be put together.... They suffer emotionally, they suffer academically, they suffer in their work life and personal life. And he had several symptoms....

They are going to defer things, they procrastinate, they wait til the last moment til panic hits them....

Follow through is a major problem.... Procrastination, the fear of failure ...

One of the things that adult ADHDs of high IQ are good at is variety, novelty and thrill. This is one of the impulse acts. This is the spur of the moment. They get bored with things that are desk work, written work, things like that.

His wife Valerie's reaction to the diagnosis of ADHD was described in the pre-sentence report: "She said, in hindsight, she realizes that indices of this disorder appeared in some of the behaviour exhibited by Mr. Matheson, in that while he commanded attention and was able to speak to anyone, he had no business sense and while his intentions were often good, he would procrastinate and fail to follow through on given tasks. Also, in support of Mr. Matheson were his two sisters, who said some of the characteristics exhibited by their brother were now, they believed, a result of this disorder. They spoke of his procrastination, his preoccupation, and his failure to follow through on tasks." The judge quoted at length from a book on ADHD that argued that "this disorder is fundamentally a mental problem of self-control."

Reeves Matheson, suffering from ADHD, was given a conditional sentence—two years less a day, to be served in the community (a sentence commonly referred to as "house arrest.") He was required to make restitution to the Nova Scotia Barristers' Society for the amount the society had reimbursed his former clients—about $117,000. The Crown appealed the sentence as excessively lenient, but abandoned the appeal six months later. The rock solid guy dropped from sight. He didn't—as Mary

Hamood suggested—"go home to his people." Later on, try as I could, I couldn't find Reeves Matheson. Messages to his lawyer went unanswered. Reeves Matheson had gone.

NOVA SCOTIA POLITICS has never been quite like politics elsewhere in Canada. Don Ripley was a prominent fundraiser for the Nova Scotia Conservative Party for twenty-five years. In a book about his experiences, he argued that politics in Nova Scotia has been characterised by pork-barrelling and cronyism: "Not long ago, judges, prosecutors, and even jailers were chosen in Nova Scotia on the basis of their political allegiance. Those selected were often fools appointed by bigger fools."[14] An October 1999 article by Kelly Toughill in the *Toronto Star* asked, "How did the Nova Scotia legislature become a haven for alleged thugs, thieves and former addicts …? Why are Nova Scotians so tolerant of behaviour that would not only cost politicians elsewhere their jobs, but also be a severe blow to their party?"[15] Toughill answered her own questions:

Nova Scotia ridings are small. The average MLA represents just 18,000 men, women and children. Compare that to Ontario, where each MPP tries to represent the best interests of more than 110,000 people.

There are no parachute candidates in Nova Scotia. You don't usually win unless you are born and bred in the community you want to represent. And that community isn't likely to change much.

Unlike much of North America, there is no mass migration here, no waves of people propelled by jobs, social ambition or the politics of their homeland, to move again and again. Except for pockets of Halifax dominated by military families and students, people here stay put.

When voters go to the polls, the candidates are usually more than names on a ballot. They are neighbours who teased each other on the school playground as children, danced at the same weddings and cried at the same funerals.

That intimacy has given Nova Scotians a rare political luxury, the ability to judge not whether someone is perfect, but if they are up to the job. That intimacy has also helped them accept the uncomfortable, important truth that good leaders are not necessarily nice human beings.

Matheson may have been disbarred and disgraced in Halifax, but in Glace Bay, perhaps for some of the reasons given by Kelly Toughill, things were a bit more complicated. Marci Lin Melvin is a lawyer and writer. Now she works for the Nova Scotia Legal Aid Commission in Yarmouth, but not so long ago she practised law in Cape Breton. In the June 18, 1998,

"Lifestyles" section of the Halifax *Daily News*, Melvin wrote about Reeves Matheson: "Those of us who practised regularly with him were shocked and saddened by his fall from grace. To his peers, Matheson was always a gentleman. He was an excellent litigator who vehemently fought for his clients' best interests. And like most good parents, he often talked fondly of his children."[16] Melvin wrote of a "collective sadness" among Matheson's former legal colleagues. Years later she wrote to me:[17]

> I find far too many people live in glass houses, but think nothing about throwing stones at their friends, neighbors and colleagues. In some legal communities, it seems, anyone's throat is fair game; mistakes are not allowed; everyone is holier than thou. That being said, Reeves was in the wrong and his actions cannot be condoned in any way. He was in a position of trust, a position of great responsibility....
>
> I always try to see the good in others and remember feeling truly sorry for Reeves when the story became known. Everyone can make mistakes, and the reasons for those mistakes are not necessarily borne out of dishonesty.

ELEVEN

THE CRIMINALS
PICK THEMSELVES

Richard Shead

Richard Shead was a prominent tax lawyer who helped a flamboyant con artist structure and execute a complex fraud that separated many ordinary people from their life savings. Shead gained little from the fraud—modest legal fees, and a bit of excitement along the way—and lost much, ending up disgraced and in prison. By all accounts, Shead was a cold, dull, and arrogant man. It was arrogance, his victims said, that made him do it: He thought he was smart enough to get away with anything.

IN THE SPRING OF 2002, I went to Winnipeg to see Richard Shead. He was a former law school gold medalist at the University of Manitoba. He had been managing partner of the leading Winnipeg law firm of Buchwald Asper Henteleff, and a bencher of the Law Society of Manitoba. He had chaired an advisory committee to the federal Minister of National Revenue, and for many years had been an active member of the local volunteer community. When I went to see him, he was a disbarred ex-convict.

Arriving downtown from the airport, I bumped into Gerry Posner, a lawyer friend, and in the course of casual conversation asked him about Shead. "One of the most brilliant lawyers Manitoba has ever seen," Gerry said. "His firm was once a real powerhouse, back in the seventies. Izzy Asper, Gerry Schwartz, Jack London, Martin Freedman, Michael Nozick, Richard Shead—they were all partners in those days. They all went on to fame or notoriety."[1] Ingrid Chen, the infamous Winnipeg lawyer, told me some time later that she regarded Shead as "godlike."[2] Shead's arrest in 1991 and later conviction for fraud was, as Marilyn Billinkoff, deputy CEO of the Law Society of Manitoba, put it, a "huge deal, a fall from grace."[3]

How did a leading lawyer become a penitentiary inmate? It was simple enough. Shead helped a client, Norman Bruce McLeod (known as "Bruce"), defraud people of their life savings in phony real estate transactions. *The Financial Post*, in a February 1, 1996, article about Canada's biggest white-collar criminals, summed up Bruce McLeod's scam:[4]

Calling himself a developer, McLeod would approach a "client" with an offer of equity in an apartment or office building he owned. A charming and persuasive personality, he was a gifted salesman who used his skills to rope in hundreds of buyers. Typically, when the deal was done, McLeod ended up with far more money in his pocket that the property was actually worth.

The Manitoba Court of Appeal gave a description of McLeod's technique in the 1993 case of *Skimming v. Goldberg*.[5] Hugh and Donna Skimming put a second mortgage on their house so they could invest in a Bruce McLeod transaction, lost everything, and sued the mortgagee to have the mortgage set aside (they failed, because it was McLeod's fault they lost their money, and not that of the mortgagee). Mr. Justice Monnin referred to the lawsuit as "the final act of the tragedy authored by the snake oil salesman." He described how the Skimmings got involved with McLeod:

McLeod first approached the male plaintiff in October of 1986 and convinced him and his wife of the soundness of purchasing one unit in the Midtown Building for $15,625.00. As the plaintiffs did not have the disposable capital to effect the purchase, McLeod made arrangements with the Royal Bank of Canada for them

to borrow the money. McLeod acted as
go-between and basically all the plaintiffs had
to do was sign the bank documentation.

Later McLeod convinced the Skimmings to buy
three more units in the Midtown Building, and it was
then that they mortgaged their house.

Bruce McLeod was arrested by the RCMP at the
Osborne Village Restaurant in Winnipeg on January
15, 1991. He was swiftly convicted of fraud and went
to prison for five years (he was paroled after twenty-
two months). After arresting McLeod, the police
turned their attention to Richard Shead. On
February 7, 1991, the front page of the *Winnipeg
Free Press* reported, "One of the city's top tax lawyers
has been portrayed by RCMP as aiding in an
allegedly fraudulent investment deal."[6] In 1996, the
legal process having taken its usual inordinate time,
Shead was convicted on ten counts of fraud.[7] On
November 7, 1996, Justice Ruth Krindle sentenced
him to five years in prison. The *Winnipeg Free Press*
reported, "The 53-year-old smiled faintly, waved to
family members in the gallery, and was then escorted
out of the courtroom by sheriff's officers."[8]

Ken Filkow, a Winnipeg friend of mine who knew
Shead, arranged for the three of us to have lunch. As
Ken and I waited for Shead in the lobby of the Delta
Hotel on Winnipeg's St. Mary Avenue, we agreed
that he might not show up. Perhaps Shead had calcu-
lated that there was nothing in it for him except

embarrassment, the rekindling of old and unpleasant emotions and memories, and new and harmful publicity. Perhaps he had said yes to Ken's lunch invitation just to end an awkward telephone conversation.

A few minutes past noon, an inconspicuous man in late middle age came into the hotel lobby. "That's him," said Ken. Shead, tall and thin, was flushed. He was obviously nervous. All three of us ill at ease, we went into the dining room and sat down. There was small talk, and an exchange of pleasantries.

"You know," Shead said after a while, "I would welcome the chance to tell my side of the story, but maybe I need the permission of my old law firm to talk to you." Then he changed tack: "It'll be up to my wife whether I cooperate. You can imagine how hard it all was on my family, but my marriage is very strong, my wife stood by me the whole time, she'd have to agree to anything." (Alyce, Shead's current wife, was his second; his first marriage, to Elly, collapsed sometime in the early nineties.)

Had he thought about leaving Winnipeg once he got out of prison? "People in Winnipeg have been very nice to me," he said. "I was a little sheepish at first, but I got over that. I have lunch with former colleagues, that sort of thing." I asked if he planned to apply for readmission to the bar. He looked startled. "No, no," he said. "There are things in life other than law."[9] Lunch over, the three of us left the Delta Hotel. Shead said he'd think things over and get back to me.

Some time later, he sent me an email: "Alyce and I have had several long discussions about participating in your book but are finding it very difficult to come to a positive response for you—partly due to the fact that we are very private people and partly because we are not sure we want to relive some of the 'memories' and 'emotions.'"[10] He asked what topics interested me. I sent a list: What motivated him in his dealings with McLeod? How did he manage emotionally to get through the police investigation, being charged, the trial, conviction? How had he put his life back together since being released from prison? Shead replied, "Alyce and I have discussed this further and we have now discussed it with my two sons. Our feeling was that if anyone of us was uncomfortable with further 'public' exposure of the case, or any personal aspects of the whole experience, we would respect that concern and say no to becoming involved. Both my sons were very emphatic that they did not want to experience any further possible publicity about the matter."[11]

In November 2003, back in Winnipeg, I called on the managing partner of Shead's old law firm, now called Pitblado. Doug Ward, who was admitted to the Manitoba bar in 1970, is one of the province's leading insolvency practitioners. He wasn't happy to see me. "Shead is a friend of mine," said Ward. "He didn't want me to talk to you. I nearly called to tell you to forget it, not to come." Becoming a little emotional—red in the face, his voice a little shaky—

Ward went on: "Richard is a wonderful human being, straightforward, honest, always acted in the best interests of his clients and partners." He was quiet for a moment. Then: "I feel incredibly sorry for Richard."[12]

"Of course," said Ward, "no one wants to read any of what I'm telling you, I don't know why you're talking to me, no one is interested in what a wonderful guy Shead is. You know, the line is always moving; standards and perception are constantly changing. You may be on the right side of the line today, but next year when someone looks at what you did today, they decide by new standards that what you did was wrong. Now you're on the wrong side of the line."

Why had Shead stayed in Winnipeg after he was released from prison, where every day he must meet people on the street who know what happened? "Family," said Ward. "He loves his family, I mean he really *loves* them. He has two superstar sons by Elly, his first wife. His mother is still alive. He has a brother. They're all in Winnipeg."

Robert Morrison and Paul Jensen, of the Manitoba Department of Justice, prosecuted Shead. I went to see Morrison and suggested that some might regard Shead's crime as a technical offence.[13] Why did the resource-poor Department of Justice assign two prosecutors to spend a year preparing the case and then participate in an eight-month trial? Why pick on Shead with such ferocity? "We don't pick the criminals," said Morrison. "They pick themselves. Shead knew exactly what he was doing. A lot of ordinary people lost a lot of money, life savings in some cases. And Shead just didn't care."

Morrison said:

Shead thought he was smarter than we were. He was arrogant, he thought he'd done nothing wrong, and that we were just stupid. He saw the trial as a game, and completely underestimated the Crown. During breaks, at the beginning of the trial, I used to chat in the corridor with his lawyer, Richard Wolson, who I know well. Lawyers do that, we have casual social chit-chat, exchange a joke or two, it doesn't matter what side you're on, it's professional camaraderie. Shead would come up to us and try and join in, be another lawyer, one of the boys. Finally, I said to him, "Look this is inappropriate. I don't want to chat with you. I want to put you in prison."

If Shead was so smart—and everyone says he was smart—how could he get in such a mess? Morrison pointed to Bruce McLeod. "McLeod had a compelling personality," Morrison said. "Shead would go over to McLeod's house at 111 Park Boulevard in Tuxedo—it's a mansion—for coffee *every morning*!" Morrison said Shead had "Lord Nelson syndrome," putting the telescope to a blind eye to ensure that you don't see what you don't want to see.

Richard Shead certainly picked his friends poorly. *The Vancouver Sun*, on November 5, 1997, had a story about Eron Mortgage Corporation, a real estate investment business in which the investors, according to *The Sun*, were "elderly and financially unsophisticated people." Brian Slobogian was president of Eron. *The Sun* quoted part of a letter Slobogian wrote to a friend in November 1996, describing a golf holiday: "I am now on the aircraft, a King Air executive jet, alone with the pilots, flying to play golf. I think I've come a long way."[14] The friend he wrote to was Richard Shead, described by the newspaper as "an old friend and once-prominent tax lawyer who was convicted of 10 counts of fraud last year and is now serving a five-year sentence in a Manitoba jail." On May 1, 2002, *The Globe and Mail* reported that, as part of "one of the biggest fraud-related investigations in Canadian history," Brian Slobogian faced thirty-three charges of fraud, frauds in which "thousands of mainly elderly investors lost a total of $220-million."[15] In January 2005, Slobogian pleaded guilty to four counts of theft and one of fraud; in March, he was sentenced to six years in prison. Martin Chambers, a former Vancouver lawyer, was also closely involved with Eron, borrowing nearly $27 million from the company for various business projects. On December 5, 2003, a Florida court sentenced

Chambers to fifteen years for money laundering connected to cocaine trafficking.[16]

Shead was disbarred in June 1995 following disciplinary proceedings by the Law Society of Manitoba that lasted eight days, six days of which were devoted to hearing evidence.[17] Shead took the position that the disciplinary proceedings should not take place before his criminal trial since they might prejudice that trial, and refused to take part. The discipline committee's reasons referred frequently to Shead's "clearly dishonest and disgraceful conduct." His actions were "intentional, unprofessional and unethical." In its conclusions the committee said this:

> Many of the investors relied upon the reputation of Shead and his law firm. They felt that it lent the investment proposals credibility. The actions of Shead in drafting documents, talking to investors and continuing to act in these schemes when he knew the true state of affairs facilitated the ongoing fraud that was being perpetrated by McLeod.
>
> Shead's willful conduct was disgraceful, dishonourable, despicable and down-right disgusting.

Ruth Krindle, the judge assigned to Shead's trial, thought Shead was also a liar. At the beginning of her judgment[18] (115 pages long, handed down on September 30, 1996), commenting on his two weeks of testimony, she says, "I came to the conclusion that Shead was not even attempting to recall or reconstruct with truth as his object." Justice Krindle described Shead as "deliberately dishonest" and referred to "situations that cropped up during the trial with disturbing frequency in which Shead attempted to find an innocent explanation for his actions and quite simply created one to suit his purposes, attesting to it as though it were truth." In the middle of her judgment she referred to the "basic dishonesty of Shead" and writes, "I continue to be astonished by the ability of Shead to play dishonest intellectual games." And, at the end of her reasons, she says, "Shead was not a truthful witness on the stand. His testimony was characterized by manoeuvering and intellectual gamesmanship and, when no other avenue of escape presented itself, then by outright dishonesty. So apparently was his practice of law."[19]

Shead, wrote Justice Krindle, "developed a 'niche' dealing with 'work-out scenarios' for individual clients who were having cash flow problems." Bruce McLeod had a "cash flow problem." McLeod had lost a lot of money in the Florida real estate market and had huge debts. Following his failed deals in Florida, he came to Winnipeg, where he had once been a life insurance salesman, and made a series of highly leveraged real estate acquisitions, using Shead as his lawyer. In 1987, for example, one of McLeod's companies bought the Brookside Building for approximately $1.5 million; McLeod quickly placed three mortgages on the property totalling more than $1.9 million. That same year, McLeod purchased, through a numbered company, 1180 Main Street in Winnipeg. He paid $500,000 for this building and immediately placed $600,000 worth of mortgages on it.

Central to the case against Shead was the so-called Shead Mortgage on Winnipeg's Midtown Building. McLeod bought the Midtown Building in 1986 through Graham Investments Limited, a corporation he controlled. The Shead Mortgage was a million-dollar mortgage, initially unfunded, that was intended to be in second place and was registered in Shead's favour. The idea was that McLeod would sell participations in this mortgage to individual investors, like Hugh and Donna Skimming, with Shead acting as the agent for the participants.

The first participant was the Capital Bank of St. Paul, which was owed money by St. Charles Development Corporation, a McLeod company that had been involved in the failed Florida ventures. Capital Bank was aggressively pursuing St. Charles and was handed a $500,000 participation to keep it quiet. St. Charles was insolvent, but Graham Investments had many creditors. Justice Krindle concluded, "I am satisfied that Shead, in issuing the certificate of participation in his mortgage to the Capital Bank for no consideration, was a party to a fraud on Graham Investments Limited."[20] Several other payments on behalf of St. Charles, and of another insolvent McLeod company (Stockton Financial Services Corporation), were made by Graham Investments, and Krindle found all to be fraudulent.

The Shead Mortgage was supposed to be a second mortgage of the Midtown Building, but was postponed on three separate occasions to the disadvantage of those who had bought participations. Postponement required consent of the participants. Shead left that matter to McLeod. Said Justice Krindle, "Shead deliberately decided to circumvent his fiduciary responsibilities to the investors by leaving to McLeod all dealings with the participants concerning the postponements."[21] But Shead did prepare the legal documentation for the postponements, documentation that Krindle found to be materially misleading.

Shead drafted the first postponement consent to suggest that the position of mortgage participants would actually be improved by the postponement. Justice Krindle said of the postponement:

Shead dishonestly failed to disclose material information to the investors in the Mortgage at the time of their being asked to consent to its postponement, knowing that he had a duty to disclose. I am satisfied that Shead knew that the economic interests of the participants were detrimentally affected by the postponement to greater prior encumbrances. I am satisfied that

Shead's postponing the position of the Shead
Mortgage ..., an act based purportedly on
those consents, was a fraudulent act which
operated to the economic detriment of the
investors.

Similar circumstances surrounded the second
postponement of the Shead Mortgage (to a new
mortgage known as the Castor Mortgage). One
difference was that the refinancing of the Midtown
Building that required the second postponement was
intended, among other things, to benefit Buchwald
Asper Henteleff, Shead's law firm. The firm had
advanced $400,000 to Graham Investments and had
guaranteed a $100,000 personal loan to McLeod
from the Bank of Nova Scotia, and was due to be
repaid out of the proceeds of the Castor Mortgage.
Said Justice Krindle of Shead and his role in the
second postponement:

He deliberately and dishonestly, with knowledge of the relevant facts, preferred the interests of McLeod and Buchwald Asper and
Henteleff to the fiduciary duty to the participants and left the risk with the participants.
    I find beyond reasonable doubt that Shead
committed an act of fraud on the participants
of his mortgage when he postponed the Shead
mortgage to the Castor mortgage.

The third postponement, also found to be fraudulent, was to a mortgage held by Sun Mortgage. Sun Mortgage was owned indirectly by Shead's law partners. Said Justice Krindle, "The involvement of his partners in the mortgage that was being moved ahead of their interest is an obvious matter for disclosure."[22] No such disclosure was made. Krindle again: "Shead's partners were positioning themselves so that they could survive the possibility of collapse and were getting their substantial interest payments and bonuses up front."[23]

On March 14, 1997, the Manitoba Court of Appeal dismissed Shead's appeal of the five-year sentence given him by Justice Krindle.[24] Justice Huband for the Court said:

> It should have been patently obvious that facilitating Mr. McLeod to the detriment of the victims was bound to end tragically for all concerned.... Yet Mr. Shead continued on an illegal course that was destined to ruin his career, place him in bankruptcy, destroy his marriage, and land him in prison. His participation is all the more incomprehensible because Mr. Shead is recognized to possess unique intellectual gifts and an enormous capacity for work.

Huband noted Shead's "total lack of remorse." Shead had attended the hearing, three days before judgment was rendered, in leg irons.

Robert Morrison of the Manitoba Department of Justice, who led the prosecution of Shead, said that Shead "did well" in prison. "He quickly figured out how to get along," said Morrison. (Izzy Asper, his former law partner, visited him at Headingley Jail, near Winnipeg. By then, Asper, founder of CanWest, was one of the best-known people in Canada.) Then Morrison added, "Bruce McLeod didn't do as well. His flamboyant personality got him into trouble."

Why did Richard Shead risk so much? Justice Krindle couldn't figure it out. Referring to the Shead Mortgage, she wrote, "Shead owed a fiduciary duty to the participants. He chose to avoid its performance in order to accommodate the interests of McLeod." Later she described numerous examples of Shead negotiating and drawing agreements for McLeod that Shead knew were incapable of being fulfilled, and said, "All of them seem to have had the same object in mind—to buy time for McLeod." And, later still: "He gambled on McLeod.... He lost." But devotion to McLeod doesn't explain Shead's actions, at least not according to Krindle: "Why did Shead do it? Not friendship, although friendship may have been part of it. Certainly his relationship with McLeod was not such that he would ever have said 'I am willing to risk my professional career for you.' Yet that was ulti-mately what he did."[25]

Justice Krindle suggested a "slippery slope" expla-nation for what happened. She talked about the "evolution" of Shead's conduct, and how after a while "Shead was himself in so far that any attempt to extricate himself would have resulted in his being seriously exposed, both financially and legally." She wrote, "At a certain point, as Shead became more involved and implicated in McLeod's wrongdoings, Shead became more dependent on McLeod's ultimate success. If McLeod could somehow have worked miracles and come up with enough money to appease his creditors, Shead's exposure would have disappeared as would McLeod's."[26] At the end of her judgment, Ruth Krindle simply said, "I do not know why Shead did the things he did."

Were Shead's mistakes just technical legal errors—mistakes in drafting the Shead Mortgage postponements, for example—that could easily have been made in good faith by any lawyer? Was he a victim of shifting legal standards, being judged after the fact by standards more stringent than those in effect at the time he acted? Was Richard Shead, to use the words of his friend and one-time partner Doug Ward, "a wonderful human being, straightforward, honest"? (Another person who spoke very highly to me of Shead was Gavin Wood, a Winnipeg litigator and Manitoba bencher at the same time as Shead. "He was a brilliant and giving man," Wood told me.[27])

The trouble is that McLeod and Shead took the life savings of ordinary people. To Justice Krindle, who spent eight months listening to the evidence about what happened, both Shead's practice of law and his testimony in court were characterized by outright dishonesty. To the law society's disciplinary committee, his conduct was "disgraceful, dishonourable, despicable and down-right disgusting." To Marilyn Billinkoff of the law society, it was "as if part of his brain was missing." The facts, found by people who took care in considering what happened, and the overwhelming weight of opinion about those facts, including the opinion of almost all Shead's professional colleagues and peers, led to the conclusion that Richard Shead knew that what he was doing was wrong and did it anyway.

Why did a respected lawyer, a leader of the local bar, become a fraudster? He was not in it for the money. McLeod paid his law firm about $435,000 in fees over several years (they were hard to collect), but only a small part of that, about $30,000, went to Shead himself as his share of partnership profits. Did the law school gold medalist believe that he was smarter than everyone else and that rules made by the less intelligent and accomplished shouldn't apply to him? Did Shead live in an amoral legal world, where moving bits of paper around seemed unconnected to what happened to people? Was he under the sway of Bruce McLeod, a far more interesting person than himself?

I went to see Kim Whiteside who (together with her father) had been an investor in McLeod's schemes, and Richard Schwartz, the lawyer who had represented a large number of those who had been defrauded. (Ironically, most of the money recovered by investors came from a Manitoba legal insurance plan that Shead had helped create some years before.) We had lunch in the same hotel dining room where two years before I had dined with Richard Shead and Ken Filkow.[28]

Whiteside earns her living as an interior decorator. Schwartz is an experienced litigator with the mid-sized Winnipeg firm of Tapper Cuddy. "When I was a new law graduate looking for a job, I interviewed with Shead at the Buchwald firm," Schwartz told me. "They offered me a job, but I didn't take it. I didn't like Shead. He was cold, remote. He didn't look you in the eye when he talked to you. I got the impression he didn't like people, he just liked business deals." Whiteside chimed in. "When you telephoned him, you'd say, just to be polite, 'Hello Richard, how are you,' and he would just ignore that and ask you what you wanted. He was an arrogant man."

"And thought he could talk his way out of anything," added Schwartz. I asked Whiteside and Schwartz if Shead had fallen under McLeod's spell, as Robert Morrison had suggested. "No," said Schwartz. "Shead was too smart for that, although all the relationships were complicated."

"Part of the story here is about the Buchwald Asper Henteleff firm," continued Schwartz. "They wanted to be the biggest firm in Winnipeg. A number of the partners had invested with McLeod through Sun Mortgage, and there was a ton of McLeod-related receivables. The firm had expensive

new space, it was buying a new computer system—
suddenly there is a scandal, uncollectible receivables—there was a lot of pressure on Shead and other
people."

SOMEONE GAVE ME Bruce McLeod's telephone
number. I rang him, and right away he started talking
in a rambling way. "I knew I was dead when Bob
Morrison in his opening statement at my trial didn't
know the difference between a mortgagor and a
mortgagee. It was okay in prison. I found the most
psychotic prisoner and walked with him. You gotta
walk with the lions and not the Thomson's gazelles."
(McLeod had once spent some time in Africa.) I
asked him if we could meet. "Sure, the Holiday Inn
on Pembina Highway. There're no suits there to
eavesdrop. Tomorrow at 3 p.m."

McLeod, sixty-five years old, had a white beard
and was wearing a jacket with "Bruce's Marina,
Gimli, Manitoba" on it. An undischarged bankrupt,
he was doing a little property management for a
friend. I asked him if Shead was under his thumb, as
Morrison had suggested. He fell back in his chair and
laughed a lot. "Well, why did Shead come round to
your house all the time?" I asked. "That's where my
office was," he replied. "We used to work by the
pool, in bathing suits, with my secretary." When I
told McLeod that Robert Morrison said he had a bad
time in jail, he got angry. "Most of the information
you have is bullshit," he said. "I thoroughly enjoyed

my time in jail. My best friend was an axe murderer. I played chess and read a lot. I read *The Joy of Yiddish*."[29]

THE NEXT MORNING I was at the airport, leaving Winnipeg, and my cell phone rang. "It's Bruce. Listen, I spoke to my guard at Stony Mountain, and he'll talk to you, and tell you that things went well for me in prison. And by the way, I'm looking forward to working with you. I've been thinking about writing my autobiography."

TWELVE

LAW PRACTICE TO PET FOOD

Martin Wirick

Martin Wirick facilitated the biggest legal fraud in Canadian history. He didn't make any money out of it. According to his law society, the whole thing happened because Wirick was unfit to practise law in the first place. A judge thought it was attributable to "weakness of character." What was Wirick's explanation? "I did it because I was unhappy," he said. "I didn't care."

MARTIN WIRICK GRADUATED from the University of British Columbia law school in 1978. When he became notorious, twenty-five years or so later, newspaper reporters and law society officials spoke to his classmates, trying to find out something more about the person responsible for a massive fraud. No one remembered him. Today, his physical appearance and personality remain nondescript. It is hard, the day after meeting him, to recall exactly what he looks like. Talking to him is pleasant enough but leaves no great impression. He cannot easily be conjured up in the imagination.

Wirick was born in Burnaby, a suburb of Vancouver, in 1954.[1] His mother died when he was ten. His father, a supervisor at Burnaby's Shell refinery, died at Christmas in 1993. He has one sister, Lynn, born in 1951. Wirick and his sister don't see each other very much anymore. When they do meet, they are careful not to talk about what happened when Martin Wirick practised law.

As a child and young adult, Wirick apparently led a happy and quiet suburban life in Burnaby. He did well in school. He went to the University of British Columbia for his undergraduate education and got good marks. Studying law seemed a natural thing to do once he finished his first degree. He says now that he did not feel a particular vocation for the legal profession, but in some vague way was attracted to a job that he thought would let him help people. As he remembers it, his marks in law school were a little above average.

Wirick was admitted to the bar in 1979 and started a solo legal practice in downtown Vancouver. At first, he specialized in "whatever walked through the door." In 1982, he moved his office to south Vancouver. After a while, his practice settled down to a mix of residential real estate conveyancing and bad debt collections. For most of his career he practised alone, sometimes sharing office space and expenses with one or two other lawyers, although for a time he was in partnership with a lawyer called David Klassen. That partnership ended, says Wirick, when Klassen decided to give up the law and go to the United States to study philosophy. In 1985, Wirick married Karen Nygaard, a legal secretary whose father was a senior executive with the Toronto-Dominion Bank.

The years went by uneventfully, but not happily. Wirick did not enjoy practising law as much as he had anticipated. Depression and resentment built within him. He has written about his feelings:[2]

> I didn't enjoy most aspects of practicing law.... I often thought about what I could do if I quit law.... I wasn't happy, and wanted to quit law.... I basically felt trapped in a job I hated. The longer it went, the less and less happy and the more stressed I became. I didn't take vacations over a week or two in length each year because I felt I had too much work to do.

Then, sometime in 1996, he acted for a client who lent money to a Vancouver real estate developer called Tarsem Singh Gill. Reporter Wyng Chow described Gill and his business in a September 21,

2002, story in *The Vancouver Sun*: "Those who know Gill or had business dealings with him—including several who said they have been 'stiffed' by Gill—describe him variously as a 'super nice guy,' 'a good family man,' a sports enthusiast, and someone who gives generously to the Ross Street Temple. Real estate sources say Gill typically builds 50-to-60 houses a year, particularly in East Vancouver."[3] Even today, Martin Wirick describes Gill (he always refers to him as "Mr. Gill") as "good-looking, charming and persuasive," although he reluctantly adds "and a user of people." Wirick and Mr. Gill got along well together, and Gill asked Wirick to act for him in routine conveyances of residential real estate properties that he was developing.

In the summer of 1999, while working on a Gill transaction, Wirick made an accounting error.[4] He underestimated by about $20,000 the amount needed to discharge existing mortgages on a property that Gill had built and was selling. When he realized his mistake, Wirick called Gill and asked for the extra money. Gill didn't have it. He told Wirick that he was finishing construction of a second property, and, when that second property was sold, some of the proceeds could be used to pay the outstanding mortgage on the first property. He asked Wirick, in the meantime, to hold in trust the insufficient funds, about $60,000, already on hand to pay the first property's mortgage. Wirick agreed to all this. It seemed reasonable enough. After all, he thought, the wait for funds to make up the shortfall should only be about a month. Gill told Wirick not to worry. He said, "There is enough equity to pay everybody."

Two weeks later Gill came to Wirick's office and asked to borrow the $60,000 held in trust. He said he needed the money to finish the second property. Wirick, desperate that the second property be finished and sold so that the mortgage on the first property could be discharged, handed the trust funds over. Much later, Wirick said that releasing these trust funds was his key mistake. "I knew it was wrong," he said. "I knew I was heading for big trouble." When asked why he did it, Wirick replied, "I was tired, emotionally drained. My marriage was collapsing. I hated practising law. I just thought, fuck it, I don't care. Also, I thought, nothing bad has ever happened to me, and never will. I'll just put the whole thing out of my mind. It'll be alright." The current of events carried a tired and depressed Wirick along.

When the second property was finally sold, some of the proceeds, as planned, were used to pay off the first property's mortgage. But now there were not enough proceeds from the sale of the second property to pay off the second property's mortgages. Don't worry, said Gill, that could be done from the sale proceeds of a third property. Gill repeated his reassurance, "There is enough equity." The relationship between Martin Wirick and Tarsem Singh Gill slid into farce.

Gill kept building and selling properties (by the end, Wirick had acted for Gill in about three hundred separate transactions over a three-year period), "borrowing" the proceeds from one deal to pay off obligations arising from previous ones. Wirick kept telling Gill that he must stop and to settle all the outstanding mortgages. Gill kept assuring Wirick that, overall, he had sufficient equity to pay off everything. But the money was not coming in fast enough from the sales of new properties to pay off the mortgages on the old properties. Purchasers were asking for particulars about the discharge of old mortgages. Banks holding those mortgages began to get suspicious. The Law Society of British Columbia, nervous about rumours, conducted a spot audit of Wirick's practice, which, surprisingly, turned up nothing. Meanwhile, to raise money, Gill began arranging new "first" mortgages on property without paying off existing first mortgages. Wirick became increasingly upset. Later he said, "We were always one property or more behind. I kept saying to Mr. Gill, sell, sell, sell, let's deal with this. But Mr. Gill didn't see it as a problem to be fixed. He thought of it as an opportunity, as a financing method."

Finally, Wirick brought matters to a head. On Saturday, May 18, 2002, at Wirick's instigation, Wirick and Gill met in Wirick's office and tried to figure out exactly what was owed. They added up the unpaid mortgages. They calculated the so-called equity. They were $32 million short. Gill

broke down and cried. Wirick knew that it was
over.

The following Monday, May 20, Wirick sent a
letter of resignation to the law society. It began:

> This letter is to report that I have made serious
> errors in my practice of law. I intend to resign
> as a member of the Law Society of British
> Columbia as soon as possible.
>
> In the summer of 1999, I made a simple
> error in calculating a Statement of Adjustments
> for a long time construction client of mine,
> named Tarsem Singh Gill. At that time, I was
> experiencing financial and emotional stress and
> depression from practicing law, and had not
> taken a vacation longer than one week a year in
> approximately 8 years.

The letter described the chain of events in detail.
Wirick described the position he took with his client:

> I told him [Gill] many times to stop buying, to
> sell the properties he had picked up in order to
> reduce his indebtedness, and he would always
> agree, but then he would carry on doing the
> same things, saying the only way out of our
> situation was to build large projects and many
> houses. I felt helpless to stop what was
> happening, and too far in to do anything but

cooperate and pray that it would work out eventually.

The letter concluded:

I have not taken one cent except in legal fees for work actually done. Mr. Gill did not offer me money to do what I did, and I did not ask for any or take any. I honestly have no idea where that much money could possibly have gone.

Obviously, I am unfit to practice law and I will do everything in my power to wind down my practice or turn it over to the Law Society as quickly as possible.... I wish to say that, except in the matters concerning Mr. Gill, I have always acted properly on my files and complied with all undertakings and trust conditions placed upon me. I am very ashamed of my actions in this matter, and wish to take this opportunity to apologize to the lawyers, notaries, financial institutions and individuals whose trust in me has been betrayed.

The law society arranged for judicial appointment of a custodian for Wirick's practice. Stories about the catastrophe started to appear in the newspaper. Criticism and abuse were heaped on Wirick's head. But Wirick felt a sense of relief. The nightmare seemed to be over.

The Law Society of British Columbia quickly began the largest audit and investigation in its history. It took two months just to photocopy all of Wirick's files and accounting records. The photocopy paper cost $11,000 and the accounting documents—client ledger cards, cancelled cheques, cheque stubs, bank deposit books, bank reconciliations, and bank statements—filled sixty-four large binders. Many of the investigated transactions were very complex (in one case, for example, the proceeds of a single conveyance were traced to more than forty other transactions). The law society team of five forensic accountants, an investigator, a staff lawyer, and a legal assistant, ended up focusing on about 870 of Wirick's files. The Vancouver police assigned two detectives and a senior sergeant to the case, retained a forensic accounting firm, and sought assistance from the RCMP commercial crime section (eventually the Vancouver police created a special unit—the Lower Mainland White Collar Crime Unit—to investigate the Wirick affair). Jim Matkin, then CEO of the law society, was quoted by David Baines of *The Vancouver Sun* as saying, "It's like an earthquake. For many years you never have a problem, then you have a problem that is so enormous it is quite frightening."[5] Martin Glynn, president of HSBC Bank Canada, was reported in *The Lawyers Weekly* as saying that what Wirick had done "affected every lending institution in British Columbia," terming the losses "unprecedented."[6]

In July 2002, Wirick filed for bankruptcy, listing debts of more than $50 million and assets of $467,859. He gave as the reason for filing "failing to pay out mortgages pursuant to my undertakings, but instead paying monies to my client on his promise to pay out the mortgages but who failed to do so." The largest creditors were VanCity Savings Credit Union, with a claim of about $14 million; CIBC Mortgages, $5 million; Canadian Western Trust, $3 million; and Toronto-Dominion Bank, $1.3 million. Tarsem Gill had himself filed for bankruptcy the month before.

The Law Society of British Columbia was now under tremendous pressure. Angry people who had bought houses in Gill-related transactions were frightened that their titles were in question. Lending institutions had apparently lost millions of dollars. Standard real estate conveyancing practices stood revealed as vulnerable to fraud. There was no point in any one suing Wirick because he was bankrupt. The law society faced huge claims against its special compensation fund. The society was forced to remove the $17.5 million cap on annual aggregate payments from the fund. The amount payable by each B.C. lawyer to the fund in 2003 was increased to $600 from the 2002 amount of $250.

In June 2002, the law society struck a task force to look into the issues raised by what it delicately called Wirick's "practice irregularities." Wirick later said that what bothered the law society most was his dramatic demonstration of weaknesses in the conveyancing system. He'd shown "how easy it was to screw up." The first report of the task force (called the "Interim report") came quickly, on August 6. It proposed a two-cheque system in conveyancing: "Purchasers' lawyers would deal directly with vendors' encumbrances and, on closing, would provide separate cheques payable to the respective parties entitled to receive the proceeds." It suggested a special new fee on all real estate transactions to pay for the cost to the law society of the Wirick inquiry and of making restitution to all those who had been cheated.

But the law society had stumbled. The reaction to the task force's August report was hugely negative. Lawyers in British Columbia made clear that they did not want the two-cheque system.[7] They did not want to be treated as if they were children or dishonest. What they wanted was restoration of confidence in the integrity of solicitors' undertakings (to some extent, the lending community shared this sentiment). And the public (as reported in the newspapers) was outraged by the proposal that the huge costs of Wirick's defalcations should, by way of a transaction fee on new real estate transactions, be paid by innocent clients who were not at all involved in what had happened. Faced with all this, the law society seemed frightened and confused. The president, Richard Gibbs, in his September 2002 message in the *Benchers' Bulletin*, wrote, "Is Wirick a 'one-off' or do his misappropriations tell us that we were gulled into thinking the base level of misappropriation was different from what it really is? Are there other defalcations out there as yet undetected? The last 15 years' experience tells us the answer is almost certainly 'yes.' We don't know what we will experience, but we do know there is a risk—and it is a bigger and different risk than we thought it was earlier this year."

In December 2002, the chastened task force issued a new report (called the "Second interim report") with a completely new set of recommendations. Now it proposed a so-called transparency response, requiring a vendor's solicitor to provide to a purchaser's solicitor, within forty-eight hours of the completion of a transaction, evidence that the vendor's solicitor has repaid existing encumbrances on title. It recommended a "30-30 Rule," which would allow a maximum of thirty days for a financial institution to provide a mortgage discharge and a further thirty days for the solicitor receiving the discharge to process it through the Land Title Office. And it recommended innocent party insurance coverage for future losses (the insurance scheme that was proposed would not pay for losses already incurred), funded by a combination of a general insurance levy assessed against all practising lawyers and a transaction fee for client matters. These recommendations seemed to be received favourably, the law society moved to adopt them, and the immediate hubbub died down.

That same month, on December 16, 2002, Wirick was formally disbarred (law societies retain the ability to discipline members even though they have already resigned).[8] The law society disciplinary panel said this:

> The Respondent has brought much shame upon the legal profession. He has misconducted himself to a level that is unprecedented in our history. His actions have had consequences beyond all reasonable contemplation of the Benchers and staff of the Law Society. He has brought significant hardship and harm to a large number of members of the general public.
>
> The members of the Law Society will be paying for the consequences of the Respondent's misconduct for years to come.... The Respondent's conduct has been, at all levels, inexcusable.
>
> ... Any system can be abused. The real lesson of Wirick is that it went on so long and involved so much money. Lawyer theft at historical levels we can absorb. The Wirick misappropriations challenge our ability and our willingness to save the public harmless.

With Wirick's disbarment, a very bad year for the Law Society of British Columbia mercifully came to an end. On January 1, 2003, a new president of the society, Howard Berge, took office, marking, it was hoped, the beginning of better times. When he became president, no one knew that the previous October Berge had driven his Volvo into a brick wall at the Kelowna Golf and Country Club, and that, when the police gave him a Breathalyzer, he blew nearly twice the legal limit. The story broke in B.C. newspapers in January. Once again, the law society was in crisis. On October 9, 2003, Berge pleaded guilty in Provincial Court to driving without due care and attention and had his licence suspended. The judge was highly critical of his conduct immediately after the accident, and as a result Berge resigned as president of the law society.[9] On June 30, 2004, the law society issued a citation against its former president[10] and scheduled disciplinary hearings. Over a year later, on July 14, 2005, a hearing panel found Berge guilty of conduct unbecoming a lawyer.[11] On October 21, the penalty was pronounced: Berge was suspended from the Law Society of British Columbia for one month.[12] Berge has since appealed his suspension.

Some time in the summer of 2003, Wirick and Karen separated (there were no children). They divorced in 2004. In September 2003, Wirick applied to the court for discharge from bankruptcy (discharge relieves the bankrupt from debts incurred before the bankruptcy). The law society and others opposed his application, arguing that there should be no discharge because he was guilty of a fraudulent breach of trust. In August 2004, Justice Sigurdson of

the Supreme Court of British Columbia decided that
creditors opposing a discharge were entitled to a
finding that Wirick was guilty of a fraudulent breach
of trust, and that accordingly, under the law, Wirick
was not eligible for an absolute discharge of bankruptcy.[13] In February 2005, Justice Sigurdson ruled
that Wirick's discharge application should wait until
the law society had completed its audit in the Wirick
matter and full information was available to the
court.[14] Finally, in June 2006, Justice Sigurdson
granted a discharge, but on the condition that Wirick
consent to a $500,000 judgment in favour of the law
society (Wirick did consent). Said the judge, "There
is no evidence that Mr. Wirick misappropriated any
funds for his personal benefit.... Mr. Wirick's fraudulent breach of trust was more a product of weakness
in his character than it was greed on his part."[15]
Justice Sigurdson added, "Perhaps the only way that
Mr. Wirick will ever pay anything to the Law Society
is if he wins the lottery." Wirick considers that he was
badly treated by the law society in his attempt to win
a bankruptcy discharge. "I cooperated completely,"
he says. "I did what I could to make it better. They
were just trying to punish me by opposing my bankruptcy discharge. They wanted to make an example
of me. I couldn't even get a credit card. And the
law society is pushing the police to lay charges. It's
not fair."

By December 2005, the total number of Wirick
claims made to the law society was about 555, worth

in excess of $80 million (some claims overlap, filed by both a bank and a property owner in connection with one transaction, and others are duplicate claims). About 495 claims valued at $75 million had been considered, and payment from the special compensation fund of $32.5 million had been authorized in respect of those claims. What happened to the money? No one seems to know. There is no evidence that Wirick derived any personal economic benefit (other than $600,000 in legal fees over the whole period). Brad Daisley, public relations officer for the law society, says that "in the forensic audit and in the special fund compensation cases, we have found no evidence that Mr. Wirick profited from his misappropriations."[16] Tarsem Singh Gill, when questioned about the money in August 2003 by a reporter for *The Province*, said, "I don't know, you ask Wirick."[17] Wirick thinks a lot of it went to the banks, as interest on unpaid loans. "The only real victims," says Wirick, "were the lawyers of British Columbia, who had to make it all good through the compensation fund." A chartered accountant hired by the law society reported in September 2005 that there were no off-shore bank accounts, or identifiable sources of recovery for the law society other than the Gill estate in bankruptcy.[18]

At the end of 2006, the Vancouver police and RCMP were apparently still investigating, although at a glacial pace. Wirick reported that he was anxious to cooperate, but, he said, the police officers who started the investigation had retired, and the new people on the file didn't understand the complex facts. As well, computer systems have crashed and data has been lost. It's not clear whether charges will be laid. Wirick says he is prepared to go to jail, if he must. "I'm ready," he says, "but I'm not hearing anything from the police. I've even telephoned them, and asked if they want me to come in, but they say, not yet. They seem to have lost interest."[19] In November 2005, he reported, "Everything has been quiet."[20]

Trying to explain what happened, Wirick now says, "It was laziness. I just didn't care. I didn't do it for money. I didn't get any money. I did it because I didn't care. The worst thing for me was not complying with my undertakings, the betrayal of trust." Then he added, "I didn't want to be a lawyer. Four or five years before all the trouble, I said to Karen, I want to do something else, quit law, write a book or something. She said no. She wouldn't let me quit."

As for Tarsem Singh Gill, Jim Matkin suggests that there was a "Robin Hood" element to his behaviour.[21] Matkin says, "Gill's business plan was, to say the least, faulty. He was selling houses at less than it cost him to build them. Some purchasers, who realized what was happening, thought of him as a hero." Gill was quickly back in the property development business. On August 29, 2003, *The Province* reported:[22]

Tarsem Gill, the developer at the centre of Vancouver's largest ongoing commercial-crime probe, appears to be back in business.

Gill is popping up at construction sites in east Vancouver and Surrey, including a row of four new homes in the 2500-block East 40th Avenue, where The Province photographed him meeting with work crews one July morning.

He has also been seen all summer long applying for permits at city hall.

... Contacted by phone this week, Gill said none of the projects are his own.

"I'm not doing anything right now, because I was forced into the bankruptcy. I'm just working for somebody, that's all."

Gill says he works sporadically for a number of friends.

"One month I work for this guy, one month I work for another guy. If somebody asks me, 'Could you help me to go to city hall?' I go there."

Local developers were amazed to see Gill at building sites.

Wirick started a new job in June 2002, working as a manager at Koko's Gourmet Pet Foods in North Vancouver for $12 an hour. "I used to take my dog there," he says. "They offered me a job when all the trouble happened. I like running a small business. That was the only thing I liked about my legal practice, running a small business. There's good potential in gourmet dog food." In October 2005, Wirick remarried, to a "wonderful lady" who had worked as a bookkeeper at various Vancouver law firms for twenty years.

Early in December 2005, Wirick's new wife was fired by the law firm where she had worked for the past two years, without warning and with no reason given. She was told to turn off her computer and was escorted off the premises by two senior partners. Wirick often bumps into lawyers, some who know him already, and some who realize who he is when they hear his name; he used to say that they all treated him well. Wirick's new wife has suggested that he change his last name, but so far he has resisted.

Lawyer Jim Matkin, the executive director of the law society who steered the society through the Wirick affair and the Berge embarrassment, became embroiled in controversy himself and resigned his position at the end of 2004. The intrepid David Baines of *The Vancouver Sun* revealed that Matkin, while executive director, also served as president and chairman of a company associated with persons who had been sanctioned for serious securities offences.[23] The law society launched an investigation and, on November 25, Matkin was placed on paid leave. By December 6, Matkin had had enough; he quit and the law society called off its inquiry. A formal complaint of Matkin's conduct was made to the society by a member; in April 2005, the discipline committee resolved to take no further action. Matkin says, "I feel a victim of a rotten system. It's as if I was walking down the street and a lump of ice fell off a building and hit me on the head."[24]

THIRTEEN

BELLETRISTIC THEORETICIAN

Marvin Singleton

Marvin Singleton is a gifted man. He is a graduate of Yale and Berkeley law school. He wrote a good book about the U.S. journalist H.L. Mencken. He is intelligent and intellectually sophisticated. In 2006 he was in a U.S. maximum security prison fighting extradition to Canada.

MARVIN KENNETH SINGLETON, once a lawyer in Nelson, British Columbia, later became an English teacher in Wichita, Kansas. He taught introductory composition courses at Wichita's Butler Community College, and was a part-time librarian at nearby Rose Hill High School. On the evening of Monday, August 30, 2004, after a busy day in the classroom, Singleton was watching television in his modest basement apartment in a house on Wichita's west side. There was a knock at the door. It was Deputy U.S. Marshal Logan Kline and his partner, come to arrest him.

The Government of Canada had requested Singleton's extradition from the United States in a diplomatic note dated July 9, 2004. In the eyes of Canadian officials, Singleton, charged with theft and fraud, had been a fugitive from justice since 1993. On August 26, 2004, the United States Attorney's Office for the District of Kansas, acting on behalf of Canada, obtained a warrant for Singleton's arrest. "He was pretty surprised when we arrested him," Deputy Kline said, "but he was a real gentlemen. He was no problem. We let him get dressed properly, and get his vitamins. It seems like he took a lot of vitamins."[1] Singleton, denied bail, was put in the Sedgwick County Jail. He began a long and mysterious fight against extradition to Canada. He hasn't been back to his apartment on the west side of Wichita since the night he was arrested.

Singleton is a tall man, slim and fit, now largely bald, with intense eyes.[2] When he was young, he was, by all accounts, handsome, with dark and wavy hair. Those who know him well say he is articulate, witty, and fond of plays on words. He has a big vocabulary. He once put up a sign on his office door that said "belletristic theoretician." He has a high opinion of himself. He is described as an intuitive, rather than a linear, thinker. Friends say he has a quick temper, bad judgment about people, and takes opposition very personally. He loathes those in authority, and instinctively sides with the underdog. Some suggest he exhibits the classic symptoms of manic depression. Singleton has always preferred the company of women to men, and is sometimes referred to as a "ladies' man." A long-time friend and admirer, a woman who lives in Nelson, describes him as "an intelligent and wise man, brilliant." He has been married twice. He separated from his first wife in the mid-eighties. His second marriage was brief.

Marvin was born in Kansas, on February 4, 1933, to Kenneth and Bessie Singleton. The Singletons have been described as a large and poor Depression-era farm family, very careful about saving and spending. (Marvin says that his father once worked for the U.S. Department of Defense as an early computer specialist.) Singleton got a bachelor of arts degree from Yale University ("certainly the first boy from these parts to go to Yale," somebody said), and then a master's degree and doctorate in English at Duke University in Durham, North Carolina. His doctoral thesis, on H.L. Mencken, the famous Baltimore journalist, writer and editor of the magazine *American Mercury*, was published in 1962.[3] He then went to the University of California at Berkeley law school.[4] Someone who knows Singleton well says he wanted a law degree "because of some paranoid thing about needing to defend himself." While at Berkeley, Singleton protested against the Vietnam war, and was an outspoken critic of the Warren Commission's report on the assassination of

President Kennedy. He still believes that the FBI and CIA were implicated in the plot to kill Kennedy. Today he refers to himself as "a law/humanities person." He describes research he has conducted over the years as showing "unsurpassed, advanced law/humanities reflection ... interdisciplinary ability unmatched conceptually."[5]

In 1967/68, Singleton was Fulbright Professor at the University of Oslo in Norway. He then immigrated to Canada (as part of the "Norwegian quota," he says), not wanting to return to a United States still embroiled in Vietnam. His first Canadian job was teaching history at the University of Manitoba. Then, in 1971, Singleton took a job teaching English at Notre Dame University in the small city of Nelson, in British Columbia (population about ten thousand). Nelson is in the Selkirk Mountains on the extreme west arm of Kootenay Lake and is generally regarded as a particularly charming town. It is home to a number of erstwhile Americans, some of whom came to Canada as draft dodgers. Singleton describes Nelson as "a rather resplendent little city."[6]

In 1977, the B.C. government closed Notre Dame University. Singleton was passionately opposed to the closure and fought it for years, earning the enmity (he believes) of many powerful government figures. He wanted to stay in Nelson: He liked it there, and cut something of a figure around town, known as both a serious ladies' man and a genuine eccentric. He turned to the best thing that seemed available to him—the practice of law. He passed a handful of exams required by the Law Society of British Columbia for those with foreign law degrees, and articled for the Nelson law firm of Ferguson and Ferguson. In 1978, Singleton was admitted to the B.C. bar. He describes himself as having been an "edgy litigator," someone who "occasionally tested the edges in litigation because of my California (Berkeley) cultural background, including my research into the late San Francisco tort activist Melvin Belli's career." He adds that his stance was flagged by the Law Society of British Columbia as "too American," and that the law society was bitter toward him because he had a role in uncovering serious professional negligence of a large Vancouver firm.

Singleton resigned from the Law Society of British Columbia, at age fifty-seven, in October 1990. The reason for this unusual step is unclear (he says he never planned to practise law for more than about ten years—it was all part of his education as a "law/humanities" person). Following his resignation he still maintained the office where he had practised law. He continued to exercise power of attorney over the affairs of Miss Haroldine Copp, an elderly lady living in a nursing home (Copp died in 1991 at age eighty-four, and Singleton became executor of her estate), and remained executor of the estate of a retired millionaire farmer from Alberta, called John George, who had lived with his mother north of

Nelson in an $8,000 trailer. It was how he behaved in these two appointments that later led to charges of fraud and theft.

In 1988, Singleton had what he calls a "bright idea." He decided to develop an upscale residential compound near Nelson. Money was transferred from the Copp and George estates into the bank accounts of two companies incorporated by Singleton, 433 Winchester Management Corporation, and Silvertip 1000 Enterprises Ltd. These companies bought 140 acres of raw land, and, as Singleton proudly describes, a $90,000 D-8 Caterpillar with ripper and three blades to clear snow, build ponds, and improve roads. Singleton claims that "433 Winchester" and "Silvertip" were owned by the Copp and George estates when these purchases were made. At the very least, he says, the Copp and George estates clearly had equitable ownership of the assets that had been acquired. Others—including the police—said that Singleton owned the companies, and the Copp and George money had, in effect, been stolen. Singleton seems to have been the sole director and officer of both companies. His idea, or its execution, turned out to be not so bright after all, and the real estate venture failed. It is not clear what happened to the 140 acres.

"Where's the money, Marvin?" asked a Vancouver newspaper article in 1994.[7] A local Nelson lawyer, Don Skogstad, who had replaced Singleton as executor of the Copps estate, decided that funds

were missing.[8] Allegations were made that Singleton
had stolen about $80,000 from the Copp estate, and
perhaps $400,000 or more from the George estate.
It is unclear, but it seems that Singleton also lost his
own money in the failed real estate venture. He
speaks of his economic ruin, and the need to
re-establish himself financially. The question was not
only, where's the money? It was also, where's
Marvin? In 1993, Singleton had disappeared
(although he maintains that he was registered with
the U.S. Social Security Administration and would
have been easy to find at any time).

After Skogstad's discovery that funds were
missing, Sergeant Doug Haddow of the Nelson City
Police opened a file. Constable Marty Misner of the
RCMP local commercial crimes unit was interested.
After six weeks spent reviewing Singleton's files, the
two officers decided that his administration of the
Copp and George estates had been fraudulent. Theft
and fraud charges were laid under the Criminal
Code.[9] A Canada-wide warrant, and then an international warrant, were issued for his arrest. But where
was Marvin? Later, the *Nelson Daily News* described
what happened after the Canada-wide warrant was
issued:[10]

Despite his run from the law, the two officers
managed to track Singleton down.

"We had him pinned down in Texas, a place
called Nocona."

The town's sheriff was "keeping an eye" on Singleton on the local cops' behalf.

"Marvin at the time was living under a bridge," Haddow recalls. "In a holiday trailer under a bridge that separated Texas and Oklahoma."

But by the time an international warrant was issued for the arrest, the Texas sheriff had retired and local police lost Singleton's trail.

Where had Singleton gone after Nocona? Mexico, some thought. But the trail went very cold. In January 1995, the Law Society of British Columbia announced that it had paid $559,878 to the George estate, the amount it concluded had been stolen by Singleton. In a press release, the law society said, "While acting as executor of the George estate, Mr. Singleton received approximately $1,070,000 of the estate's assets, but paid only $500,000 of bequests. By the time an administrator was appointed, the estate account had been virtually emptied, and Mr. Singleton had left the country." In August, $77,710 was paid to the Copp estate by the law society. That seemed the end of the matter. The files were put in a drawer. It was yesterday's business.

Singleton was destitute. For a time, he worked as a combine operator and trucker in the Kansas wheat harvest. From what he earned from the harvest, he bought a bright blue three-quarter-ton windowed 1978 Ford van. Parked first on the bank of the Red

River near Nocona, Texas (where the local sherriff apparently kept an eye on him), and then on the streets of Wichita, Kansas, the van was his home. It had a camp stove, and a sleeping bag on the steel floor. Singleton's only income was $292 a month from U.S. Social Security. While he lived in the van, says Singleton, he wrote two unpublished novels, what he describes as a "wheat" novel and a literary western (he is still polishing the western, which he hopes in due course will win a Golden Spur Award from the Western Writers of America). He says he has also written an unpublished trilogy called *The Cyprian Epic*.

In 1998, Corporal Luc Quenneville of the RCMP's commercial crime division was posted to Creston, British Columbia, about 125 kilometres from Nelson.[11] Reviewing cold cases in the region, he came across the dusty Marvin Singleton file. He decided to look at it once a year, just in case something came up. In the late summer of 2004, browsing once more through the file, he noticed something he hadn't noticed before—the name of Singleton's estranged daughter, Solveig, his only surviving child (by his first wife).[12] He searched "Solveig Singleton" on Google. He found a high-powered lawyer and right-wing lobbyist in Washington, D.C., with that name.[13] He emailed her and asked if she was Marvin Singleton's daughter. Yes, was the reply. He telephoned her and asked if she ever heard from her father. "Yes," she said, "every two or three years. He's in Wichita, Kansas."

Corporal Quenneville began filling in extradition papers. Soon, Deputy Marshal Kline was at the door of Singleton's basement apartment.

Singleton was denied bail. The Sedgwick county jail became his home. He decided to fight extradition to Canada, acting as his own lawyer. Sometimes he says he is fighting extradition because the lengthy delay in his case, as well as the antagonism of the Law Society of British Columbia and many Canadian lawyers and high government officials, preclude effective legal representation and a fair trial in Canada. He says that the charges against him have been revived, and Canada is seeking extradition, because powerful forces in Canada harbour great hostility toward him. They are hostile because he is American, because there is prejudice against people from the B.C. "interior high country" that he regards as his real home, and because he was active in protesting the closure of Nelson's university (which, he alleges, was closed partly because of the strong American presence in its faculty). He says of the Canadian attempt to extradite him that "here was a politically-charged opportunity to bait in Canada an individual perceived as an American, and two precarious Liberal governments—one Provincial and one Federal—decided in the late Spring of 2004 some advantage might accrue from publicity even a weak case [sic]." He also believes that U.S. authorities have political motivations in his case. He writes, referring to himself in the third person:

A Portland, Oregon lawyer named Brandon
Mayfield, wrongly charged as a principal in the
Madrid Train bombing early in 2004, was thoroughly investigated. This investigation of
Mayfield's Kansas roots led through a cousin to
the cousin's girlfriend, who had a tenant ...
Singleton. That information alone, according
to Singleton, might not have led American
authorities to throw him up to be baited by
Canadian nationalists. But there may have been
more. By June, 2004, Singleton, at the request
of a Kansas attorney representing a Florida man
who was attempting to sue Henry Kissinger for
War Crimes, provided the man with a number
of books and articles.... These mailings by
Singleton were known because the disabled
Vietnam veteran seeking international law
indictment of Kissinger ... had his mail from
Singleton opened and scrutinized. In any
event, the State Department decided to draw
Canada's attention to a man Canada could
have located in less than an hour for the past
8 years, if they had wanted to. Singleton
believes the United States wants Canada to
reciprocate by sending down Canadian
nationals of near-Eastern origin for the United
States to interrogate. The United States
suddenly had a rare bargaining chip to throw to
the previously-uncooperative Canadians.[14]

Singleton has also suggested that the FBI and CIA, still concerned about his belief that they were involved in the Kennedy assassination, were "delighted to induce Canadian elements to reactivate old charges ... and finally set up an extradition."[15] The Canadian authorities, he says, acted out of "an embattled, insecure nationalism that could brand an American as a sort of Captain Alfred Dreyfus." He adds, "No one figured Singleton being his own Zola in his Dreyfus case."[16] Singleton also believes that U.S. and Canadian authorities do not understand, and are attempting to misapply, basic notions of extradition law, and says he is not willing to be a party to "anything goes" law.[17]

Singleton's extradition hearing was held on December 20, 2004, before Magistrate Donald Bostwick of the U.S. District Court for the District of Kansas. He appeared before Magistrate Bostwick in an orange jumpsuit and wearing leg shackles. For reasons that are not clear, Singleton dropped his earlier application for bail. At the hearing he argued that the request for extradition did not give an adequate statement of the facts of the case or provide the text of relevant Canadian laws to support extradition. He argued that there should be no extradition because the offence for which extradition was being sought was of a political character. He argued that there was severe misconduct by the prosecution when it presented certain inappropriate materials to the court, particularly "inflammatory" press clippings from Canadian newspapers that were part of a "press campaign" against him (these materials were withdrawn by the Government of Canada and did not form part of the record of the case). On February 25, 2005, Magistrate Bostwick rejected all of these arguments. Singleton was ordered to be held without bail, pending his surrender to Canada.

Singleton did not give up. He appealed Magistrate Bostwick's decision, delaying his release to Canadian authorities. He continued to deny that he was subject to extradition, and sought release from custody, filing a petition of habeas corpus. There was a flurry of further supplemental filings by Singleton in the summer, autumn, and early winter of 2005, amending and reamending his habeas corpus petition and related filings, and making elaborate and emotional attacks on Magistrate Bostwick's judgment. In one of these filings, Singleton accuses Bostwick of "palpable errors" and refers to the "Defendant's annihilative, obliterative, total rebuttal of the naked conclusory charges in Canada's affidavits."

On September 16, 2005, Singleton was moved to the Leavenworth Detention Center, a maximum security prison, where a prisoner does "hard time"; the cells are very small, the mattresses are very thin, the food is bland, and there are lots of rules. When he first got to Leavenworth, there was a confrontation with guards, and he was put in solitary confinement (known as "the hole') for two weeks. Singleton told me that he liked "the hole": He was by himself and could concentrate on his studying and writing. Now he shares a cell with three other prisoners. He spends a lot of time playing cards and chess with other inmates. Singleton is allowed visitors for two hours every Friday evening, and one international call a week for fifteen minutes. He can't have much correspondence, because stamps are in short supply. He says the food is better at Leavenworth than at Sedgewick, and there is a better law library. He can get vitamins (they were not available at Sedgewick). He can trade chocolate bars for oranges, which makes him happy. Singleton has lost twenty pounds since being transferred to Leavenworth. Other inmates call him "the very old man." He says that he expects to live another twenty-five years.

At the end of 2006, Marvin Singleton's habeas corpus application was still pending (early in 2006 Singleton seemed willing to withdraw his application, waive extradition, and consent to be transferred to Canada, but subject to conditions that were not acceptable to the U.S. Department of Justice). He spends his time in prison working on his legal arguments, writing "prison poems" (in which, he says, he puts "quite a bit of stock"), and working on his literary western. (A source of annoyance is that he is not allowed a laptop computer.) Jim Cross, public affairs officer for United States Attorney Eric Melgren, District of Kansas, said, "Mr. Singleton has explored every legal means to stay where he's at."[18] When asked why he had done so, particularly since the general view is that Canadian justice and jails are more agreeable than those in the United States, Mr. Cross said, "Everything about Mr. Singleton is a mystery." Some simply suggest that his judgment is impaired, and that he needs psychiatric help. Others say that he does not want to be dragged back to Nelson for trial, allowing local friends and acquaintances to judge his guilt or innocence for themselves. One person wrote to me, "His fantasy that he is being persecuted for crimes he did not commit is fragile, and if confronted by actual evidence he would have to account to himself for what he has done. Perhaps he prefers to live in his fantasy." Someone else said that Singleton wants to come back to Nelson as a free man, not dragged back in shackles. Part of the explanation may be his simple bloody-mindedness. He wrote to me, "My problem is: I can't 'let go of the tiger's tail.'"[19]

Singleton has written, "Everyone assumed that extradition is a facile power-politics ritual, grinding down defendants from a grouping unable to cope with U.S. hard-time jail conditions and supposedly passive in the face of defence-counsel collusion in massive prosecutorial and judicial misconduct."[20] He continues:

> I did not want to slide along with a bad extradition a politicized fiddle ... and because the Justice Dept. relies on "white-collar" types simply being unable to hack jail conditions, jail

conditions they are responsible for generally. In a larger sense, as a child of the 20th century, it is my turn to be the individual caught up in being a "d.p."/political pawn whipsawed by 2 sovereign states which feed on little human victims of crude, bullying/"stereotyping."… [I] want to show the two "States" that an individual can put up a fight.

And then, on a different tack:

I have come upon the truth that a Law/ Humanities Authority must recognize the importance of *Injustice* as a key dimension of Law/Humanities wisdom-of-value. I believe "Injustice" can only be understood by persons incarcerated for not less than a year under dubious, politically-influenced charges. Thus my prison experiences, and reflections thereupon, were the required "Post-Doctoral" regime I had to personally experience.

I decided to go to Leavenworth and see him. I wrote, saying that I wanted to come and visit. Singleton seemed reluctant. He wrote back that at any moment his habeas corpus application might be successful, and he would be gone from prison; I risked a futile trip. Anyway, he said, he could give written answers to any questions that I asked in writing: Wouldn't that be better? I persisted. He put

me on his visitors' list. His case manager sent me the
visitation rules; in particular, I should not wear
orange clothing that might make guards, in an emer-
gency, confuse me with an inmate. The only time
Singleton could be seen was six-forty-five on a Friday
night. One Friday, in January 2006, I got on a flight
to Kansas City. When I got there, I rented a car and
drove west, out of Missouri, into the farm country of
Kansas, on my way to Leavenworth.

The Leavenworth Detention Center is
surrounded by two high razor wire fences. Each has
a remote-controlled gate that opens once you have
been studied and approved on closed-circuit television. The second gate will open only when the first is
closed, which means that for a time, coming or
going, the visitor is caught in a kind of no-man's land
between razor wire. Once inside the building, you
must produce identification and register. No
"personal property" is allowed—that includes books.
No "contraband" is permitted—that includes
obvious items like guns and drugs, and puzzling
things like photographs. You wait in a waiting room
for your name to be called. I was the only white
person there. Most of the waiting visitors were black
women with small children, presumably going to
visit partners and fathers inside. While I waited, an
old white man went past, going (he said) to teach
"creation science" to a group of inmates. There are
about eight hundred prisoners in the Leavenworth
Detention Center. I discovered later that, as I waited

in the prison, Vice-President Cheney was across the road at Fort Leavenworth, a U.S. Army installation, pinning medals on soldiers.[21]

After a long wait, a guard shouted, "Visitor for Singleton!" I went through a metal detector into a room lined on three sides with thick windows, with a telephone and a chair in front of each window. Behind each window was an inmate. In front of the window were the inmate's visitors. On the fourth side of the room was a guard who watched everyone. The room was full of the noise of shouted one-sided conversations and crying children. Behind one of the windows was an old, white man. It was Marvin Singleton, once a member of the Law Society of British Columbia, wearing orange clothing, waiting for me.

We talked for an hour over the telephone. He told me his story, much as I have told it. I asked what it's like for an old white one-time lawyer to be in a place like this. "If you have certain social skills, you can get along," he said. What about violence? "I've had to threaten to mix it up a couple of times," he said, "just to make a point." He seemed good-humoured about prison, and cheerful. The guards are like hotel clerks, he said. I wonder, Does he like living in Leavenworth? Does he relish his predicament, which marks him as a rebel who fights the establishment on points of principle? He said he finds being in prison "irksome." He said that he resents looking out of the window and seeing razor wire.

I asked him if he's made a serious miscalculation. He'd been fighting extradition for almost eighteen months. He may well lose, and be taken back to Canada in chains, having spent a long time in a harsh U.S. prison for nothing. He admitted that could happen. Meanwhile, he polishes his legal arguments and works on his prison poems.

Visiting time is over. The guard tells us all to leave. I say goodbye to Marvin Singleton. As I go, I see his slightly smiling face behind the thick glass. He waves. I wave back.

Later Singleton wrote to me, "Your visit earlier in the month is very much appreciated. Speaking with you opened up my 'siege mentality' and helped me think more realistically."[22] But it would not be long before he decided that I should be added to the list of those who had done him wrong. In May 2006, I published an account of my visit to Leavenworth in the magazine *Canadian Lawyer*.[23] It brought forth a long letter of outrage from Singleton.[24] "[I]t was likely you would represent me in the Canadian trial," he wrote. "This led me to discuss freely with you matters I did not want publicized." He accused me, among other things, of breaching solicitor-client privilege, elaborately sustaining a deceit, baiting him into correspondence, and violating the ethics of literary journalism. I replied:[25]

There was never any suggestion by me that I was prepared or able to represent you.... What someone tells a writer and journalist who is interviewing him may obviously end up in print....

I am sorry you feel the way you do. I enjoyed meeting you, and all along have felt sympathy for your plight: I thought that might have been evident from my magazine piece. I wish you the best, but must say that this correspondence is now finished.

FOURTEEN

GUERRILLA FIGHTERS

Eric Belhassen and Christina Finney

A woman fell in love with a con man. He moved in, and they got married. When the woman discovered the truth about her new husband, she threw him out and sought legal recourse. She and the lawyer representing her estranged husband became bitter enemies. Long after the con man disappeared into an Egyptian prison, the woman and the lawyer waged an intense battle that seemed to last forever. The struggle eventually became one between the woman and the Quebec Bar Association which, she said, was negligent in responding to her complaints about the lawyer. Many years later, the Supreme Court of Canada agreed. In the end, the story is not so much about two men who behaved badly, as about how poorly the legal profession can be governed, and how one person who feels the victim of injustice can be ferocious in response.

CHRISTINA FINNEY met Samir Badr in 1986.[1] Christina was fifty-one years old and recently divorced. She lived in Lachine, Quebec, and taught music at St. Thomas High School in Pointe Claire. Samir was a fat, bald Egyptian, sometimes described as "charismatic," who claimed to be a businessman and a scientist. In a July 17, 1994, feature article in Montreal's *Gazette*, reporter Susan Semenak described what happened shortly after Christina and Samir met: "He would call her 10 times a day. When she saw him, he'd play love songs on the stereo and they would talk for hours. He told her she was the smartest, the most beautiful woman in the world, and it wasn't long before they were lovers."[2] Samir moved into Christina's house in Lachine, a two-storey stone cottage full of antiques. They married soon afterward.

Samir persuaded Christina to buy two rental properties with him, a fourplex in Pointe Claire and a duplex in Lachine (Christina was interested in real estate, and already owned several buildings). Samir and Christina both contributed to the modest down payments on these properties, but somehow only Samir's name appeared on the titles. Without telling Christina, Samir quickly remortgaged the fourplex and duplex. He pocketed the mortgage proceeds, and put the properties up for sale.

Samir Badr had a lawyer friend called Eric Belhassen. In May 1990, Jasson Finney, Christina's son, was involved in a contract dispute involving his

music band, and needed legal advice.[3] Samir told
Christina that Belhassen could help Jasson. She gave
Belhassen a $2,000 advance on his fees. Soon, both
Jasson and his mother were dissatisfied with
Belhassen's work, and asked for their money back.
Jasson complained to the Quebec Bar Association
about the $2,000 advance. Christina complained
separately, and was told by bar officials that Belhassen
was a lawyer in good standing and that she should
settle with him. Belhassen's response to her
complaints was to sue her for $6,800, which he
claimed she owed him for work relating to her real
estate investments. (Four years later, a court
dismissed this claim.) Belhassen, described by some
as a "madman," had chosen a formidable opponent.
Christina Finney was tough, vindictive, energetic,
and emotional. She never—ever—gave up.

In 1990, Christina split up with Samir Badr. She
had discovered that he kept an apartment in Pointe
Claire where he saw other women. She had found
out that he already had a wife, and six children, in
Plattsburgh, just across the Quebec–New York
border. She had discovered that he had a criminal
record, in both Canada and the United States.
Christina went to see a lawyer, Robert Francis.
Francis sent Badr a letter demanding that Badr hand
over Christina's share of the Lachine and Pointe
Claire properties. Francis had the properties seized so
that they could not be sold until the dispute was
resolved.

Badr reacted angrily. Susan Semenak reported in *The Gazette* that he "sent a bailiff with a restraining order to [Christina's] door, alleging that she had hit him in the head, spit in his eye and broken his finger."[4] He filed several civil suits against Christina seeking damages. One claimed that she had tried to burn down the Pointe Claire fourplex. Others asserted that she owed him money for construction work he had done on her properties. As part of the general onslaught, Samir Badr's lawyer, Eric Belhassen, initiated bankruptcy proceedings against Christina's lawyer, Robert Francis (the petition in bankruptcy was later withdrawn).

In 1992, the Quebec Superior Court resolved the dispute over the fourplex and duplex in Christina Finney's favour, awarding her $179,000. A gas station owned by Badr was sold in a sheriff's auction so that Finney could be paid. Eric Belhassen saw a notice of this sale posted in the courthouse. He contested the distribution of the sale proceeds. He claimed that Badr owed him $62,500 for legal services that had not yet been billed. Finney was paid only $112,000, with the balance being frozen until Belhassen's claim could be resolved. The bitter feelings between Christina Finney and Eric Belhassen increased. Belhassen alleged that in October 1993, Finney approached him outside a courtroom and threatened to kill him. In August 1994, she was acquitted of these charges. In November 1993, Finney's new lawyer, Joan Benson, was threatened by

Belhassen when they bumped into each other outside Montreal's Alexis Nihon Plaza. Belhassen told Benson, "You know, if I were you, I wouldn't be involved. You've got five children and why would you want to be involved in something like that … with me?"[5] Frightened, Benson withdrew from the file.

Samir Badr spent eight months of 1992 in a New York State prison, for defrauding the Clinton County welfare system of $20,000. In February 1993, he tried to cross the Canada–United States border at Derby Line, Vermont, but was arrested as an illegal immigrant and sent to Montreal's Parthenais jail. There he stayed until October 1993, when the refugee board denied him refugee status and ordered him deported to Egypt. When he arrived in Cairo, Egyptian authorities promptly put him in prison (the reason is not known). Susan Semenak reported that, in January 1994, Samir wrote to Christina from his Cairo cell, professing love, and asking for $5,000 to be sent to him as soon as possible.[6] He was not heard from again. Christina Finney was through with Samir Badr. The fight with Eric Belhassen was only beginning.

Belhassen already had a long disciplinary history with the Quebec Bar Association, beginning shortly after he became a lawyer.[7] In 1979, he served phony lawsuits on tenants engaged in a rent dispute with their landlord, telling the tenants that the suits would be dropped if the rent was paid. He was given a severe reprimand by the bar association. In 1983, he was again reprimanded, this time for negligence and making needless presentations in a court case. In 1985, he was reprimanded once more, and his right to practise law briefly suspended, for falsifying information on a seizure order. Also in 1985, he was disciplined for having taken out abusive proceedings against an insurance company. The bar's professional inspection committee began an investigation into his practice in 1985; it took five years to complete. The committee's report in April 1990 concluded, "Not only does the incompetence of Mr. Belhassen put the rights of his clients in peril, but it discredits the lawyer's profession and undermines the authority of the courts.... It is urgent to suspend the right of Eric Belhassen to practice." In June 1992, he was ordered by the bar's executive committee to report all his activities to a supervising lawyer. Meanwhile, he continued to practise law, and complaints about his conduct and competence continued to be made. Despite this long history, when Christina Finney complained to the bar in 1990, she was simply told that Belhassen was a lawyer in good standing.

In May 1994, a two-member disciplinary committee of the Quebec Bar Association considered twenty-three misconduct charges that originated in complaints filed against Belhassen by Finney in 1993. It concluded that he had been waging a "judicial guerrilla war" against her. It found that his bankruptcy proceedings against Robert Francis had been initiated "for the sole purpose of harming this colleague and his client." It ruled that Belhassen's suit against Badr, claiming unpaid legal fees, was "manifestly unreasonable." The committee described Belhassen's conduct as "seriously compromising the public good" and suspended his right to practise pending further investigation, promising a final decision by the end of June.[8] When he was suspended in 1994, Belhassen, forty-seven years old, had been a member of the bar since 1978. The first complaint about his behaviour had been made in 1979.

Belhassen quickly challenged the committee's ruling before the Quebec professions tribunal. In January 1995, the tribunal upheld the committee's decision. In February, Belhassen was able to get the next disciplinary hearing, intended to resolve finally the matter of his disbarment, put off until September 5. Belhassen told the disciplinary committee, "I know that it's very important to get me disbarred completely, but I have other obligations." Christina Finney expressed outrage at the delay.[9] In September, the disciplinary proceedings began again. Geoff Baker of Montreal's *Gazette* reported:[10]

Belhassen, representing himself without a lawyer, had to be warned repeatedly about his tone, tactics and attitude by the two lawyers presiding at the hearing.

... When Belhassen asked that Finney be excluded from proceedings Thursday because she is to be called as a witness later, she attempted to speak but was told, rather abruptly, to leave the room. She could later be heard shouting in a corridor as the Bar's prosecutor, Jacques Fournier, tried to calm her down.

Finney has expressed concern that Belhassen is trying to delay the proceedings long enough to get the charges dropped because the case is taking too long.

In an interview Thursday night, Belhassen said he has not ruled out that tactic.

A few days later, Albert Janin, one of the two members of the disciplinary committee, discovered that for technical reasons he was not qualified to hear the case, and resigned. Adjournment followed adjournment. The fight between Belhassen and Finney continued in intensity. In October and November 1996 Belhassen sent bailiffs to Finney's house on eleven occasions, armed with seizure orders and bills for court costs from earlier litigation. Most of these bills were later thrown out by the court. The file before the disciplinary committee grew to thirty-seven volumes, with 8,636 pages. In April 1998, eight years after Finney first complained to the Quebec Bar Association, and one year after the disciplinary hearings ended, the bar association reached a final decision: Belhassen was guilty of misconduct and was permanently disbarred. His appeal to Quebec's professions tribunal was unsuccessful. They say that he now sells real estate. Late in 2005,

Christina Finney reported that she saw him on the street, and he looked "very prosperous."

Eric Belhassen may have been disbarred, but Christina Finney was not done. She now turned her wrath on the Quebec Bar Association, its director general, Pierre Gauthier, and two of its "syndics" (benchers). She began a lawsuit against all of them in January 1996, arguing that the bar had been negligent in not protecting her from Belhassen. She said that she had been forced to take early retirement because of stress, and that her finances had been destroyed by Belhassen's legal harassment. She sought almost a million dollars in damages. The French-language trial took place in September 1998, with Finney representing herself, often accompanied by her mother in a wheelchair offering moral support. (Finney's French is not good; later she said the bar exploited her language difficulties, and the bar's lawyers laughed at her during the trial and made disrespectful jokes about her in French.) During the trial, counsel for the bar denied wrongdoing, but also cited the immunities granted by the legislation that governs the professions in Quebec. In December, Justice Jean Normand delivered his verdict.[11] Because of the immunity granted to the bar by section 193 of Quebec's Professional Code,[12] Finney had to prove intentional wrongdoing, which, said Justice Normand, she had failed to do.

The Quebec Court of Appeal heard Finney's appeal in September 2001. A newspaper account described her presentation as "impassioned, emotional—sometimes angry."[13] Giving its judgment in June 2002, the Court of Appeal said that Belhassen posed a threat to the public, and the bar knew that this was the case. It found that the time that elapsed between Finney's complaints in 1993 and action by the bar was inexcusable. The bar, said the court, had failed to protect the public, as required by section 23 of the Professional Code, which states, "The principal function of each corporation shall be to ensure the protection of the public," and accordingly did not enjoy s. 193 immunity. Christina was awarded $25,000 for "moral damages."[14] The Quebec Bar Association appealed to the Supreme Court of Canada.

The Supreme Court considered the case in February 2004. It was now almost twenty years since Samir Badr moved in with Christina Finney. This time Finney was represented by Guy Pratte, eminent counsel and son of a former Supreme Court of Canada judge.[15] Justice LeBel delivered the court's judgment on June 10.[16] He began:

An independent Bar composed of lawyers who are free of influence by public authorities is an important component of the fundamental legal framework of Canadian society. In Canada, our tradition of allowing the legal profession to regulate itself can largely be attributed to a concern for protecting that independence and to lawyers' own staunch defence of their autonomy. In return, the delegation of powers by the State imposes obligations on the governing bodies of the profession, which are then responsible for ensuring the competence and honesty of their members in their dealings with the public.... Subject to the limits defined by the applicable legal rules and principles, a law society will be liable for a breach of this supervisory duty. Such cases are indeed rare, but one has arisen in this instance.

Justice LeBel emphasized that, under the Quebec Professional Code, the primary objective of professional organizations is to protect the public, and that the monopoly enjoyed by lawyers was not created for private purposes, but rather to recognize their social importance. That monopoly, he said, carried with it the obligation to monitor competence and supervise conduct. And then:

The Court of Appeal passed harsh judgment on the conduct of the Barreau, particularly in respect of its lack of diligence and its slowness to act, not to say its lack of action, in its handling of McCullock-Finney's complaints. In my view, that judgment was justified. The attitude exhibited by the Barreau, in a clearly urgent situation in which a practising lawyer represented a real danger to the public, was one of such negligence and indifference that it cannot claim the immunity conferred by s. 193. The very serious carelessness it displayed amounts to bad faith, and it is liable for the results.

After the judgment was announced, Finney said, "It's really something ... for someone to get the 20,000-member Barreau single-handedly."[17] She kept the $25,000 the Court of Appeal awarded; the Supreme Court ordered the bar to pay her reasonably incurred costs of the litigation. In an editorial on June 15, Montreal's *Gazette* commented, "This unambiguous ruling ... should make all of the provinces 40-plus professional organizations start combing through their files for any incompetent or criminal members they may have failed to deal with.... Professional bodies are not unions or social clubs. They are legally obliged to uphold professional standards and to monitor their members' compliance with these standards." The decision in favour of Finney was noticed outside Quebec. Beppi Crosariol, writing in *The Globe and Mail* on August 16, 2004, said that it "has sent a chill through the corridors of the provincial law societies that police the conduct of lawyers."[18] Christina Finney was something of a hero.

Still she was not finished. In January 2001, Finney had commenced a new action, alleging "abuse of power," against the Quebec Bar Association, its director general Pierre Gauthier, and the lawyers who represented the bar in the earlier trial (Jean Saint-Onge and the firm of Lavery, deBilly). She sought $3.5 million dollars in damages—a million dollars for loss of enjoyment of life, $500,000 for attacks on her honour, and $2 million in punitive and exemplary damages.[19] Finney alleged that Justice Normand (the trial judge) was biased because of his earlier involvement with the Quebec Bar Association, particularly as *bâtonnier* of Trois-Rivières (a *bâtonnier* is the elected representative of the local bar); that documents under court seal (Belhassen's medical records) were improperly produced by lawyers for the bar; and that she was denied the services of an interpreter.[20]

The action against the bar association and the other defendants was finally tried in Quebec Superior Court in January 2006.[21] The trial took nine days, with Finney—once again—representing herself. Justice Carole Hallée gave her thirty-one-page judgment on March 14. She rejected all Finney's accusations and awarded costs against her. She said that the Supreme Court of Canada had already decided the relevant issues. Justice Hallée, nonetheless, went on to comment on the particulars of Finney's accusations in order, she said, to remove any doubt. On the question of improper production of documents under seal, after a detailed analysis of what happened, the judge said that Saint-Onge and Lavery, representing the bar, had behaved in an exemplary fashion. On the language issue, the judge said the result would have been no different had the trial been held in English. Allegations about possible bias of the trial judge were rejected out of hand. Finney, said the judge, had made her fight with the legal profession a full-time job. She claimed to want a full and fair hearing, but she wanted it only according to her own agenda. She blamed all her troubles and worries on her fight and on persecution by lawyers. But, said the judge, only she can stop it all.

At the end of the trial, leaving the courtroom and realizing that things had not gone well, Finney shouted out, "See you all in the Court of Appeal."[22]

WHY DOES CHRISTINA FINNEY DO IT? "I want justice," she told me just before the January 2006 legal proceedings began. "I am protecting Canadian democracy and the system of justice. As for the bar, I was the first one to break into that little club of theirs. They don't intimidate me," she says. Then she adds, "Although, sometimes I do get a little scared. There are days when I feel very depressed. My children tell me, it's enough, I should stop now. But, you know what? I want justice. That's what I want. I'm not giving up."[23]

FIFTEEN

THE LAST HOPE

Angie Codina and Harry Kopyto

Angie Codina and Harry Kopyto were lovers. They were also each other's lawyers. They were clever, aggressive, unreasonable, intemperate, and irritating. They were committed to a romantic and old-fashioned concept of class struggle. They fought what they called "the Establishment." They had no respect for the courts or the legal profession, which reciprocated their hostility. The Toronto newspapers, particularly *The Globe and Mail*, for a time followed their every step, almost adoringly; there were front-page stories and lead editorials written about them, and op-ed pieces that they wrote themselves. But, in the end, Angie and Harry were consumed by their bad judgment, febrile emotion, and absurd rhetoric. They lost support and respect. They became figures of fun to some. They were hated by others. They were disbarred. When Kopyto was kicked out of the Law Society of Upper Canada in November 1989, the headline in Vancouver's *Province* newspaper was "Famous lawyer ousted."[1] In 2000, Angie went to prison in New York State.

ANGELINA MARIE CODINA was born in Uruguay. Her family immigrated to Canada in 1965. She graduated from the University of Ottawa law school in 1983. Harry Kopyto describes her as a "brilliant technical lawyer." She called herself a Marxist. In May 1989, the *Toronto Star* reported that she flew to Beijing and gave a ten-minute speech before a crowd of five hundred thousand protesters in Tiananmen Square. She described her speech to the newspaper: "I told them that their protest was vital to the development of democratic principles within a socialist state."[2] Harry says that he was dazzled by Angie and her lifestyle. "She would spend $10,000 on jewellery at the drop of a hat," he says. "She was building an international immigration law empire." They met in 1984—"I was bowled over," says Harry.[3]

On Monday, August 7, 1989, the RCMP waited at Pearson International Airport to arrest Codina. Thirty-one years old, she was on her way back from the Portuguese colony of Macau (now part of China) where she had lived on and off since 1987. Codina fainted when the RCMP took her into custody. She was charged under section 95 of the Immigration Act with counselling a foreign resident to misrepresent a

material fact to Canadian immigration officials.[4] She
spent her first night back in Canada in a Metro
Toronto police cell. In the morning, she was released
on $50,000 bail, secured by the seven-bedroom
Forest Hill house where she had lived for some time
with Kopyto. Three weeks later, the house on
Dunvegan Road, one of the most fashionable residential streets in Toronto, was up for sale—asking
price, $1.76 million. Kopyto, a self-described
Marxist-Leninist, told the *Toronto Star*, "Here I am
living among a class of person I have class hatred
for."[5] Perhaps his inability to meet the $11,000 per
month mortgage payments was more significant than
his class hatred. For years, Codina had paid the mortgage and the heating and food bills. But now,
Codina's immigration law practice was in difficulty
and money was scarce.[6]

On April 1, 1993, a jury found Codina guilty of
immigration fraud. In May, a judge sentenced her to
six months in jail. She immediately appealed her
conviction and was released on $25,000 bail.
Codina, aided by eminent criminal defence lawyers
Clayton Ruby and Alan Gold, fought ferociously and
with considerable skill. In January 1995, the Court
of Appeal quashed her conviction on the grounds
that the judge may have misled the jury on important
areas of evidence, and directed a new trial.[7] On
February 27, 1997, she was convicted a second time
by a jury and fined $5,000. But in February 1999,
the Ontario Court of Appeal set aside the second

conviction, finding, yet again, that the jury had been improperly charged.[8] Justice Goudge giving judgment said, "The event giving rise to the charge took place well over eleven years ago. The appellant has been prosecuted twice without success. The charge, while important, is not among the most serious. In the circumstances, it is appropriate that these proceedings be stayed and I would so order."[9]

A different kind of trouble for Angie Codina had begun in 1991. Two young lawyers who worked in her law firm were assigned files funded by the Ontario Legal Aid Plan. A docket form was stapled on the inside of each file folder, and all work performed on the file was reported on the docket. When a file was completed, the folder was given to Codina, who would send an account to Legal Aid. The two young lawyers discovered that many accounts sent to Legal Aid contained numerous entries of time spent by Codina, time they believed was bogus. They went to the audit and investigation department of the law society. A criminal investigation began. On June 18, 1992, search warrants were executed at Codina's office and at the house on Dunvegan Road (which, despite Harry's class hatred of his neighbours, had not been sold). Alan Gold, acting for Codina, went before the Ontario Court of Justice and attacked the validity of the search warrant. Justice Humphrey was not impressed by Gold's arguments.[10] He said:

The justice would have been fully justified in
issuing a search warrant on the lawyers' statements alone. In their statements they describe
how Ms. Codina's spouse, Harry Kopyto, a
former lawyer who was disbarred because of
irregular billings to Legal Aid, was virtually
practicing law through Ms. Codina and in fact
he was preparing the accounts to Legal Aid,
which were then certified by Ms. Codina and
tendered for payment. There was also information from the lawyers that trust monies were
deposited in the general account which was
barely in the black and often cheques written
on that account were NSF. There was evidence
from the lawyers that Ms. Codina was living
hand to mouth since she was paying enormous
amounts of money on the mortgage on her
Dunvegan Road home. There was evidence
from the lawyers that bogus interpreter fees
were claimed on the Legal Aid accounts and
that the actual interpretations were done by
staff who were not paid for that service or
through a bogus company....

With respect to the scope of the warrant, in
light of the information the justice had about
the goings on at the law firm with Harry
Kopyto acting as the Wizard of Oz behind the
scenes, and considering that the lawyers
described serious concern about the number of

unethical and illegal activities, the justice might well have issued an authorization less restrictive than the one he authorized.

Added Justice Humphrey:

I know that Mr. Gold's brilliant, lofty and engaging argument deserves better treatment by me. While initially during the argument I showed some enthusiasm for his arguments, on more mature consideration and reflection the feeling passed as the reality of the situation settled into my thoughts.

The search warrant question answered, Codina was then charged with defrauding the Ontario Legal Aid Plan of about $20,000 in 1991 and 1992, billing for about 270 hours of work she never performed. Her trial was not until late 1997. She was found guilty on two counts. The judge described her behaviour at the trial as "arrogant and aggressive." In January 1998, he sentenced her to six months in jail. The judge said that "she presented herself as a legal Joan of Arc but the evidence I heard does not support this." He called her "devious, very aggressive and dishonest." Finally, in 2002, because of this conviction, Codina was disbarred in Ontario.[11] In Canada, at least, Codina's legal career was over.

Meanwhile there was serious trouble for Codina in another part of what Harry Kopyto had called her "international immigration law empire." In 1996, she had opened a law office in New York City, with a staff of sixteen (four of them lawyers), in the elegant Helmsley Building on Park Avenue. Several of her clients at that office, who had paid fees in advance, claimed that they had not received promised legal services, and reported her to the New York bar. When it was discovered that she was not qualified to practise law in New York State, the bar complained to the New York Attorney General's office. On March 20, 1998, the Attorney General executed a search warrant and seized files from Codina's office. (It was two months after her conviction in Toronto, and Codina believes that the New York prosecution was initiated by the Canadian authorities, annoyed that she had slipped from their grasp, under a reciprocal agreement between the two jurisdictions.) In May 2000, following a ten-day trial in Manhattan, she was convicted of fraud, larceny, and practising as a lawyer in New York State without being admitted to the bar. The judge described her as "a cold calculating repeat offender who refuses to acknowledge and take responsibility for her criminal behaviour, and, thus, presents no hope of rehabilitation." Codina called her conviction "politically motivated."[12] Sentencing took place in July. A triumphant July 24, 2000, press release issued by Eliot Spitzer, now the New York Attorney General, announced:

Angie Codina, who fraudulently portrayed herself as an immigration lawyer and victimized hundreds of people seeking to become United States citizens, was sentenced to a term of 9 1/3 to 28 years in prison and ordered to pay $108,840 in restitution by Manhattan State Supreme Court Judge Laura Visatacion-Lewis....

Testimony at the trial indicated Codina defrauded as many as 1,000 victims. Witnesses testified they each lost from $7,000 to $178,000 and that Codina stole more than $260,000 in legal fees from the 17 victims named in the charges against her. One victim who was scheduled to testify was unable to do so because he was stranded in the Czech Republic as a result of an exclusion procedure for which he had originally sought Codina's legal assistance.

But the legendary Spitzer, like others before him, had underestimated Codina. She appealed, and in September 2002 the appellate division of the New York Supreme Court quashed her conviction and ordered a new trial.[13] The 1998 search warrant had been improperly issued. The evidence obtained pursuant to the warrant was inadmissible. The new trial took place in April 2003, and Codina was convicted again, but given a lesser sentence. When last heard of, she was prisoner number 66854, in

"E Pod" of the Monmouth County Correctional Center, Freedhold, New Jersey.

On September 10, 1985, Codina and Kopyto published an article in *The Globe and Mail* about prison.[14] It began:

> Imagine a city of 12,000 people ruled by a faceless bureaucracy that determines to whom they speak, what they eat, what they read and where they work. There is no privacy, not even for bodily functions. There is no right to vote, to decide what to buy or what to wear. Sex is forbidden. Any form of disobedience can result in disassociation in primitive isolation cells without ventilation, where every breath comes with difficulty. Despite such repression, a cycle of anger and frustration leading to violence burst out periodically.

> This is the city where Codina herself lived fifteen years later. She told a journalist that her capacity for "intellectual abstraction" allowed her to make the transition from lawyer to prison gardener and hospital porter.[15]

HARRY KOPYTO was born in a displaced persons camp in Ulm, Germany, on December 13, 1946. He says that more than a hundred of his relatives died in the Holocaust. He came to Toronto with his parents in 1952, living in the College and Spadina area (where his office is today). His mother, Frieda, went to work in a factory. His father, Israel, worked as a tailor. Harry graduated from Osgoode Hall Law School at York University in 1970.

Kopyto first attracted public attention in December 1980, in what the *Toronto Sun* called the "Chanukah Caper." He was representing a man charged with trafficking in narcotics. Kopyto asked that the jury trial be adjourned because it fell on the same day as the Jewish holiday of Chanukah. The judge granted the adjournment. On the day in question, a gowned Kopyto was spotted in another court room. Crown counsel in the trafficking trial told Kopyto he intended to tell the judge that Kopyto had misled the Court. Kopyto reacted angrily; he later testified that he felt a Christian was attempting to interfere with his rights as a Jew. He had requested an adjournment, said Kopyto, because if the trial went ahead on the scheduled day, he would be unable to celebrate Chanukah with his family in the traditional way the evening before, since trial preparation would have to be done. The judge ordered that Kopyto appear later in the week to explain what happened. Kopyto didn't show up, sending his secretary instead. Now it was the judge who was angry. He found Kopyto guilty of two charges of contempt. Responding to emotional evidence given by Kopyto at the contempt hearing, the judge said, "What this case has absolutely nothing to do with … is Mr. Kopyto's right to live his life as a Jew; it has

nothing to do with his having been born in a
displaced persons' camp; it has nothing to do with
Nazi persecution."

But, on appeal, Kopyto's convictions in the
Chanukah Caper were set aside.[16] Justice Brooke for
the Ontario Court of Appeal said that, although
Kopyto's conduct was unreasonable and unprofessional, there was doubt that he intended to mislead
the judge, and that subsequently the judge was
wrong to treat as inappropriately qualified an
apology that Kopyto gave the court. The Ontario
Attorney General promptly appealed the acquittal to
the Supreme Court of Canada. Kopyto responded by
saying that "the universal feeling in the legal community is that they're out to get me." The Supreme
Court declined to hear the appeal.

By March 1982, Harry Kopyto was considered
interesting enough to be featured in a front-page
story in *The Globe and Mail*:[17]

"Harry Kopyto," Harry Kopyto says, "does
not sue persons unless they are very wealthy
and establishment people. I sue major corporations and I sue the government. I sue the
police."

... He has no friends in the legal profession,
whose membership he describes as "self-
important, egotistical, egomaniacal in some
cases, materialistic.... They think they're God's
gift to the world, they have overblown evalua-

tions of themselves, they are more concerned with how much money they can make than with serving their clients."

... "The people I represent," he says, "wouldn't be represented by anyone else. I'm the last person they come to. I am the dead end. After me there is nothing. Oblivion. I am the last hope."

One of Harry Kopyto's closest friends was Ross Dowson (Dowson died in 2002). An avowed follower of Leon Trotsky, Dowson was a full-time Canadian political agitator for a succession of organizations, particularly the Revolutionary Workers Party, the League for Socialist Action, and the Socialist League. In his obituary, *The Globe and Mail* noted that Dowson "managed to make a significant mark on the Canadian political scene from the sidelines, in part by being a thorn in establishment's [*sic*] side."[18] In the seventies, allegations were made that the RCMP had improperly investigated the activities of the League for Socialist Action and of Dowson.[19] Kopyto, Dowson's lawyer as well as his friend and a political sympathizer, got busy. In 1982, after the failure both of an action against the RCMP for defamation and of an attempt to have criminal charges brought against RCMP members, Kopyto, as a final effort, commenced civil proceedings in small claims court. In 1985, Judge Zuker dismissed the claim, in part on the grounds that the action was not brought within the statutorily prescribed limitation period.

When Zuker dismissed Dowson's claim, Kopyto gave an angry interview to Kirk Makin of *The Globe and Mail*. Makin's story, published on December 18, 1985,[20] quoted Kopyto at length: "This decision is a mockery of justice.... It stinks to high hell. We're wondering what is the point of appealing and continuing this charade of the courts in this country which are warped in favor of protecting the police. The courts and the RCMP are sticking so close together you'd think they were put together with Krazy Glue." (Kopyto later admitted that these were not impromptu remarks; in particular, he says that he had carefully prepared the Krazy Glue comment the night before.) Ian Scott, the Attorney General of Ontario, was not amused. On February 7, 1986, Kopyto was charged with "scandalizing the court." In another interview, after he was charged, Kopyto told Makin, "This may be the biggest freedom of speech case of the decade.... I think I'm being persecuted for my views.... It's incredible that a person should face jail for expressing an opinion.... I give voice to the secret world of the dispossessed and the oppressed.... Most lawyers are fixers and manipulators of the system."[21]

By April, Makin was reporting that "the fight to acquit Harry Kopyto has grown to include lawyers of all political stripes, fringe-party activists and supporters from the arts and media."[22] At an April fundraising party at his house, Kopyto read a poem titled "Ode to Krazy Glue." (Harry fancies himself a poet. "When I was in Spain one time," he told me, "I wrote a poem about how a lobster feels when it is put in the cooking pot.") In September, Robert Priest and his band, The Great Big Face, gave a benefit concert for Kopyto at Lee's Palace, a nightclub on Bloor Street West in Toronto.

The trial, with Harry facing the obscure and archaic charge of scandalizing the court, began on Monday, September 22. On Tuesday, Drew Fagan in *The Globe and Mail* was reporting that "the trial of outspoken lawyer Harry Kopyto for contempt of court appears destined to provide a wide-ranging examination of the criminal justice system."[23] On Wednesday, Kopyto, giving evidence on the freedom of conscience section of the Charter of Rights and Freedoms, told the court that the principle that guided him in practising law was "to give body and flesh to the deep thirst I have for equality." He told the now familiar tale about losing most of his relatives in the Holocaust, and being born in a displaced persons camp. On Friday, while Angie Codina as one of his defence lawyers was questioning Attorney General Ian Scott, Kopyto rushed out of the prisoner's box and demanded to question Scott himself. Justice Montgomery refused, and the trial was adjourned until Monday, amid chaos.

On Wednesday of the next week, Justice Montgomery refused to allow the defence to call evidence attempting to prove that the courts were biased, on the grounds that it would be contrary to the public good. "I can't allow this proceeding to turn into a circus," he said, perhaps a bit too late. The trial concluded on Friday, October 3, with an impassioned address by defence lawyer Charles Roach, who compared Kopyto to Socrates.

On Friday, October 17, judgment was given. Kopyto was found guilty of scandalizing the court. On November 6, he was sentenced. Justice Montgomery ordered him to apologize for his remarks, and said that until such an apology was made Kopyto could not appear before the courts. Supporters of Kopyto in the courtroom responded with catcalls. Leaving the courthouse with his eleven-year-old son, Marc, and nine-year-old daughter, Erica, Kopyto said he would not apologize and would appeal. A lead editorial in the November 7 edition of *The Globe and Mail* commented that "any sentence for this law is too harsh, because the law itself should not exist.... The public interest will be far better served by respected lawyers and others challenging Mr. Kopyto's assertions than by using the weight of the law to silence him.... Once the state gets into the business of punishing people for their opinions, where does it stop?"[24] On November 27, 1987, the Ontario Court of Appeal, although highly critical of Kopyto's behaviour, overturned his conviction on the charge of scandalizing the court, with a majority of the judges holding that the offence was contrary to the guarantee of freedom of expression found in the Charter of Rights and Freedoms.[25]

The Law Society of Upper Canada still wanted to discipline Kopyto. "They were out to discredit the radical lawyer movement," he later told me. "The pursuit of me was part of an attack on activist lawyers in general. And there was an institutional antipathy towards me personally." A variety of disciplinary proceedings against him continued.[26] At first, the law society's principal charge was based on the statements about Kopyto's unprofessional behaviour made in the Court of Appeal judgments that acquitted him of scandalizing the court. Then, in January 1989, allegations of a different sort were made. It was said that Kopyto had deliberately submitted inflated bills to the Ontario Legal Aid Plan. It was alleged that, among other things, he had billed the plan for more than twenty-four hours' work on a single day, and for over a thousand phone calls made on behalf of a single client.

In an agreed statement of facts, Kopyto unexpectedly admitted that he had overbilled Legal Aid, saying that overcharging was a result of poor bookkeeping, guessing, and estimating, by an extraordinarily overworked lawyer who turned no one away and was working forty-five hundred hours a year. Why did he suddenly give in? "My political supporters dropped away," he told me. "They felt I had betrayed them. Suddenly it wasn't about justice, fighting for the little guy, it was about stealing money. I became isolated. And I had to admit that I'd been sloppy. But not crooked!" The disciplinary committee promptly found him guilty of professional misconduct and recommended to the law society that he be disbarred. In a front-page story on July 25, *The Globe and Mail* reported Kopyto's reaction: "I only admitted to doing what hundreds and hundreds of lawyers do."[27] On September 17, there was a rally for Kopyto outside Queen's Park. About sixty people showed up. Frances Kelly described the scene the next day in the *Toronto Star*:[28]

> Harry Kopyto loving Harry Kopyto. The downtrodden loving Harry Kopyto. The blind, the disabled, the abused, the dispossessed and the poor loving Harry Kopyto.
>
> ... "We're on the edge, but we haven't gone over it yet," Kopyto shouted to applause and cheers of "God love ya, Harry," and "Victory to Harry Kopyto" from the crowd.
>
> "It ain't over until the fat lady sings," he shouted.

On November 8, the law society accepted the disciplinary committee's recommendation and disbarred Kopyto for fraud. An outraged Kopyto said he was betrayed: "There was clear agreement I had been negligent, not fraudulent. There were no facts that said I was fraudulent."[29] His daughter Erica sat weeping beside him as the decision was announced.

"The fight has just begun," he said. "Now, they've got me real angry." *The Globe and Mail* reported that "Kopyto trudged off, hugging his daughter and hefting a briefcase covered with a sticker saying, Boycott South Africa, Not Nicaragua."[30] Later Kopyto said that eighty inmates in Toronto's Don Jail were going to skip their lunch in solidarity with him. On November 14, Kirk Makin reported in *The Globe and Mail*:[31]

In a telephone linkup at the prison, Mr. Kopyto and *The Globe and Mail* [*sic*], inmate Patrick McCarman led a series of group cheers for the embattled lawyer.

"Okay, guys. How do you feel about Harry?" Mr. McCarman hollered down the cell-block.

"Yayyyy," chorused the inhabitants.

"Wait a second," Mr. Kopyto interrupted feverishly. "Where is my damned tape machine?"

"I may not be all that popular with the law society," Mr. Kopyto said afterwards, "but if I was in the Don Jail I would be king. They may even be starting a club for me soon."

Kopyto's disbarment took effect on November 19, 1989.[32] The rules of professional conduct do not allow a lawyer to share premises with a disbarred lawyer. Codina's disbarment was yet to come. On the instructions of the law society, a wall was built in the office they shared, separating Harry and Angie.

HARRY'S INTIMATE RELATIONSHIP with Angie is long since over; she is far away, in prison. Now Harry lives with Geraldine Bowman, who teaches mathematics at Seneca College in Toronto. He met her forty years ago, when they were both students at York University. But, Harry reports, he often speaks to Angie on the telephone.

He works as a legal agent in Toronto. He doesn't seem to be engaged in great civil liberties issues anymore. He doesn't seem to be fighting injustice and oppression. On April 22, 2005, the *National Post* reported, "A Dalmatian that was turned over to the Toronto Humane Society while his owner was on an extended trip to Greece was yesterday ordered back into the care of the man who says he lovingly shared his pizza and doughnuts with the dog."[33] Kopyto represented the dog's owner at a Small Claims Court hearing. In June 2005, he was again in Small Claims Court, this time representing a ten-year-old suing the Applewood Hockey Association, who was kicked off his house league team because of conflict between his father and coaching staff.[34] Harry would passionately deny a description of what he now does as trivial. "I'm fighting injustice every day," he told me. "I'm doing what I always did."

One September afternoon, I visited Harry at his office in downtown Toronto, on the second floor of a nondescript building on College Street just off Spadina Avenue, in the neighbourhood where his family lived when they moved to Toronto in 1952. The sign on the door said "Resnick Services" ("my holding company," Harry later explained, "named after my ex-wife.") The office, small and scruffy, looked like the office of a struggling member of the bar. There were law books piled on bookshelves, and the room was furnished with the battered red leather chairs that, for some reason, lawyers favour. Harry came out to greet me. He looked old (he was born in 1946). His grey hair was braided in a pigtail. He wore a black T-shirt, shorts, socks, and sandals. We sat down in his cluttered office. I asked him about the political philosophy that has informed his life. He started talking, rapidly and passionately. "My creed," he said, "is deconstructionism. Ruthless criticism of everything. My job is to destroy injustice. I use law as a political weapon. I use it to educate. The legal profession deals in law. I deal in justice."

"Today as a legal agent I have exactly the same practice as I had before," Harry told me. "When it disbarred me, the Law Society clipped my wings, but I can still fly!" He called to his secretary, "Get me page 6!" She didn't have to ask what page 6 he was talking about, and pulled out the dissenting reasons of bencher Thomas Carey in the disbarment proceedings, the reasons that favoured Harry's case. The next morning I listened to his weekly morning show on a Toronto radio station. He was, yet again, attacking the police. "The police are just a gang of Crazy Harrys," he said. Then, at the end of the program: "Do you need legal advice? Call me." And he gave his telephone number.[35]

SIXTEEN

THE SEARCH FOR JUSTICE

How much justice can the average Canadian afford? None.[1] For financial reasons, he is denied use of the legal system and courts, key institutions of government and democracy. It is as if the right to vote in a general election were given only to those with an income above a certain level. Do not look to the legal profession to solve this problem. The answer will not be found within legal culture.

In 2004, average after-tax earned income for a "non-elderly" male living in Canada (a Statistics Canada category) was $28,300; for a "non-elderly" female, $24,400.[2] If this is how much money you make, you won't get legal aid (available only to those who are really poor), and will almost certainly be denied the pro bono legal services that socially concerned lawyers occasionally offer.[3] If you need a lawyer, you'll have to dig into your own pocket. In the cities, even a junior lawyer charges $200 or more for an hour's work. A routine matter can cost as much as a mid-priced car. Fees of this magnitude are beyond almost everybody's ability to pay.

Young people go to law school to improve or consolidate their social and economic position. Horatio Alger told us that hard work and virtue can overcome adversity and lead to great wealth and respect.[4] Law school can put the child of a poor immigrant into a Bay Street bank tower. It can make the son of a Cape Breton coal miner into someone to be reckoned with. It can give a reputation to the child of parents who could barely read and write. It can make the daughter of immigrants from Taiwan into a professional. It can gratify a father who is a pillar of the church and the community. (None of this necessarily prevents eventual disaster and disgrace, as we have seen.)

Law school encourages cosmopolitan desires and pursuits. It reaffirms traditional values. It teaches what the economist Paul Seabright has called "the narrative."[5] Students are encouraged to anticipate wealth and power; they are told how to serve the rich, for it is only the rich who can afford lawyers;[6] they are taught rules, technique, and toughness, and learn to avoid emotional involvement or moral judgment. This is what law students, and those who will eventually employ them, want. Access to justice is not on the agenda. The one-time young idealist who backpacked through Asia and dreamed of a better world becomes a tax lawyer; the youthful environmentalist who once supported the Green Party, general counsel to an auto-parts company. As Michael Gorra has written of characters in Ward Just's novel *Forgetfulness*,[7] "They have discovered that a career creates its own requirements, which are often at odds with the ideals that led to the choice of that career in the first place. At their outer edges, the compromises people make become ... Lebenslüge, the lie that allows one to live."[8]

Every year an army of law school graduands disperses into society and the workplace.[9] These new lawyers are clever and educated, ambitious and aggressive. With few exceptions, they seek to participate in what their predecessors have established, not to reform what is there. They will make their way in the world as they find it. They will adopt its ways and eschew change. They will be reluctant to turn away clients, no matter who they are and what they want. They will be helpful, not judgmental. They want to work hard and be successful (although, as I have described, some will stray). They will serve their rightful masters. Their masters do not include the poor, or even the middle class.

As the stories I have told show, a lawyer in practice, whether he is by himself or with a handful of others or in a large firm, has much to contend with. Harsh economic imperatives promote inefficient work habits and even bad behaviour (overbilling, for example, or other forms of cheating). There is no moral compass, for it is not the job of the lawyer to pass moral judgment. Professional mastery of legal rules, and the need to manipulate them on behalf of clients, may encourage disrespect for values that are found in the law. Almost all of its practitioners see law as a business (the judgment of the B.C. Court of Appeal in the Strother litigation notwithstanding[10]). And there is extensive psychological baggage. To quote Martin Seligman once more, "Lawyers are trained to be aggressive, judgmental, intellectual, analytical and emotionally detached. This produces predictable emotional consequences for the legal practitioner: he or she will be depressed, anxious, and angry a lot of the time."[11] Lawyers are also pessimistic. And sometimes, as some of my stories show, a lawyer descends into what can only be called a kind of madness, exhibiting psychopathic and other deviant behaviour. None of this favours justice in the broader community.

Many new lawyers join the great Canadian law firms and stay there for many years, even for their entire careers. In these great firms, which serve the economic elite (corporations, governments, a few rich individuals), a lawyer's work is as challenging as it gets; his prestige, considerable; his income (in due course), huge. Many of these firms are very large, with multiple offices in Canada and overseas. They have enormous overheads. They are businesses. Their need and desire for profit is relentless. Abusive billing practices are common. Oversight of quality and integrity is difficult, if not impossible. The partners and associates hardly, if at all, know each other. Knowing and trusting your partner or colleague is unusual and unnecessary; firm size, geographic spread, and organizational and legal structures (such as the limited liability partnership, creating what David Cay Johnston calls a "moral hazard"[12]) ensure that this is the case. A law firm has little concern for access to justice by the man on the street.

Who will give us access to justice? Will the provincial law societies, explicitly charged with regulating the legal profession and protecting the public interest, do it? They have made some attempts to address the issue, principally by permitting contingency fees and class actions.[13] In October 2002, the then treasurer of the Law Society of Upper Canada announced a new conduct rule for contingency fees. He said, "The strength of our legal system lies in its ability to be accessible to all people."[14] (The new rule was prompted by the judgment that year of the Ontario Court of Appeal in *McIntyre v. Attorney General of Ontario*, which held that contingency fee arrangements are not necessarily illegal.[15]) In 2004, a news release by the Ontario Ministry of the Attorney General announced some technical amendments to the rules governing contingency fees in the Solicitors Act. The treasurer of the Law Society of Upper Canada commended the Attorney General "for moving ahead with contingency fee legislation in Ontario, designed to enhance access to justice."[16] But the amended rules seem restrictive more than anything else,[17] and few lawyers are ready to give up substantial and largely guaranteed hourly rates to gamble on contingency arrangements.

I have described the often ineffective and confused treatment by regulators of lawyers gone bad. Sometimes egregious conduct leads to disbarment; sometimes, to a token reprimand. Sometimes a disbarred lawyer is easily readmitted to legal practice (after cooling his heels for a few years); sometimes he will remain forever beyond the pale. Sometimes sex with a client is regarded as acceptable; sometimes, not. The distinction between one case and the other may be elusive, and the discrepancies from one province to another considerable. Sometimes a law society's disciplinary process is completely ineffective. On some occasions, confronted with a big problem, a law society seems simply baffled.[18]

Law societies are run by lawyers, according to the world view and temperament of lawyers. It is no surprise that they have the same agenda and attitude as their members. Law societies are by nature conservative and protective of the status quo. They nourish their own and are the voice of the establishment. A law society member who is different risks severe criticism and marginalization.[19] It is not the law societies of Canada that will change things. Among lawyers themselves there is growing resistance to the expanding concept of "professional misconduct," and to the idea that law societies should be wide-ranging policemen of lawyers' lives, supplementing, if not supplanting, everything from the teachings of the church to the strictures of the criminal law. This is particularly seen in the way law societies have dealt with sexual transgressions by lawyers.

Sir David Clementi has said, of the current British system of regulating the legal profession and of the radical new system that he has proposed, "The current regulatory system is focused on those who provide legal services: the new framework will place the interests of consumers at its centre."[20] As described earlier, the 2004 Clementi Report contained four main sets of recommendations. It proposed that the legal profession be overseen by a new legal services board with a lay majority chaired by a non-lawyer and accountable to Parliament. It recommended that the profession lose its powers to investigate complaints against lawyers, and that a new independent office be created for that purpose. It recommended that lawyers should be free to enter into partnerships with non-lawyers. And it proposed what quickly became known as the "Tesco law," allowing outside companies or individuals to own and manage a law practice (named after the British supermarket chain that offers do-it-yourself divorce and will kits, legal forms and agreements, and law books for the layperson, and that is expected to offer traditional legal advice once the Clementi reforms are implemented).

It is time for very similar reforms in Canada. There are no good arguments for the view that only lawyers can regulate lawyers, and many good arguments for the contrary position. Disciplinary action should be in the hands of an independent body; for a law society to investigate, prosecute, and judge violates elementary principles of justice. Above all, it is time to put the interests of the consumer at the centre of the system, making the legal system and the courts available to all. Only the government can do these things.

There will always be lawyers who go bad, no matter what the legal system. But the legal system should have no tendency to create, encourage, or permit transgressions. Those will inevitably come from the vagaries of human nature, which cannot be escaped.

EPILOGUE

I finished writing *Lawyers Gone Bad* in December 2006. The book tells stories of lawyers who got into serious trouble. It discusses broad themes suggested by those stories—problems in legal culture and education, the inadequate governance and discipline of the legal profession, and extremely poor public access to the legal system, mostly because of the high fees that lawyers charge. This introduction to the paperback edition, written at the end of April 2008, brings readers up to date with recent developments.

What is the fundamental duty of a lawyer to his client? That was the question at the heart of the Robert Strother case (Chapter 6). Strother, after a retainer letter with one client expired, acquired a financial interest in another client in the same line of business, whose interests he then preferred. The first client took exception and sued. Did Strother's duty of loyalty to the first client survive the expiry of the contractual obligations found in the retainer letter? The trial judge said it didn't, the court of appeal unanimously said it did, and it was left to the Supreme Court of Canada to decide this fundamental issue, one way or another, once and for all.

But, in *Strother v. 3464920 Canada Inc.*, the Supreme Court decided one way and another, stumbling badly. Judgment was handed down on June 1, 2007. Five justices (Binnie, Deschamps, Fish, Charron, and Rothstein) took an expansive view of a lawyer's fiduciary duty and thought that Strother had behaved improperly. The other four disagreed fundamentally. To make matters worse, the majority eviscerated their harsh assessment of Strother's conduct by dramatically limiting the consequences for him of what he had done. Instead of having to hand over $30 million to his erstwhile client, as the court of appeal said he should, Strother had to disgorge only a million dollars, possibly less. The result of this unappetizing Supreme Court of Canada stew was that although Strother, in a strict legal sense, lost the case, he was able with some justification to issue a press release that, in effect, claimed victory.

Justice Binnie gave the discursive majority judgment in Strother. He wrote, "Fiduciary duties provide a framework within which the lawyer performs the work and may include obligations that go beyond what the parties expressly bargained for." Lawyers, he said in a colourful sidebar, are professional advisers, not used-car salesmen or pawnbrokers. A lawyer's duty of loyalty, in some circumstances (where he is motivated by a personal financial interest, for example), may extend beyond contractual obligations found in a retainer letter.

Chief Justice McLachlin, writing for the minority, had a completely different point of view. She considered that "whether a conflict between two clients exists is dependent on the scope of the retainer between the lawyer and the client in question. The fiduciary duties owed by the lawyer are moulded by this retainer, as they must be in a world where lawyers represent more than one client." It was not open to the court, said the chief justice, "to superimpose a broad fiduciary obligation independent of and inconsistent with the retainer." Later in her reasons, she commented, "If the duty of loyalty is described as a general, free-floating duty owed by a lawyer or a law firm to every client, the potential for conflicts is vast." Finally, she referred abstrusely to the "underlying difficulty" in Justice Binnie's majority judgment: "The reasons do not ask whether there was a direct conflict between Strother's duties under his retainer ... and what he was doing, but rather whether there was a decontextualized potential or past conflict." After all the huffing and puffing and hand-wringing about Robert Strother over the past few years, the Supreme Court gave us something for everyone and nothing much for anyone.

What's happened to Ingrid Chen? The one-time Winnipeg immigration lawyer (Chapter 4) is most famous for hiring members of a motorcycle gang to intimidate clients who upset her. "It has to be one shot and then gone," she instructed her Los Bravos contact in a telephone conversation monitored by police. In 1999, in her first encounter with the law, Chen was arrested and charged with drug and immigration offences. The Law Society of Manitoba suspended her almost immediately. It was not until May 2006, however, that a disbarment hearing was held, and not until March 14, 2007, that the discipline committee finally threw her out of the legal profession. Ingrid Chen's disbarment appeal was dismissed by the Manitoba Court of Appeal on January 18, 2008.

Toronto lawyers Simon Rosenfeld and Peter Shoniker, both wild and crazy guys (Chapter 5), were convicted separately of money laundering. Shoniker was sent to prison in September 2006 and was given early release in January 2007. In March 2005, Rosenfeld was sentenced to three years in jail; his appeal is expected to be heard later in 2008, and in the meantime he has been free on bail. Shoniker liked to hand out business cards describing himself as Sir Peter Shoniker, O.B.E., and was recorded by police as saying (inaccurately, as it turned out), "There isn't a fucking judge in the city who would grant an authorization [tap] on my line." As for Rosenfeld, he invited an undercover RCMP officer to a golf game where, he claimed, there would be naked women at every hole. Remarkably, both Shoniker and Rosenfeld are still lawyers, members of the Law Society of Upper Canada, although each has undertaken not to practise law until the law society agrees. Meanwhile, Canadian lawyers continue to be exempt from statutory requirements that suspicious cash transactions be reported to FINTRAC, a federal government agency, although the federal government has indicated that new regulations, to take effect at the end of 2008, will put lawyers on the list of those subject to record keeping and government scrutiny of suspicious financial transactions.

What's the latest on sex with clients (Chapter 7)? There have been interesting developments in the cases of Gary Neinstein and George Hunter. In 2004, the Law Society of Upper Canada wanted to disbar Neinstein because of his sexual relationship with a client. In June 2007, the law society, battered and bruised after a long battle with Neinstein, finally settled for imposing the lesser penalty of a twelve-month suspension. The reasons of the original Neinstein panel, the one that wanted him disbarred, were in part:

> We ask: how can it be in this day and age, given the public interest and expectation that a lawyer will be disbarred for stealing a client's money, save exceptional circumstances, that the solicitor will not face the same fate when he/she commits sexual harassment, a breach of trust which violates the dignity and self-respect of a client or employee?

That panel was chaired by George Hunter, who went on to become treasurer of the Law Society of

Upper Canada and president of the Federation of Law Societies. But Hunter, who pursued Neinstein with such sanctimony and enthusiasm, was a man with a secret. In February 2007, his hidden life unravelling, Hunter himself admitted sexual misconduct with a client. On March 28, 2007, a law society hearing panel summoned up all its fortitude and suspended him for sixty days. The reasons of the Hunter hearing panel had quite a different tone from that of the Neinstein panel chaired by Hunter:

> The member should not be treated more harshly as a result of his former status as Treasurer and as a bencher. Nor, of course, should he receive favoured treatment, although he is entitled to make the important point that his entire career is incompatible with this misconduct and that, therefore, this misconduct can be regarded as "out of character." We have no difficulty in so finding.

No doubt Hunter, his blue-chip law firm, and the law society hoped that was the end of the matter, but it was not to be. In December 2007, the client with whom Hunter had an affair brought a legal action against him and his law firm, seeking $1.4 million in damages. George Hunter was back in the public eye. "Hunter and firm sued over steamy affair," said one headline in early 2008. "Ex-law society head, firm sued over sex with family law client," said another. There was no comment from Gary Neinstein.

Michael Bomek (Chapter 9), once an admired criminal defence lawyer practising in northern Manitoba and Saskatchewan, was convicted of sexual assault, drug trafficking, and making child pornography. I thought his story was over when he went to jail in January 2007, but in February 2008, Bomek was back in the news, hauled out of jail to be tried for obstruction of justice. Former Saskatchewan provincial court judge Terry Bekolay testified that in 2003 Bomek asked him for a favour in a bail hearing for Norman Custer, a twenty-seven-year-old charged with aggravated assault. In December 2003, Bomek and Bekolay had coffee at Tim Horton's, and Bomek allegedly tried to give Bekolay a nude photograph of Custer. Bekolay said he refused the photograph and was not influenced in his bail decision (bail was granted). According to news reports, Bekolay testified that he had often gone for coffee with Bomek, who would show him pictures of naked men, and that he had sex with some of them at Bomek's home in a room called the Boom-Boom Room. Bekolay, a former president of the Saskatchewan NDP, was suspended from the bench in 2006 and resigned in 2007. On February 29, 2008, Bomek was given an additional year in prison, on top of time he was already serving, for attempting to obstruct justice.

Between 1999 and 2002, Martin Wirick (see Chapter 12) was part of the biggest fraud in

Canadian legal history. In January 2006, David Baines of the Vancouver Sun wrote, "The magnitude of the fraud perpetrated by former Vancouver lawyer Martin Wirick ... is breathtaking. So is the amount of time it is taking police to investigate the case." Baines predicted that it would be two years before charges were laid. At the end of 2006, the Vancouver police and RCMP were still looking into the matter; Wirick told me then that he was ready to go to jail, but no one seemed interested in putting him away. In November 2007, Baines wrote, "Despite a large and costly apparatus for dealing with commercial crime, few white collar criminals in B.C. end up in jail." In early 2008, notwithstanding Baines's prediction in 2006 that there would be charges in 2008, the police are still investigating the Wirick affair. Is Wirick still ready to go to jail? I doubt it.

In January 2006, I went to Kansas and visited Marvin Singleton in Leavenworth prison (see Chapter 13). Singleton once practised law in Nelson, British Columbia. When I went to Leavenworth, Singleton was inexplicably fighting extradition to Canada on charges of theft and fraud committed while a lawyer. He seemed to prefer a jail cell in Kansas to a trial in Canada. But on September 5, 2006, he unexpectedly appeared in Provincial Court in Nelson and was released on bail. A local journalist told me that he has since been spotted at the local museum and the courthouse library. Someone else reports that he spends every Wednesday at the courthouse, presumably working on his defence. Crown counsel says that Singleton's trial date, on charges of theft and fraud, will be set soon. Apparently, the trial is being delayed by a large number of pre-trial motions brought by Singleton.

Meanwhile, Harry Kopyto (see Chapter 15), a disbarred lawyer who has worked for many years as a paralegal, continues an idiosyncratic fight against what he considers "injustice." In January 2008, for example, it was reported that Kopyto was considering taking the case of a client called Ron Guild to the "United Nations human rights committee." Guild, says Kopyto, was discriminated against when the federal government compensated victims of tainted blood transfusions. But time may be running out for Harry and his quixotic causes. In May 2007, the Law Society of Upper Canada, no friend of Harry's, was granted the power to regulate and licence paralegals. The law society is now implementing the licencing process. Harry has applied, but the speculation is that he will be denied a licence because he is not "of good character." Harry has been quoted as saying, "They will eat me alive and pick their teeth with my bones." In November 2007, the law society formally reprimanded a lawyer, Joseph Markin, just for associating professionally with Harry Kopyto. The law society made Markin undertake "that he will not associate in any way with Harry Kopyto … until he has approval from the Committee of Convocation to do so." The omens are not good for Harry Kopyto.

Robert Strother has walked away from the Supreme Court of Canada, bloodied a bit but largely unbowed. Peter Shoniker and Simon Rosenfeld, convicted money launderers, remain on the rolls of Ontario lawyers. George Hunter, once treasurer of the Law Society of Upper Canada, who wanted to disbar Gary Neinstein for sexual indiscretions with a client, has been suspended for two months for his own sexual misadventures. Bomek is once more in the news. Martin Wirick is still waiting to hear from the police about the biggest legal fraud in Canadian history. Marvin Singleton, fresh from Leavenworth prison in Kansas, is back in British Columbia, busy in the courthouse library preparing his defence against theft and fraud charges. Harry Kopyto confidently expects that the law society will not allow him to practise as a paralegal.

At least, the Law Society of Manitoba has finally disposed of the troublesome Ingrid Chen.

SOURCES AND
ACKNOWLEDGMENTS

The primary written sources for this book are court records, including trial and appellate judgments and transcripts, reports of law society disciplinary proceedings, and, in some instances, private documents to which I had access. I also rely, from time to time, on journalistic reporting, principally newspaper accounts.

I interviewed many people, some in person and some by telephone. I identify them, and the date and place of interview, except in the case of a few who did not want to be named. The people I interviewed included many of the lawyers I write about. Only two, Bob Donaldson and Robert Strother, refused to speak to me.[1] Martin Pilzmaker died some years ago.[2] Angie Codina did not reply to the letter I sent her in a U.S. prison. I couldn't find Reeves Matheson and Eric Belhassen. I did not speak to Simon Rosenfeld and Peter Shoniker; both were before the courts on criminal charges at the time I was working on this book. I spoke to anyone else I thought could help me understand the lawyers and stories I was writing about, including colleagues, friends, family members, and clients of the lawyers in question, law society representatives, Crown prosecutors, police officers, a moral philosopher, a psychiatrist, and journalists.

I am indebted to many people. Those who helped in various ways include Mary Adachi, Toronto; Walter Bachman, New York; Rodger Beehler, Victoria; Marilyn Billinkoff, Winnipeg; Michael Bomek, Prince Albert; Beth Brock, Nelson, British Columbia; Steven Bulut, Toronto; Lois Burke, Flin Flon; Dennis Cann, North Battleford; Stephen Cheikes, Vancouver; Ingrid Chen, Winnipeg; Patricia Chisholm, Toronto; Kirby Chown, Toronto; Daniel Cooper, Toronto; Paul Copeland, Toronto; Jim Cross, Wichita, Kansas; Brad Daisley, Vancouver; Kristin Dangerfield, Winnipeg; Avrum Fenson, Toronto; Ken Filkow, Winnipeg; Christina Finney, Lachine, Quebec; Michael Fitz-James, Toronto; Sol Goldstein, Toronto; Arnold Goodman, Watrous, Saskatchewan; Scott Gray, The Pas; Douglas Haddow, Nelson, British Columbia; James A. Hodgson, Toronto; Albert J. Hudec, Vancouver; Gillian Lewando Hundt, Leamington Spa, England; Karl Jaffary, Toronto; J. Agnew Johnston, Thunder Bay; Logan Kline, Wichita, Kansas; Henry Kloppenburg, Saskatoon; Harry Knutson, Vancouver; Harry Kopyto, Toronto; Freya Kristjansen, Toronto; Dan Le Dressay, Vancouver; Earl Levy, Toronto; W.R. (Bill) Majcher, Vancouver; James Matkin, Vancouver; Bruce McLeod, Winnipeg; Marci L. Melvin, Yarmouth, Nova Scotia; David Merrick, Vancouver;

Lore Mirwaldt, The Pas; Robert Morrison, Winnipeg; Jonathon Naylor, Flin Flon; Andrew and Janine Pavey, Vancouver; Alfred Petrone, Thunder Bay; Julian Porter, Toronto; Gerry Posner, Winnipeg; Richard Potter, Toronto; Guy Pratte, Ottawa; Gordon Pullan, Winnipeg; Luc Quenneville, Creston, British Columbia; Eileen Ryan, Fredericton; Arthur Scace, Toronto; Richard Schwartz, Winnipeg; Ian Scott, Toronto; Richard Shead, Winnipeg; Marvin Singleton, Leavenworth, Kansas; Donald Skogstad, Nelson, British Columbia; Doug Ward, Winnipeg; Kim Whiteside, Winnipeg; Martin Wirick, Vancouver; Gavin Wood, Winnipeg; and Gene Zazelenchuk, Winnipeg.

I spent the (Canadian) winter of 2006 as a visiting professor of law at the University of Cape Town in South Africa. There I tried out many of the ideas and stories in this book on my colleagues and students, and on members of the local bar. South African lawyers knew exactly what I was talking about when I described the perils of practising law. My particular thanks go to professors Mike Larkin, Julien Hofman,[3] Christina Murray, and Graham Bradfield, and to Laurie and Lourens Ackermann.

A few of these stories, in earlier and shorter versions, and some of my ideas about lawyers have appeared in *Canadian Lawyer* magazine over recent years. In particular, Chapter 1 incorporates several thoughts that have appeared in my monthly column "Law & Money." I indicate, by endnote, if I have written before on the same subject, in *Canadian Lawyer* or elsewhere.

This book was finished on December 31, 2006, and attempts to be current as of that date. Some of the cases I describe were not then over. The Law Society of Manitoba had not decided whether to disbar Ingrid Chen. Simon Rosenfeld's appeal against his conviction on money laundering charges had yet to be heard. We awaited the Supreme Court of Canada's judgment in the Strother litigation. And Marvin Singleton, sitting in a cell in Leavenworth, Kansas, where I visited him early in 2006, continued his mysterious fight against extradition to Canada.

NOTES

Epigraph

1. Sybille Bedford, *Quicksands: A Memoir* (London: Hamish Hamilton, 2005), 46.

One: Money, Sex and Madness

1. A man who kills his wife or mother in a fit of rage, or becomes a pimp, may be a lawyer, but his crime probably has little to do with his being a member of the bar. Lawyers, even in Canada, do kill their wives or mothers, or become pimps. In 1989, Maurice Sychuk, an Alberta law professor, was convicted of murdering his spouse; he had stabbed her twenty-two times in a fit of rage. In 1999, Sychuk applied for readmission to the Alberta bar. His application was unanimously rejected by the hearing committee. In 1990, Sébastien Brousseau killed his mother, stabbing her forty times; while on parole, Brousseau went to law school, and in 2006 Quebec's professions tribunal decided that he could attend the bar admission course and then be admitted to the practice of law. In 2000, Gary Wayne Patterson, a lawyer in Toronto, was convicted of pimping.

2. Steven Lubert, professor of law at Northwestern University, writes (after a reference to the famous opening line of Leo Tolstoy's *Anna Karenina*—"happy families are all alike; but every unhappy family is unhappy in its own way"):

> There is no great literature about happy families, because happiness is uninteresting and, worse, there is nothing we can learn from it. To increase our knowledge, to deepen our understanding of the human condition, we must instead turn our attention to grief. That is why physicians study pathology, engineers study disasters, psychologists study psychoses, and card players endlessly replay lost

hands. It can be helpful to identify the things you did right, but it is critical to recognize how things went wrong.

Steven Lubert, *Lawyers' Poker: 52 Lessons That Lawyers Can Learn from Card Players* (New York: Oxford University Press, 2006), 242.

3. *Samuel Ciglen v. Her Majesty the Queen*, [1970] S.C.R. 804.

4. Leger Marketing, *How Canadians Perceive Various Professions* (Montreal: 2004).

5. HarrisInteractive, "Doctors, Dentists and Nurses Most Trusted Professionals to Give Advice, According to Harris Poll of U.S. Adults," *The Harris Poll 37*, 10 May 2006, www.harris-interactive.com/harris_poll/index.asp?PID=661 (accessed 20 July 2006).

6. www.flsc.ca/en/lawSocieties/statisticsLinks.asp (accessed 20 July 2006).

7. This perception is continually fuelled by newspaper stories—for example, the story about the lawyer for one of those accused in the Air-India bombing who put his client's children on the publicly funded legal defence team. See Robert Matas, "Lawyer suspended, fined over Air-India billings," *The Globe and Mail*, 27 April 2006, A13. The phenomenon is universal. On holiday in the African country of Namibia, in April 2006, I picked up the local newspaper and read about "revelations this week that our legal practitioners can (and do) charge about N$240 to read an A4-size typewritten page at N$120 per 100 words. This may not constitute what we know as corruption, but it sure is daylight robbery!" See Gwen Lister, "Political perspective," *The Namibian*, 13 April 2006, 6. A Namibian dollar is worth about twenty Canadian cents.

8. (New York: Harper Paperbacks, 1999).

9. Cameron Stracher, "After (Billable) Hours," *The Wall Street Journal*, 24 March 2006, W19.

10. Jack Katz, *Seductions of Crime: Moral and Sensual Attractions in Doing Evil* (New York: Basic Books, 1990).

11. Robert Hare, *Without Conscience: The Disturbing World of the Psychopaths Among Us* (New York: The Guildford Press,

1993). See 61. See also Paul Babiak and Robert D. Hare, *Snakes in Suits: When Psychopaths Go to Work* (New York: Regan Books, 2006).

12. Joe Klein, *The Natural: The Misunderstood Presidency of Bill Clinton* (New York: Doubleday, 2002). See 163.

13. Theodore Dalrymple, *Our Culture, What's Left of It: The Mandarins and the Masses* (Chicago: Ivan R. Dee, 2005), 22–23.

14. xi.

15. 35.

16. Patrick Shiltz, "Those Unhappy, Unhealthy Lawyers," *Notre Dame Magazine*, Autumn 1999.

17. Martin E.P. Seligman, *Authentic Happiness* (New York: Free Press, 2002). A 2006 U.K. study of twenty-eight occupations, conducted by the vocational awards body City & Guilds, found that lawyers were second-last in the ranking of those happy at work; they fared somewhat better in the ranking of best work/life balance, tying butchers for sixth place. See "Because they're worth it—UK beauty therapists are 'made up' about their jobs," City and Guilds, 28 March 2006, www.city-and-guilds.co.uk/cps/rde/xchg/SID-0AC0478C-04C69067/cgonline/hs.xsl/9543.html (accessed 20 July 2006).

18. 178. It has been reported that a study conducted at the Virginia law school found that pessimistic law students outperformed optimistic students on traditional measures of achievement, such as exam results. See Danny Lee, "Depressed? You should be," *Times Online*, 4 October 2005, www.timesonline.co.uk/article/0,,8163-1806176,00.html (accessed 6 September 2006).

19. 181.

20. *Law Society of Upper Canada v. Codina*, [2002] L.S.D.D. No. 84.

21. Jonathan D. Glater, "Caught Between Doing Well and Doing Good," *The New York Times*, 18 November 2005, C6.

22. Thus making what social psychologists call the "fundamental attribution error," ascribing success to innate characteristics when what really counts is context.

23. In 2006 federal prosecutors in the United States began laying securities fraud charges in connection with stock option backdating. It is thought that a considerable number of Silicon Valley technology companies may have indulged in this practice. *The New York Times* noted, "As scores of Silicon Valley firms went public in the late 1990's, there was enormous pressure on many accounting firms and law firms to keep their newly minted clients happy." The story went on to quote Michael S. Melbinger, an executive compensation lawyer at Winston & Strawn in Chicago: "'These guys were dancing on leather table-tops in their leather pants.... The rules didn't apply to them. They were the new Masters of the Universe. If they called one firm and they wouldn't do it, you'd have firms lining up to take their business.'" Gary Rivlin and Eric Dash, "Silicon Valley Firms Scrutinized on Stock Option Policies," *The New York Times*, 22 July 2006, B1. In a subsequent Times story, Gary Rivlin focused on the possible role of Larry W. Sonsini, "Silicon Valley's most feared and sought-after lawyer." Rivlin noted that "Mr. Sonsini's firm provided legal counsel on corporate governance issues like the proper handling of stock options to roughly a dozen of the 25 Silicon Valley area companies implicated so far in the widening probe." Gary Rivlin, "A Counselor Pulled from the Shadows," *The New York Times*, 30 July 2006, 3-1.

24. Julie Hilden,"Scummery Judgment: Why Enron's sleazy lawyers walked while their accountant fried," Slate, 21 June 2002, www.byliner.com/story/?id=53621 (accessed 6 September 2006).

25. *Report of the Review of the Regulatory Framework for Legal Services in England and Wales*, December 2004.

26. *The Future of Legal Services: Putting Consumers First*, presented to Parliament by the Secretary of State for Constitutional Affairs and Lord Chancellor, October 2005 (Cmd. 6679).

27. David Cay Johnston, *Perfectly Legal: The Covert Campaign to Rig Our Tax System to Benefit the Super Rich—and Cheat Everybody Else* (New York: Portfolio, 2003), 275.

28. Letter to the editor in *Canadian Lawyer*, August 2005. The author's article on the Wirick affair appeared in the magazine's May 2005 issue.

29. See Michael Asimow, "Bad Lawyers in the Movies," *Nova Law Review* 24 (Winter 2000), 533. See also the book by Asimow and Paul Bergen, *Reel Justice: The Courtroom Goes to the Movies* (Kansas City: Andrews McMeel, 1996).

30. See review at www.mshepley.btinternet.co.uk (accessed 19 December 2006). This is a website called "The Missing Link," devoted to classic horror movies.

31. There is even a scholarly treatise on jokes about lawyers—Marc Galanter, *Lowering the Bar: Lawyer Jokes and Legal Culture* (Madison: University of Wisconsin Press, 2005). Galanter groups lawyer jokes into four categories: "The Lawyer as Economic Predator," "Lawyers as Fomenters of Strife," "The Lawyer as Morally Deficient," and "Death Wish Jokes." He observes that jokes about lawyers sharpened when the profession introduced hourly billing. A sample joke given by Galanter: "An ancient, nearly blind old woman retained the local lawyer to draft her last will and testament, for which he charged her two hundred dollars. As she rose to leave, she took the money out of her purse and handed it to him, enclosing a third hundred-dollar bill by mistake. Immediately the attorney realised he was faced with a crushing ethical question: Should he tell his partner?"

32. Robert Verkaik, "Unmasked: Author who exposed lawyers' antics," *The Independent*, 27 August 2005, http://news.independent.co.uk/uk/legal/article308360.ece (accessed 6 September 2006).

33. The back jacket of *Fish Sunday Thinking* (Bury St. Edmunds: Arima Publishing, 2005) describes what the book is about: "In a large London law firm, trainee solicitor Denton Voyle contemplates why he is pursuing a career in law. Every Sunday afternoon ... he questions his miserable, listless, alcohol-fuelled existence and wonders if the pursuit of being the big fish could ever really satisfy him." Criticism of the law and the legal profession in books, including serious literature, is a long-standing and powerful tradition. An outstanding example is *Bleak House* (1852–53) by Charles Dickens. "The one great principle of the English law is, to make business for itself," wrote Dickens (Chapter 39). The lawyer is described as "smoke-dried and faded, dwelling among mankind but not consorting with them, aged without experience of genial youth, and so long used to

make his cramped nest in holes and corners of human nature that he has forgotten its broader and better range" (Chapter 42). A contemporary example (one of a large number) can be found in Hilary Mantel's memoir, *Giving Up the Ghost* (London: Harper, 2004): "When I was eighteen I left home to go to the London School of Economics. My course was law, and my burning desire for equity made me peculiarly unsuited to the subject" (154). Professor Julien Hofman of the University of Cape Town has drawn my attention to a lengthy passage about the legal profession in *The Reverse of the Medal* by Patrick O'Brian (London: HarperCollins, 1997), in which Stephen Maturin makes this comment among many others: "I do not say that all lawyers are bad, but I do maintain that the general tendency is bad" (226).

34. www.anonymouslawyer.blogspot.com.

35. Jeremy Blachman, *Anonymous Lawyer* (New York: Henry Holt, 2006). In a representative passage, the book's central character describes the real meaning of phrases used in bills sent by his Los Angeles firm to clients: "'Research' is code for surfing the Internet, 'drafting' is code for eating in your office, 'misc. legal forms' is code for ordering gifts online, and 'preparing for a meeting' is code for taking a crap. Everyone knows. It's no big deal" (56).

36. Beppi Crosariol, "Bay Street veterans play law life for laughs," *The Globe and Mail*, 9 November 2005, B10. Crosariol describes "well-dressed, ambitious young women and men working in close proximity late into the night to ratchet up the tension."

37. Andrew Ryan, "And justice for all," *The Globe and Mail*, television section, 19–25 November 2005, 6.

38. "'Boston Legal' represents a new low in pop culture's portrayal of the legal profession … the main characters … are really disgusting people," Mark Donald, "Lawyer Prestige Hits New Low with Fall TV Season," *Texas Lawyer*, 12 August 2004, www.law.com/jsp/law/LawArticleFriendly.jsp?id= 1101738508222 (accessed 8 August 2006).

39. Alessandra Stanley, "First, Kill All the Lawyers? Nah, Give 'Em Therapy," *The New York Times*, 14 September 2005, www.nytimes.com/2005/09/14/arts/television/ 14stan.html? (accesssed 6 September 2006).

40. 183. Lawrence Joseph, *Lawyerland: What Lawyers Really Talk About When They Talk About Law* (New York: Farrar, Straus & Giroux, 1997). *Lawyerland* records many highly critical comments of the legal profession, made by lawyers themselves. In another example, a federal judge says, "Lawyers know too much. If you know too much, how don't you lie? Everything you say has another meaning. The posturing, the playacting, arguing over the smallest things, the narcissism, the beyond-belief egomania" (72).

Two: The New Age

1. I have drawn on several published accounts of the Pilzmaker scandal. *The Globe and Mail*, and in particular reporter Victor Malarek, gave the story extensive coverage over two years. (Ironically, *The Globe and Mail*'s coverage of the Lang Michener affair contributed to that newspaper's receiving in 1988 the Michener Award for disinterested and meritorious public service journalism.) Malarek also wrote about the affair in his book *Gut Instinct: The Making of an Investigative Journalist* (Toronto: Macmillan Canada, 1996). Michael Crawford focused on the Lang Michener and law society "cover up" angle in "The Lang Michener Affair," *Canadian Lawyer*, April 1990, as did Margaret Cannon in "The whistle-blower," *Saturday Night*, October 1990.

2. See note 1.

3. See note 1.

4. 174.

5. 217.

6. Victor Malarek, "4 lawyers' aid to Hong Kong immigrants investigated by RCMP and law society," *The Globe and Mail*, 21 June 1988, A1.

7. Victor Malarek, "14 lawyers at top firm investigated," *The Globe and Mail*, 6 July 1988, A1.

8. Victor Malarek, "Charges averted after smuggling uncovered at law firm," *The Globe and Mail*, 8 July 1988, A1.

9. Victor Malarek, "Judge orders immigration lawyer to pay $75,000 bail, stay in Ontario," *The Globe and Mail*, 7 July 1989, A4.

10. Journalist Lynda Hurst has given an exhaustive account of what went on inside Lang Michener. See "The saga that set Ontario's legal world abuzz," *Toronto Star*, 22 July 1990, B1.

11. 206. Claude Thomson, lawyer for four of the five lawyers, was reported in the *Toronto Star* as telling the disciplinary committee that "media reports were sensationalized and distorted, and the five received more bad publicity than 'disbarred Harry Kopyto.'" Rick Haliechuk, "Five lawyers given a tongue-lashing for misconduct," *Toronto Star*, 19 January 1990, A2. See Chapter 15 for the story of Harry Kopyto.

12. Victor Malarek, "Panel reprimands 5 Lang lawyers as penalty," *The Globe and Mail*, 19 January 1990, A1.

13. My account of the Donaldson affair is drawn from the public report of the law society discipline committee and other public documents. See *Law Society of Upper Canada v. Donaldson*, [1992] L.S.D.D. No. 60.

14. Tracey Tyler, "Lawyer guilty of misconduct over billings," *Toronto Star*, 21 May 1992, A6.

15. Dan Westell, "Crude justice served," *The Globe and Mail Report on Business*, 28 May 1991, B1.

16. "Lawyers in Ontario mindful of misconduct: Change in attitude cited as high-profile member disbarred," *The Vancouver Sun*, 19 September 1991, A6.

17. The discipline committee's decision described Bob Donaldson's life, based on the evidence given to it, in this way:

- the Solicitor was at work very early in the morning (in the range of 5:00–7:00 a.m.) and left very late at night
- he worked seven days a week
- he was able to spend more weekend time at home or his country property when the fax machine made his offices in those locations more accessible
- he was almost invariably available to clients and others, if not instantly, within hours, regardless of the day of the week or the time of the day
- he illustrated his travel commitments by explaining that in one given week, he travelled to and from Vancouver three times because he had a deal in each place; he took Valium

and alcohol to facilitate sleep on the airplane so as not to lose valuable time resting upon arrival at each destination
- he rarely took holidays, and if he did, he was always preoccupied with work or work-related activities
- ... the Solicitor spent one hour per week with his wife.

18. See note 13.

19. Melnitzer is now a respected legal commentator and writer who, turning adversity to his advantage, has written books about the frauds he committed and his subsequent prison experiences. See *Maximum Minimum Medium: A Journey Through Canadian Prisons* (Toronto: Key Porter Books, 1995), and a novel in which Melnitzer thinly disguises some of his experiences, particularly in prison—*Dirty White Collar* (Toronto: ECW, 2002). See also Brian Martin, *Never Enough: The Remarkable Frauds of Julius Melnitzer* (Toronto: Stoddart, 1993).

20. *Law Society of Upper Canada v. Rovet*, [1992] L.S.D.D. No. 24.

Three: Just Building Up an Art Collection

1. An earlier version of this story appeared as "Deconstructing Daniel," the cover story of the February 2004 issue of *Canadian Lawyer*. I interviewed Daniel Cooper in Toronto twice, on February 26, 2002, and April 3, 2002. At the second meeting, he told me he was applying for readmission to the bar, and asked me not to pursue his story until the law society had dealt with his application, after which he promised to cooperate. I held off, Cooper was readmitted, and thereafter, despite his promise, he refused to communicate with me.

2. The Donaldson and Cooper stories played out about the same time. On May 28, 1991, the same page of *The Globe and Mail*, B2, had separate stories about each lawyer.

3. Peter Whybrow, *American Mania: When More Is Not Enough* (New York: Norton, 2005), 57.

4. For the story of Dome Petroleum, see Jim Lyon, *Dome: The Rise and Fall of the House That Jack Built* (Scarborough: Avon, 1983), and Peter Foster, *Other People's Money: The Banks, the Government and Dome* (Toronto: Collins, 1983).

5. See Christopher Moore, *The History of McCarthy Tétrault* (Toronto: Douglas & McIntyre, 2005).

6. See Stephen Strauss, "Computer lawyers: Explorers chart course into a new legal maze," *The Globe and Mail*, 25 September 1980, T1.

7. My account of the immediate events leading up to Dan Cooper's resignation from McCarthy Tétrault is based on an interview with Arthur Scace. Interview by Philip Slayton, Toronto, 28 May 2003.

8. Cooper's major client at the time was Global Resorts International, which was attempting with Cooper's advice to establish a cable television network in Serbia. Cooper sat on Global's board of directors. Apparently, Global later sued McCarthy Tétrault, alleging that Cooper had been negligent in his representation of Global and had breached his fiduciary duty. The law firm is believed to have settled this claim.

9. See Chapter 2.

10. See, for example, "Lawyer quits over $200,000 payments," *The Record* (Kitchener-Waterloo), 13 November 1990, B8.

11. "Lawyer quits firm over misuse of funds," *The Globe and Mail*, 13 November 1990, A5.

12. The May 28, 2003, interview with Arthur Scace.

13. A McCarthy Tétrault senior partner later told me that, before Scace sent this letter, a partnership meeting was held to discuss whether sending such a letter was appropriate.

14. *Law Society of Upper Canada v. Cooper*, [1991] L.S.D.D. No. 93.

15. Deborah Chesnie Cooper, interview by Philip Slayton, Toronto, 25 August 2003.

16. See Re Weisman, Report to Convocation, 27 January 1997. The Weisman criteria are frequently applied in readmission cases. See, for example, the 2004 Law Society of Upper Canada cases of *Robert Charles Watt*, [2004] L.S.D.D. No. 10, *Bruce Allan Clark*, [2004] L.S.D.D. No. 6, and Henry Peter Steponaitis, [2004] L.S.D.D. No. 16.

17. The conditions required Cooper: To obtain the law society's approval of an eighteen-month plan of supervision; to pass the

bar admission course examinations in business law and professional responsibility; and to restrict his practice to corporate,
commercial, and technology law (the secretary of the law society
was allowed to approve expansion of Cooper's practice to other
areas). Order of The Law Society of Upper Canada,
21 November 2002, file no. READ03/02.

Four: A Kid Who's Been Beat Up Bad

1. Patti Edgar, "Doctor-lawyer-trekker dies in sleep at 29," *The Gazette* (Montreal), 20 July 2001, D11.

2. *The Queen v. Ingrid Yin Yu Chen*, Provincial Court of Manitoba, transcript of proceedings before The Honourable Judge Lismer, 30 June 1999, 1.

3. Transcript of 30 June 1999 proceedings, 29.

4. Ingrid Chen, interview by Philip Slayton, Winnipeg, 10 November 2005.

5. In *Chen v. Law Society of Manitoba*, [1999] M.J. No. 546. This was Chen's appeal from the decision of the law society to suspend her from practice. The appeal was dismissed.

6. Much of Justice Shulman's account comes from the June 30, 1999, bail hearing. For example, at page 21 of the transcript of that hearing, Maniella is describing the wiretap of one of the conversations between Chen and Patrick Armstrong:

> Ms. Chen says ... "I want a quote on a price."
> Mr. Armstrong says, "Well, if I break a leg, a leg is
> $1,000. You don't want something like that." Ms. Chen
> says, "No, I want them to fuck off and leave me alone.
> The thing is I have a list of about four guys right now.
> There is two I'm debating on and two I've completely
> made up my mind." The conversation goes on. Ms. Chen
> says, "I'm going to get a list together and shit and write
> down all what I want. I want you to give me prices on
> this. I'm looking for results. I've had it."

7. *Chen v. Law Society of Manitoba*, [2000] M.J. No. 230. Chen and her lawyers have made much of alleged procedural unfair-ness in the law society hearings. In this judgment, the Court of Appeal noted the following:

Potentially of ... concern to this Court is the allegation
that the committee had before it significant and important
documents, copies of which were not provided to the
applicant or her counsel. There can be no doubt that the
committee, but not Ms Chen or her counsel, was in
possession of a 21-page investigation report—with attach-
ments. The report consisted of a summary of events,
including the bail hearing, an extract from the transcript of
intercepted private communications (part of the Crown
bail brief).

Examination of the investigation report reveals that
with one exception—a memorandum respecting the
disposition of the $3,400 U.S. retainer—the report
simply and accurately summarizes the facts contained in
the bail hearing transcript and the Crown bail brief that
were already in the possession of the applicant and her
counsel. With respect to the retainer, there was other
evidence, well known to the applicant, to much the same
effect as the memorandum.

There is equally no merit to the alternative position,
emphasized by Ms Chen's counsel at the reconvened
hearing before this Court, that it was in some way
improper for the committee to have before it the bail
hearing transcript and Crown bail brief including the
entire transcript of the wiretap information. All of this
information was known to the applicant, and known to be
in the possession of the Society. It was of obvious and critical relevance to the committee's deliberations on July 8th.

In the result, the fact that the applicant was not in
possession of the summary provided to the committee did
not operate to the prejudice of the applicant. That is to
say it did not deprive her of a fair hearing.

8. Ingrid Y. Chen and Rodney Graham, *Protect Yourself from
Your Lawyer: Unveiling the Benefactors of Misery* (Winnipeg:
Ingrid Chen and Rodney Graham, 2002). In the book's introduction, Chen writes, "Publishing this book may disbar me for
life. This book will offend, outrage, anger and even frighten
many lawyers." That is unlikely; the book is poorly written and
devoid of substance. Chen's view of life is perhaps shown in

another part of the introduction: "In a grown up world those you think you can rely on all to [*sic*] often betray you, mislead you, and use you."

9. The *Winnipeg Free Press*, in a number of its stories about Ingrid Chen, incorrectly reported that she had been convicted of falsifying immigration documents, and later that she had been disbarred (sometimes describing her as an "ex-lawyer"). Chen has threatened a defamation suit. The newspaper, in its archives, has prefaced these stories with a correction, which sometimes adds, "We apologize for any confusion this may have caused."

10. Mike McIntyre, "City job news to woman seeking visa," *Winnipeg Free Press*, 20 November 2003, B3.

11. Mike McIntyre, "Ex-lawyer gets conditional sentence," *Winnipeg Free Press*, 15 May 2004, B3.

12. *R. v. Chen, R. v. Guevarra*, 2004 MBCA 194 (CanLII).

13. Amended statement of claim, 23 August 2005, paragraph 11.

14. *R. v. Chen*, 2006 MBQB 241 (CanLII).

15. Attempts by Chen to quash her committal to stand trial, arguing on procedural grounds, have failed. See *R. v. Chen*, [2006] M.J. No. 198.

16. Carol Sanders, "Agent, web firm in dispute," *Winnipeg Free Press*, 28 July 2005, B1.

17. Carol Sanders, "Police review web firm complaints," *Winnipeg Free Press*, 13 August 2005, B6.

18. Ingrid Chen, "Attention Ingrid Chen," email message to author, 24 October 2005.

19. Ingrid Chen, "Arrangements," email message to author, 26 October 2005.

20. Ingrid Chen, "Arrangements," email message to author, 4 November 2005.

21. Ingrid Chen, "Thanks," email message to author, 15 November 2005.

22. Ingrid Chen, "Hi there," email message to author, 25 November 2005.

Five: Wild and Crazy Guys

1. Bermuda Short had two parts. In part one, FBI and RCMP undercover agents posed as members of the Columbian Cali cocaine cartel who wanted to launder drug proceeds. Part two featured a fictitious foreign mutual fund; posing as a fund employee, an FBI agent approached business executives and stockbrokers offering to buy stock at above market rates in exchange for kickbacks. A prime target of Bermuda Short part one was Martin Chambers, once a Vancouver real estate lawyer. In December 2002, Chambers was convicted by a Florida court of laundering purported cocaine trafficking money and was sentenced to almost sixteen years in prison. He received the upper range of possible sentencing, despite the contention by defence lawyers that he is "dedicated in [sic] making sure the natural resources, the trees, the fishing rights and native Indian rights have been preserved." It is reported that, when sentenced, Chambers talked about how much he loved his common-law wife, known as "Queenie," and began sobbing in court.

2. Bill Majcher, interviews by Philip Slayton: Toronto, 2 February 2005; Vancouver, 17 February 2005; Toronto, 17 March 2005; and Toronto, 16 August 2005.

3. www.thefiftybest.com (accessed 14 December 2005).

4. This seizure of documents led to two cases on solicitor-client privilege—*R. v. Law Office of Simon Rosenfeld*, [2003] O.J. No. 834, and *R. v. Law Office of Simon Rosenfeld*, [2003] O.J. No. 5821. The first case was an important one about the proper procedure to be followed in determining whether seized documents are the subject of privilege.

5. *Re Rosenfeld*, [2002] O.J. No. 3158. Rosenfeld's appeal from this decision was dismissed—*Re Rosenfeld*, [2004] O.J. No. 2459. See also *Iamgold Ltd. v. Rosenfeld*, [1998] O.J. No. 4690, and *Rinaldo v. Rosenfeld*, [1999] O.J. No. 4665, both dealing with allegations of a fraudulent conveyance of property by Simon Rosenfeld to his wife in order to defeat and defraud creditors. The Iamgold case settled. Rinaldo's action was dismissed. Rosenfeld has generally been very litigious; see, for example, *Rosenfeld v. Iamgold International African Mining Gold Corp.*, [1997] O.J. No. 3770.

6. See U.S. Securities and Exchange Commission, Litigation Release No. 16932, 14 March 2001.

7. Adrian Humphreys, "Tripped up by $1, lawyer jailed for money laundering," *National Post*, 31 March 2005, A4.

8. David Baines, "Frustrated inspector looks elsewhere," *The Vancouver Sun*, 21 May 2005, H5. Baines reported in December 2005 that Majcher's lawyer had sent a letter to the RCMP stating that the force's conduct toward Majcher "has been egregious, reckless and, in some cases, defamatory of him and has caused him undue emotional, professional and financial harm." David Baines, "Two years later, not much to show," *The Vancouver Sun*, 10 December 2005, H2.

9. Betsy Powell, "Launderer lost a game with RCMP; Brokers applaud Dirty Money inventor: How-not-to-do-what-I-did was topic," *Toronto Star*, 29 September 2005, A16.

10. Betsy Powell, "A reputation built on connections; Family ties opened doors for Shoniker, Ex-crown accused of money laundering," *Toronto Star*, 3 July 2004, A1.

11. John Barber, "Let's hope this 'untouchable' is put where he belongs," *The Globe and Mail*, 23 August 2006, A8. In his article, Barber also wrote that Julian Fantino was "more or less excised from the body politic." He was wrong. On October 12, 2006, Fantino was named commissioner of the Ontario Provincal Police, starting on October 30.

12. Christie Blatchford, "High-powered friends duck for cover," *The Globe and Mail*, 26 June 2004, A17.

13. A version of this discussion first appeared in my "Law and Money" column, *Canadian Lawyer*, August 2005.

14. In R. v. Campbell, the Supreme Court of Canada adopted what it described as the "functional" definition of solicitor-client privilege set out in *Descôteaux v. Mierzwinski*, [1982] 1 S.C.R. 860 at 872: "Where legal advice of any kind is sought from a professional legal adviser in his capacity as such, the communications relating to that purpose, made in confidence by the client, are at his instance permanently protected from disclosure by himself or by the legal adviser, except the protection be waived."

15. *Federation of Law Societies of Canada v. Attorney General of Canada*, [2002] O.J. No. 17.

16. Put into force by amendments to the Rules of Professional Conduct and to by-laws 18 and 19.

17. Stephen Schneider, *Money Laundering in Canada: An Analysis of RCMP Cases*, Nathanson Centre for the Study of Organized Crime and Corruption, York University, 2004, 67–73. Schneider is co-author with Margaret E. Beare of *Money Laundering in Canada: Chasing Dirty and Dangerous Dollars* (Toronto: University of Toronto Press, 2007). One of the most convincing accounts of money laundering is to be found in Shana Alexander, *The Pizza Connection: Lawyers, Drugs and the Mafia* (New York: Weidenfeld & Nicolson, 1988). See especially Chapter 4 in Alexander's book.

18. Steven Chase, "Scope of dirty money problem balloons," *The Globe and Mail*, 4 October 2006, A4.

19. Department of Finance, "Canada's New Government Toughens Anti-Money Laundering and Anti-Terrorist Financing Regime," 5 October 2006.

Six: A Small Army

1. David Cay Johnston, *Perfectly Legal: The Covert Campaign to Rig Our Tax System to Benefit the Super Rich—and Cheat Everybody Else* (New York: Portfolio, 2003). See 263.

2. Lynnley Browning, "Lawyers Face Scrutiny in Tax Inquiry," *The New York Times*, 25 January 2006, C1.

3. *The Role of Professional Firms in the U.S. Tax Shelter Industry*, report prepared by the Permanent Subcommittee on Investigations of the Committee on Homeland Security and Governmental Affairs, U.S. Senate (Washington: U.S. Government Printing Office, 2005). See 96 and 99.

4. See http://levin.senate.gov/newsroom/release. cfm?id= 260030 (accessed 1 August 2006). See *Tax Haven Abuses: The Enablers, The Tools and Secrecy*, Minority and Majority Staff Report of the Permanent Subcommittee on Investigations of the Committee on Homeland Security and Governmental Affairs, U.S. Senate (Washington: U.S. Government Printing Office, 2006).

5. See David Cay Johnston, "Tax Cheats Called Out of Control," *The New York Times*, 1 August 2006, C1. The role of lawyers in

tax shelters is multifarious. A newspaper story begins, "A former senior partner at the law firm of Greenberg Traurig has formally resigned from the New York bar after admitting that he took $1.3 million in kickbacks for steering wealthy clients ... to questionable tax shelters." Lynnley Browning, "Lawyer Tied to Kickbacks Quits the Bar," *The New York Times*, 16 November 2006, C3.

6. "... the opulence of a professional waiting room that soothes the visitor's anxiety about how much it is all going to cost with the subliminal assurance that nobody who makes this much money can be peddling unsound advice." Paul Seabright, *The Company of Strangers: A Natural History of Economic Life* (Princeton: Princeton University Press, 2004), 85.

7. Davis & Company declined to discuss the Strother affair with me, giving the reason that "the matter is still before the courts." Strother also declined to be interviewed, giving the same reason. I interviewed Harry Knutson and David Merrick, of Monarch Entertainment Corporation, in Vancouver on November 22, 2005. Views and quotations attributed to Knutson are from that interview. I have several times written about the Strother affair in *Canadian Lawyer*, and some of the language and ideas in this chapter are drawn from those columns.

8. *In 3464920 Canada Inc. v. Strother, Davis & Company, et al.*, 2002 BCSC 1179, Justice Lowry gave a full explanation of how TAPSF worked:

> [4] What was referred to as tax-assisted production serv-ices financing was a concept that served to enhance the advantages of producing American-made films in Canada by providing for investors a 15 year (and after 1994 a 10 year) tax deferral. The concept was not a government-sponsored, legislated tax incentive to attract American film business. It was developed by Stephen Cheikes, an American attorney who practised law in the Los Angeles motion picture industry for some years before coming to Canada in 1987.
>
> [5] Utilizing a limited partnership in a complex struc-ture to facilitate the flow of funds between investors, lending institutions, the studio involved, and other neces-sary on-and-off-shore entities, investors would notionally produce a film for a studio in return for a fee, paid over

time, which was contingent on the success of the film. The application of Generally Accepted Accounting Principles (GAAP) yielded a loss to the partnership because of a mismatch between the expenses it incurred in producing the film and the part of the fee it received at the outset of the life of the investment. The loss was flowed out to the investors to be deducted from their unrelated income which was thereby sheltered.

[6] The concept was based on the advantage to be taken of the court-sanctioned view that the right to receive income at some future date is not a capital asset. As a result, expenditures made for that purpose do not become non-deductible capital expenditures: *Asamera Oil (Indonesia) Limited v. The Queen* (1973), 73 D.T.C. 5274 (F.C.T.D.). They could be used as income tax deductions without offending the provisions of the *Income Tax Act*, R.S.C. 1985 (5th Supp.), c. 1 including, in particular, those provisions which prevent technical reliance on a part of the statute in a manner at odds with its overall purpose: s. 245, the General Anti-Avoidance Requirements (GAAR).

[7] An investment in the production services of a film held a limited prospect of profit. For the investor, the principal attraction of the concept was the sheltering of income achieved by deducting losses from income on which tax would otherwise have to be paid. Tax would eventually have to be paid on the balance of the fee revenue when it was received, but that would not be for many years and the investor enjoyed the use of the money in the interim. Hence, a production services investment provided what could be a valuable tax deferral.

[8] The American studio, which paid no tax in Canada, shared in the tax benefit achieved by the deferral through effectively selling to the Canadian investors the expenses of making the film for a price that then served to reduce its cost of production. The promoter of the tax shelter would incur the expenses of securing a film to be produced, assembling and marketing the investment transaction which most often would be done by a public offering, and attending to the administration required over the life of the investment. The promoter derived its

profit as a middleman from the difference between what the investors actually paid as part of their investment for the production expenses and the price the studio received.

9. Patricia Best and Ann Shortell, "Stopping the puck," *The Kingston Whig-Standard*, 4 January 1986, 1.

10. See Katherine Gay, "Feds take aim at 'abusive' tax shelters," *The Financial Post*, 12 September 1995, 17. In that article, Gay observes that "tax shelter brokers are a never-say-die breed, able to slip through hairline cracks in tax rules and revered by clients for doing so." Perhaps the best recent explanation of what constitutes an "abusive" tax shelter is found in The Role of Professional Firms in the U.S. Tax Shelter Industry, report prepared by the Permanent Subcommittee on Investigations of the Committee on Homeland Security and Governmental Affairs, U.S. Senate, (Washington: U.S. Government Printing Office, 2005). Its introduction explains:

In its broadest sense, the term "tax shelter" is a device used to reduce or eliminate the tax liability of the tax shelter user. This may encompass legitimate or illegitimate endeavors. While there is no one standard to determine the line between legitimate "tax planning" and "abusive tax shelters," the latter can be characterized as transactions in which a significant purpose is the avoidance or evasion of Federal, state or local tax in a manner not intended by the law.

The abusive tax shelters investigated by the Subcommittee were complex transactions used by corporations or individuals to obtain substantial tax benefits in a manner never intended by the Federal tax code. While some of these transactions may have complied with the literal language of specific tax provisions, they produced results that were unwarranted, unintended, or inconsistent with the overall structure or underlying policy of the Internal Revenue Code. These transactions had no economic substance or business purpose other than to reduce taxes. Abusive tax shelters can be custom-designed for a single user or prepared as a generic tax product sold to multiple clients. The Subcommittee investigation focused on generic abusive tax shelters sold to multiple clients as opposed to a custom-tailored tax strategy sold to a single client.

11. The B.C. Court of Appeal's first decision in the case is *3464920 Canada Inc. v. Strother*, 2005 BCCA 35.

12. In his *Strother* trial judgment, Justice Lowry explained the basis of the new ruling Sentinel Hill relied on:

> [26] The exceptions to the Rules were first published at the end of July 1997 in what appears to have been a final draft of the amendments to the Act. Although clearly none of the exceptions were intended to foster the resurrection of the tax shelters, the exception given by s. 18.1(15)(b)—the one upon which Sentinel Hill had sought the advance tax ruling (the "15(b) exception")—proved to accomplish exactly that. As enacted, it effectively provided that the Matchable Expenditures Rules would not apply where more than 80% of a right to receive remuneration was realized before the end of the year in which an expenditure was made. Its purpose appears to have been to accommodate service providers where a relatively small part of their income is contingent on events and is earned over time, but it actually served to facilitate the tax-sheltered financing of American motion picture and television films being made in Canada until 2001.
>
> [27] Prior to the Matchable Expenditures Rules, a tax-assisted production services investment was predicated on the investors' contingent fee being paid by a studio in two parts. The first part, equalling 50% of the expenditures, was paid early in the life of the investment while the remainder, amounting to the balance of the expenditures, and perhaps more, if any investment profit was to be realized, was deferred to the end. The investors' loss deduction lay in the 50% of the expenditures not recovered when the first part of the fee was paid.
>
> [28] Once the Rules came into force, tax-sheltered financing had to be undertaken on a different basis. To fall within the 15(b) exception, the investment had to be predicated upon the investors receiving a non-contingent

or fixed fee of 80.1% in the year in which the expenditure was made (commensurate with the production of the film), and a further fee at the end of the investment. This meant that, instead of 50%, only 19.9% of the expenditures could be deducted, and two-and-a-half times as much film production was required to achieve the same amount of deduction. In addition, the scope for investment was reduced because the government's tax credit program effectively removed Canadian labour expenses from the amount of production available. Hence only non-Canadian labour expenses (NCLE) were available to be purchased from the studios because it was always more advantageous for a studio to take the tax credit benefit where Canadian labour was employed.

13. There are some similarities between the Strother story and the fabled tale of U.S. tax shelter lawyer Paul Daugerdas. See Paul Braverman, "Helter Shelter," *The American Lawyer*, 5 December 2003, 65. Daugerdas and Diversified Group Inc. (DGI), a company that made and sold tax shelters, entered into a business arrangement. Daugerdas, then with the Chicago law firm of Altheimer & Gray, worked with DGI to develop and sell a shelter called COBRA. Daugerdas wrote opinion letters for the buyers. Profits were split fifty-fifty. Braverman writes, "In 2000 DGI sued Daugerdas, claiming that he was using DGI's idea but not giving DGI its cut. Daugerdas, who had since moved to Jenkens & Gilchrist, responded that no agreement prohibited him from using the shelter, adding that it was based on a nonproprietary strategy that anyone familiar with the tax code could figure out." The case settled after a payment by Jenkens & Gilchrist's insurance carrier. Braverman describes Daugerdas as a products lawyer: "The 'products' lawyer creates something, then goes looking for someone to buy it."

14. *3464920 Canada Inc. v. Strother*, 2005 BCCA 385.

15. Davis claims that the correct figure for fees paid by Monarch is $50,000.

16. Here is how the Supreme Court framed the issues in giving leave to appeal:

Commercial law—Barristers and solicitors—Duty of loyalty—Remedies—Accounting remedy—Court of

Appeal concluding that lawyer breached duty of loyalty to client and ordering that he account for and disgorge all profits received—Court of Appeal also ordering law firm to disgorge profits it earned in form of legal fees as a result of acting for second client in conflict with its duty to its original client—Circumstances in which solicitors and other professional fiduciaries are entitled to act for commercial competitors—Limits of duty of loyalty owed by a professional fiduciary—When disgorgement of profits through an accounting is justified as a remedy for breach of fiduciary duty—Whether no profit rule requires an order for disgorgement to one client, of profits or fees earned for services rendered to the other client—Whether disgorgement remedy can be ordered against a partnership on the basis of vicarious liability in the absence of any loss suffered as a result of a partner's wrongful act.

17. In the Supreme Court of Canada, S.C.C. File No. 30838, Factum of Robert C. Strother et al., 31 March 2006, paragraph 7.

18. For the full arguments, see Strother factum, paragraphs 66–142.

19. In the Supreme Court of Canada, S.C.C. File No. 30838, Factum of Davis & Company, 3 April 2006, paragraph 5.

20. In the Supreme Court of Canada, S.C.C. File No. 30838, Factum of 3464920 Canada Inc., formerly known as Monarch Entertainment Corporation, 30 March 2006.

21. In the Supreme Court of Canada, S.C.C. File No. 30838, Motion for Leave to Intervene of Canadian Bar Association, 2 May 2006. The CBA was initially represented by the law firm of Heenan Blaikie. Monarch objected, noting that Heenan Blaikie had acted for Strother and Darc in various capacities. Heenan Blaikie withdrew from its representation of the CBA.

22. Darc rejects all the arguments of Knutson and Monarch. See In the Supreme Court of Canada, S.C.C. File No. 30838, Factum of J. Paul Darc et al., 25 May 2006.

23. David Baines, "Courts have differing views on partnerships, loopholes," *The Vancouver Sun*, 17 December 2005, D4.

24. It was recorded by the cable channel CPAC and was broadcast a few days later.

Seven: Sleeping with a Client

1. The lawyer is always a man. To the author's knowledge, no female lawyer in Canada has ever been formally accused of having an improper sexual relationship with a client. I first wrote about this subject in a *Canadian Lawyer* cover story—"What's Love Got to Do with It?" November–December 2004.

2. *Law Society of Upper Canada v. Ramsey*, [1992] L.S.D.D. No. 47.

3. *Nova Scotia Barristers' Society v. Rose*, [1996] L.S.D.D. No. 108.

4. *Law Society of Alberta v. Adams*, [1997] L.S.D.D. No. 157.

5. *Law Society of Alberta v. Adams*, [1998] L.S.D.D. No. 139.

6. *Adams v. Law Society of Alberta*, [2000] A.J. No. 1031. Said the court:

> Professional bodies are those to whom the government has seen fit to grant monopoly status. With this monopolistic right comes certain responsibilities and obligations. Chief amongst them is self-regulation. Self-regulation is based on the legitimate expectation of both the government and public that those members of a profession who are found guilty of conduct deserving of sanction will be regulated—and disciplined—on an administrative law basis by the profession's statutorily prescribed regulatory bodies.... A professional misconduct hearing involves not only the individual and all the factors that relate to that individual, both favourably and unfavourably, but also the effect of the individual's misconduct on both the individual client and generally on the profession in question. This public dimension is of critical significance to the mandate of professional disciplinary bodies. (paragraph 6)
>
> Historians may question the origin and the history of the oft-repeated statements about the honour and integrity of the legal profession, but it cannot be denied that the relationship of solicitor and client is founded on trust. That fundamental trust is precisely why persons can

and do confidently bring their most intimate problems
and all manner of matters great or small to their lawyers.
That is an overarching trust that the profession and each
member of the profession accepts. Indeed, it is the very
foundation of the profession and governs the relationships and services that are rendered. While it may be difficult to measure with precision the harm that a lawyer's
misconduct may have on the reputation of the profession,
there can be little doubt that public confidence in the
administration of justice and trust in the legal profession
will be eroded by disreputable conduct of an individual
lawyer. (paragraph 10)

7. F.M. Christensen, *Pornography: The Other Side* (New York:
Praeger, 1990).

8. See Deborah Tetley, "Prof dismisses uproar over book on
porn," *Calgary Herald*, 2 April 2001, B2.

9. Donna Laframboise, "Scandal taints fathers' rights group,"
National Post, 17 April 2001, A8.

10. Quoted by Donna Laframboise, "Dispute erupts at rights
group for fathers," *National Post*, 30 March 2001, A5.

11. *Nova Scotia Barristers' Society v. Pavey*, [2001] L.S.D.D.
No. 3. Pavey's appeal to the Nova Scotia Court of Appeal was
dismissed with costs to the society. See *Nova Scotia Barristers'
Society v. Pavey* 2001 NSCA 165.

12. Andrew Pavey, interview by Philip Slayton, Vancouver,
24 November 2005.

13. *Law Society of Upper Canada v. Joseph*, [2003] L.S.D.D.
No. 34.

14. *Law Society of Upper Canada v. G.N.*, [2003] L.S.D.D.
No. 41

15. The sex-ban rule proposed in Ontario appeared to be
modelled on the American Bar Association's Rule 1.8(j),
adopted in 2002, which provides that "a lawyer shall not have
sexual relations with a client unless a consensual sexual relationship existed between them when the lawyer-client relationship
commenced." The weight of opinion in the United States seems
to favour such a ban (more than twenty states have flat prohibi-
tions), although a ban has received far from universal support

and different states have taken different approaches. The California rules are vague, forbidding "coerced" sex. New York only bars sex in domestic relations cases. Some states—Nevada, for example—have refused a ban. ("Adults are adults," said the chairman of a Nevada committee that considered the matter.)

16. See Kirk Makin, "Lawyer disbarred for sexual harassment," *The Globe and Mail*, 2 July 2004, A7.

17. See Michelle MacAfee, "Lawyers reject new rules restricting sex with clients," *The Globe and Mail*, 16 August 2004, A1. See also Kirsten McMahon, "CBA delegates reject guideline on romance with clients," *Law Times*, August 2004, and Peter Worthington, "Lawyers' 'dirty little secret,'" *Toronto Sun*, 17 August 2004.

18. The commentary, on rule 2.04(3) of the *Professional Rules of Conduct*, dealing with the avoidance of conflicts of interest, now reads:

> If a lawyer has a sexual or intimate personal relationship with a client, this may conflict with the lawyer's duty to provide objective, disinterested professional advice to the client. Before accepting a retainer from or continuing a retainer with a person with whom the lawyer has such a relationship, a lawyer should consider the following factors:
>
> a. The vulnerability of the client, both emotional and economic;
> b. The fact that the lawyer and client relationship may create a power imbalance in favour of the lawyer or, in some circumstances, in favour of the client;
> c. Whether the sexual or intimate personal relationship will jeopardize the client's right to have all information concerning the client's business and affairs held in strict confidence. For example, the existence of the relationship may obscure whether certain information was acquired in the course of the lawyer and client relationship;
> d. Whether such a relationship may require the lawyer to act as a witness in the proceedings;
> e. Whether such a relationship will interfere in any way with the lawyer's fiduciary obligations to the client,

his or her ability to exercise independent professional judgment, or his or her ability to fulfill obligations owed as an officer of the court and to the administration of justice.

19. *Law Society of Upper Canada v. Neinstein*, [2005] L.S.D.D. No. 3.

20. On the issue of witness credibility, the appeal panel said:

The [Hearing] Panel engaged in a credibility contest. In so doing, it erred.

The two-step approach adopted by the Hearing Panel promotes the "either/or" approach: If the member is believed, the particular is dismissed. If he is disbelieved and the complainant's evidence meets the standard of proof, there will be a finding of misconduct. The trier is not directed to examine any other possibility.

In particular, the Hearing Panel's ... method fails to direct the panel to consider the third alternative: if the trier disbelieves the member, does the member's evidence nonetheless prevent the trier, in the context of the whole, from finding clear and convincing proof?

When a decision on credibility can result in the "professional death" ... of the member, it is imperative to avoid the "oft-repeated error" of the either/or approach.

21. On adequacy of reasons, the appeal panel said:

The very length of the reasons, at first blush, suggests that they are adequate. However, a more careful review of their content reveals otherwise. While they contain a lengthy review of the evidence, there is little or no analysis of it. Nor is the basis of the Hearing Panel's decision meaningfully enunciated. There is minimal discussion of the material conflicting evidence.

22. In 2006, prominent Ontario lawyer Peter Budd was found guilty of two criminal charges of sexual exploitation involving two teenage sisters—see *R. v. Budd*, 2006 CanLII 16541. The sisters were not Budd's clients. Justice Little of the Ontario Supreme Court, in his judgment, described what happened:

The accused, the separated father of three boys, swept into the lives of the D. family in the late 1990s when he purchased a hobby farm in Napier near the D. family farm in K.[…], Ontario. The D. women, mother D.D. and daughters M.D., A.D. and K.D. were wowed by this charismatic, exuberant, high energy, generous, big city lawyer, his financial and career success, and his partying lifestyle....

The accused worked his way into being an integral part of the D. family life. He hired the girls to work for him and his firm; he attended family functions and M.D.'s high school graduation; he encouraged the D.'s to purchase a cottage near his; he advised the girls on their career choices; he commiserated with them, and advised them when they had problems and he entertained them. He took them off the farm....

He became a confidant and friend. They all looked up to him and admired him for his personality, kindness, success and wealth.

He made his residence in Toronto available to the D.s. He introduced the D. daughters to big city life. And he slept with all of them when they were over 14 and not yet 18.

23. Cristin Schmitz, "Affair with client lands lawyer in hot water," *Ottawa Citizen*, 11 September 2006, A3

24. Cristin Schmitz, "Law Society of Upper Canada investgates former Treasurer," *The Lawyers Weekly*, 15 September 2006, www.lawyersweekly.ca (accessed 15 September 2006).

25. Kirk Makin, "Ex-head of law body faces conduct review," *The Globe and Mail*, 14 September 2006, A14.

26. Nancy J. Moore, "Sex with a client: Always a violation?" American Bar Association, *GPSolo Magazine*, October/November 2002.

27. James A. Hodgson, interview by Philip Slayton, Toronto, 29 January 2004.

28. The analogous rule for the medical profession has been very clear for some time. In 1992 the College of Physicians and Surgeons of Ontario adopted, as part of a policy with the coy title "Physician-Patient 'Dating,'" a guideline that says "sexual relationships between doctors and patients during treatment are

prohibited." Other guidelines in the policy address the issue of sexual relationships after treatment is over.

Eight: An Ordinary Man

1. I interviewed Agnew Johnston, in Thunder Bay, on January 10 and 11, 2005, and also had an email correspondence with him.

2. Henry Hess, "Police probe Crown lawyer," *The Globe and Mail*, 21 June 1994, A8.

3 Ian Scott, interviews by Philip Slayton, Toronto, 20 September 2004, 19 January 2005.

4. Estanislao Oziewicz, "Thunder Bay lawyer's trial shrouded in mystery," *The Globe and Mail*, 7 October 1995, A1.

5. *R. v. Johnston*, [1996] O.J. No. 2882. See paragraph 23 of the judgment.

6. Agnew Johnston, "Update," email message to author, 19 December 2005. In December 2005, Lichtenfeld was found guilty of obstructing justice in an unrelated incident, and was put under house arrest for twenty months. Ian Scott prosecuted Lichtenfeld.

7. Four years later, Justice Labrosse, in the judgment of the Ontario Court of Appeal that dismissed Johnston's appeal from his eventual conviction, described what happened that June afternoon:

> Mr. Ross ... advised the trial judge that he was in an extremely difficult position with his client on this motion, as a result of third-party representations. He said he had a conflict between his own personal position and that of his client, and that his client was aware of his difficulties. He could only speak of generalities and was not in a position to disclose the nature of the conflict. He had sought advice from many sources and wished to seek more advice from senior counsel. He wanted the motion adjourned to July 2, 1996 (the date set for the trial). (paragraph 15)

The Court of Appeal found that the conversation between Judge Sargent and Ross gave no appearance of unfairness or of an attempt to interfere with the conduct of the defence. *R. v. Johnston*, [2000] O.J. No. 3539.

8. John Ibbitson, "Prominent citizens linked to prostitution: A well-known Crown attorney in Thunder Bay, Ont., has been

charged with soliciting the sexual services of juveniles," *The Vancouver Sun*, 5 July 1996, A4.

9. Alfred Petrone, interview by Philip Slayton, Thunder Bay, 12 January 2005. Johnston said of Petrone, "I worked for Alf for twelve years before I went to the Crown's office. He is my mentor, my trusted friend. He knows what happened."

10. See note 7.

11. *Law Society of Upper Canada v. Johnston*, [2001] L.S.D.D. No. 59.

12. *Law Society of Upper Canada v. Johnston*, [2003] L.S.D.D. No. 21.

Nine: A Lonely Time

1. I first wrote about this story in *The Globe and Mail*. Philip Slayton, "Lust and the law," 24 July 2004, F2.

2. All quotations from Dennis Cann are from an interview with the author, North Battleford, Saskatchewan, 25 May 2004.

3. All quotations from Michael Bomek are from interviews with the author in Prince Albert, Saskatchewan, on May 24 and 25, 2004.

4. (Toronto: McClelland & Stewart, 2005). In a Canadian Press interview, Siggins described her book as "a white guilt book.... The slant was very, very pro native person.... I don't find balance is very interesting." On Bomek, she said that "he is a modern day symbol of so many things that happened to the good people there." See *The Chronicle-Herald* (Halifax), 21 August 2005, "The NovaScotian/Books," 13.

5. 3. And at 286: "Once again a white man in authority, who had something valuable to offer, has instead transgressed. Bomek must now join the long line of fur traders, missionaries, teachers, judges, social workers, police officers, bureaucrats, and politicians who imposed their will on the Rock Cree and did incalculable damage in the process."

6. Leslie Perreaux, "Victims recall horror of attacks by sex predator: Crown seeks dangerous offender status for rapist," *The StarPhoenix* (Saskatoon), 14 September 2000, A7.

7. Lois Burke, telephone interview by Philip Slayton, 19 August 2004.

8. Arnold Goodman, telephone interview by Philip Slayton, 2 September 2004.

9. *Bomek v. Bomek*, [1983] M.J. No. 96.

10. *Law Society of Manitoba v. Greenberg*, [1998] L.S.D.D. No. 93.

11. In June 2004, a Saskatchewan government commission concluded that racism in police services is a major contributor to the environment of mistrust and misunderstanding that exists in Saskatchewan. The commission reported that it heard many complaints of abusive treatment of First Nations and Metis people at the hands of municipal police officers and members of the RCMP, including complaints of police abuse in the detention areas of police facilities. See "Legacy of Hope: An Agenda for Change," *Final Report from the Commission on First Nations and Metis Peoples and Justice Reform*, 21 June 2004, Chapter 5.

12. The disbarment proceedings were in Winnipeg on March 23, 2004. The author attended. See *Law Society of Manitoba v. Bomek*, [2004] L.S.D.D. No. 17.

13. See *Law Society of Manitoba v. Bomek*, [1994] L.S.D.D. No. 2, and *Law Society of Manitoba v. Bomek*, [1994] L.S.D.D. No. 139.

14. *Law Society of Manitoba v. Bomek*, Discipline Digest, Case 02-01.

15. Gavin Wood, telephone interview by Philip Slayton, 4 August 2004.

16. Lore Mirwaldt and Scott Gray, telephone interview with both by Philip Slayton, 4 August 2004.

17. "Accused of sex crimes, former lawyer sits in jail," www.cbc.ca/sask/story/bomek051109.html (accessed 10 November 2005).

18. Jonathon Naylor, "Disturbing new charges have been brought against former Flin Flon lawyer J. Michael Bomek," *The Reminder*, 21 November 2005.

19. Jonathon Naylor, "Mr. Bomek," email message to author, 9 November 2005.

Ten: Coal Miner's Son and Rock Solid Guy

1. From the poem "Cape Breton," by Elizabeth Bishop.

2. Michael Greenberg, "Freelance," *The Times Literary Supplement*, 29 July 2005, 14.

3. *Nova Scotia Barristers' Society v. Matheson*, [1998] L.S.D.D. No. 7.

4. Rachel Brighton, "Why did he do it? Glace Bay struggles to figure out its disgraced MLA," *The Daily News* (Halifax), 21 June 1998, 7.

5. *Hansard*, 5 June 1998, www.gov.ns.ca/legislature/hansard/han57-1/h98jun05.htm (accessed 2 July 2005).

6. "House no home for Matheson," *The Daily News* (Halifax), 8 June 1998, 11.

7. See note 4.

8. Cathy Nicoll and David Rodenhiser, "Matheson introduces bill to deal with likes of him," *The Daily News* (Halifax), 30 June 1998, 5.

9. David Rodenhiser, "'I'm going to sit through this session': Disgraced Matheson gets rough welcome," *The Daily News* (Halifax), 16 October 1998, 5.

10. Tera Camus, "Jobs, Matheson hot topics in C.B. East race," *The Halifax Chronicle-Herald*, 10 July 1999.

11. *Saccary v. Wilson*, 2000 CanLII 2613.

12. *The Daily News* noted that Matheson was the first MLA to face criminal charges since the eighties. In October 1986, Billy Joe MacLean, a former Nova Scotia cabinet minister, pleaded guilty to uttering forged documents. In February 1986, Port Hawkesbury lawyer and MLA Greg MacIsaac was convicted on eleven counts of fraud. Billy Joe MacLean is now mayor of Port Hawkesbury. Port Hawkesbury is in Cape Breton. Cathy Nicoll, "Cape Breton East MLA faces 12 charges," *The Daily News* (Halifax), 17 December 1998, 3.

13. *R. v. Matheson*, [2001] N.S.J. No.195.

14. Donald F. Ripley, *Bag Man: A Life in Nova Scotia Politics* (Toronto: Key Porter Books, 1993), 1. In Chapter 24 of his book, Ripley tells at length the extraordinary story of establishment

Halifax lawyer John Grant, originally from Sydney in Cape Breton, who had been president of Nova Scotia's Progressive Conservative Party from 1977 to 1983. Ripley writes that Grant "had everything: looks, a good income, a cultured and attractive wife, great kids, and a large expensive home in ritzey south-end Halifax" (188). In the late eighties, Grant came under investigation by the Nova Scotia Barristers' Society, for reasons that are not clear, and on September 19, 1988, he was found dead from stab wounds in a room in Dartmouth's Wandlyn Inn. Grant was forty-seven years old. The verdict of the medical examiner was suicide. See also Stevie Cameron, *On the Take: Crime, Corruption and Greed in the Mulroney Years* (Toronto: Seal Books, 1995), 298–304. Cameron raises the possibility that Grant was murdered.

15. Kelly Toughill, "Intimate politics allows for some hard truths; In Nova Scotia, voters know their politicians well. So the leaders don't need to be perfect, or even nice," *Toronto Star*, 2 October 1999, 1. Part of Toughill's article read as follows:

> Imagine this: The new Tory minister of education admits she was a needle-craving addict for years, that she has a marijuana conviction, that her life on the seamy side of Halifax cost her custody of her only son, that her heroin habit left her with a lifelong hepatitis C infection.
>
> The reaction? A big yawn and a little sympathy. It was forgotten in a day.
>
> The confession of Jane Purves is just the latest in a series of titillating tales about the misadventures of those who govern this land.
>
> Rookie Liberal MLA Brian "Crusher" Boudreau is in court next week, accused of pummeling his brother in a fight over family land. (The nickname is real—no kidding.) NDP MLA Reeves Matheson was charged with bilking his Cape Breton law clients last year, disbarred and slapped with 12 criminal charges, including theft, fraud and forgery.
>
> NDP leader Robert Chisholm fessed up that he had been convicted of drunk driving in his youth—but only after fibbing about the matter early in this summer's election campaign. The nomination for one riding was contested by two men who both had drunk driving convictions.

And then there is former Liberal Premier Gerald Regan. You need an abacus to keep track of how many times he has been accused of mauling young girls. He spent six weeks in court last year defending his honour with the costly help of famed Toronto lawyer Edward Greenspan. Regan has not been convicted of anything.

In March 2001, Brian (Crusher) Boudreau was acquitted of assaulting his brother. At the end of August 2005, Boudreau was charged with ninety-one counts of forgery and uttering forged documents between 1995 and 1999, when he was president of the Bras d'Or North Community Development Association. He was arraigned in October 2005, and elected trial by jury. The trial is expected to take place in 2007. Boudreau won a provincial by-election in 1999 and sat as the Liberal member for Cape Breton–The Lakes until 2003 when he was defeated.

16. Marci Lin Melvin, "She says: Matheson case stings lawyers: Time for disgraced MLA to quit House," *The Daily News* (Halifax), 18 June 1998, 30.

17. Marci Lin Melvin, "Reeves Matheson," email message to author, 27 July 2005.

Eleven: The Criminals Pick Themselves

1. The late Izzy Asper (1932–2003) is best known as founder of CanWest Global Communication Corporation. Gerry Schwartz is the founder and head of Onex Corporation, one of Canada's largest corporations. Jack London is a former dean of the University of Manitoba law school. Martin Freedman is a judge of the Manitoba Court of Appeal. Michael Nozick is a prominent Winnipeg property developer.

2. Ingrid Chen, interview by Philip Slayton, Winnipeg, 10 November 2005. For the story of Ingrid Chen, see Chapter 4.

3. Marilyn Billinkoff, interview by Philip Slayton, Winnipeg, 27 November 2003.

4. John Greenwood, "Rogue's Gallery," *The Financial Post*, 1 February 1996, 46.

5. *Skimming v. Goldberg*, [1993] M.J. No. 370.

6. "RCMP probe lawyer-fraud link," *Winnipeg Free Press*, 7 February 1991, 1.

7. *R. v. Shead*, [1996] M.J. No. 466.

8. David Kuxhaus, "Shead jailed 5 years for fraud," *Winnipeg Free Press*, 8 November 1996, 1.

9. Richard Shead, interview by Philip Slayton, Winnipeg, 19 March 2002.

10. Richard Shead, "No Subject," email message to author, 15 April 2002.

11. Richard Shead, "No Subject," email message to author, 22 April 2002.

12. Doug Ward, interview by Philip Slayton, Winnipeg, 27 November 2003.

13. Robert Morrison, interview by Philip Slayton, Winnipeg, 27 November 2003.

14. David Baines, "Eron VP stickhandled wealth," *The Vancouver Sun*, 5 November 1997, D1.

15. Peter Kennedy, "Criminal charges laid against Eron executives," *The Globe and Mail*, 1 May 2002, B1.

16. See Chapter 5 for more about Martin Chambers.

17. *Law Society of Manitoba v. Shead*, 1995 L.S.D.D. No.50.

18. *R. v. Shead,* [1996] M.J. 466.

19. paragraph 555.

20. paragraph 128.

21. paragraph 306.

22. paragraph 363.

23. paragraph 365.

24. *R. v. Shead*, [1997] M.J. No. 117.

25. paragraph 556.

26. paragraph 557.

27. Wood also spoke highly of Michael Bomek. See Chapter 9.

28. Kim Whiteside and Richard Schwartz, interview by Philip Slayton, Winnipeg, 23 March 2004.

29. Bruce McLeod, interview by Philip Slayton, Winnipeg, 23 March 2004.

Twelve: Law Practice to Pet Food

1. Martin Wirick, interview by Philip Slayton, Vancouver, 16 February 2005. Some of the personal information about Wirick is drawn from that interview and subsequent correspondence. Quotations from Wirick, unless otherwise indicated, come from the interview. An earlier and shorter version of this chapter appeared in *Canadian Lawyer*, May 2005.

2. Martin Wirick, "Follow up," email message to author, 12 March 2005.

3. Wyng Chow, "The two faces of a controversial builder: 'Pillar of community' sued more than 100 times," *The Vancouver Sun*, 21 September 2002, A4.

4. This account of what happened is largely drawn from Wirick's May 20, 2002, letter of resignation to the Law Society of British Columbia, and from an affidavit he filed in connection with his 2004 bankruptcy proceeding.

5. David Baines, "Massive fraud puts law society on hook for up to $46 million: Special fee on clients' real estate transactions will fund fraud claims," *The Vancouver Sun*, 17 September 2002, A1.

6. Michael Wilhelmson, "Real estate lawyer's actions cause shock waves at B.C. banks," *The Lawyers Weekly*, 20 September 2002, 3.

7. Brad Daisley, public relations officer for the Law Society of British Columbia, made this comment in a March 23, 2005, email to the author:

> The two cheque system was poorly received for two reasons. One was that it was seen to impose an additional burden on the way in which real estate lawyers convey property. The other was the principled argument that the two cheque system resulted in an intrusion into solicitor-client privilege.

8. *Law Society of British Columbia v. Wirick*, [2002] L.S.D.D. No.41.

9. In *R. v. Berge*, (2003 BCPC 0377), Judge Burdett said:

> Mr. Berge is a prominent member of the British Columbia Bar. He has served as a bencher of the Law Society of British Columbia for many years and is

presently the President of the Law Society. Given that, I find his conduct after the accident to be shocking.

As a lawyer, I assume he is well aware of the intricacies of impaired driving investigations. The attempt to dispose of the open beer can, the consumption of mouthwash, and the ingestion of the pills were deliberate, conscious attempts to thwart the police investigation.

... As a bencher of the Law Society, Mr. Berge is charged with upholding and protecting the public interest in the administration of justice. He owes a duty under the Canons of Legal Ethics, a duty to the State, to maintain its integrity and its law. In light of those over-riding duties and obligations, his attempts to derail the impaired investigation, in my view, are disturbing.

Berge then hired none other than Richard Gibbs, his predecessor as law society president, to appeal the suspension of his driving licence. The appeal, heard in March 2004, was dismissed. See *R. v. Berge*, (2004 BCSC 474).

10. The law society citation described the former president's conduct:

On October 2, 2002, after consuming a substantial amount of alcohol just prior to driving a motor vehicle and then causing an accident by driving without due care and attention, you removed an open can of beer from your car to dispose of it, or you acted in a manner that made it appear as if you intended to dispose of it, and you used mouthwash prior to the arrival of the police in order to mask the smell of alcohol on your breath.

11. *Law Society of British Columbia v. Berge*, (2005 LSBC 28).

12. *Law Society of British Columbia v. Berge*, (2005 LSBC 53).

13. *In the Matter of the Bankruptcy of Martin Wirick*, (2004 BCSC 1126). The applicable law is s. 172(1) of the Bankruptcy and Insolvency Act, R.S.C. 1985, c. B-3.

14. *In the Matter of the Bankruptcy of Martin Wirick*, 2 February 2005, Docket 22890 1/VA02.

15. *In the Matter of the Bankruptcy of Martin Wirick*, 2006 BCSC 1273 (CanLII).

16. See note 7.

17. Adrienne Tanner, "Developer facing probe spotted at work sites," *The Province*, 29 August 2003, A16.

18. See "The Wirick claims—an update," Law Society of British Columbia, Benchers' Bulletin, November– December 2005. The update reports on the findings of an investigation into the Wirick affair, on behalf of the law society, by MacKay Co., chartered accountants. An excerpt:

> MacKayCo confirmed that, over the four-year period, Martin Wirick paid approximately $52 million from trust to the Vanview group of companies and other related parties, primarily the operating company, Vanview Construction Ltd....
>
> Funds distributed through this Vanview Construction Ltd. account during the period totalled approximately $52.7 million. There were no funds on hand when Vanview closed....
>
> The $52.7 million distributed was disbursed as follows:
>
> $32.6 million—business expenses (development and construction costs)
>
> $12.5 million—payments to lenders
>
> $3.2 million—payments to Vanview group, Gill and related individuals
>
> $2.5 million—payments to unrelated businesses
>
> $.6 million—payments to Wirick
>
> $1.3 million—unidentified payments
>
> ... In reporting to the Benchers in September 2005, MacKayCo said that it appeared Tarsem Gill engaged in poor business practices. In particular, his Vanview group of companies exercised little control over expenses and frequently paid its suppliers round amounts. Moreover, the Law Society audit of Martin Wirick's records revealed that Mr. Gill and his companies frequently sold or resold properties for less than it cost to develop them, resulting in significant losses.

www.lawsociety.bc.ca/publications_forms/bulletin/2005/05-12-20_scf-wirick.html?h=+wirick (accessed 14 September 2006).

19. David Baines wrote in January 2006, "The magnitude of the fraud perpetrated by former Vancouver lawyer Martin Wirick and his developer client, Tarsem Gill, is breathtaking. So is the amount of time it is taking the police to investigate the case.... Nearly four years have passed, but police have not yet obtained Wirick's books and records, which are central to the whole case." David Baines, "Time taken to investigate fraud case inordinate," *The Vancouver Sun*, 25 January 2006, D1.

20. Martin Wirick, "Update," email message to author, 16 November 2005.

21. Jim Matkin, interview by Philip Slayton, Vancouver, 14 February 2005.

22. See note 17.

23. David Baines, "Law society chief linked to stock offenders," *The Vancouver Sun*, 13 November 2004, A1.

24. Jim Matkin has gone on to a new and successful career as a businessman.

Thirteen: Belletristic Theoretician

1. Logan Kline, telephone interview by Philip Slayton, 4 November 2005. An August 31, 2004, press release from the United States Marshals Service said that "as a fugitive, Singleton has lived in numerous places, but has always been able to stay out of trouble."

2. I interviewed Singleton at the Leavenworth Detention Center, Leavenworth, Kansas, on January 6, 2006. We have also had an extensive correspondence. His 2006 letters to me, following our meeting, are dated January 28, February 8, March 2, March 16, March 21, April 2, April 3, April 9, May 4, and June 24.

3. M.K. Singleton, H.L. *Mencken and the American Mercury Adventure* (Durham: Duke University Press, 1962).

4. Much of the biographical information on Marvin Singleton is drawn from a 2004 paper he wrote (in the third person)— "Background to a 2004 U.S./Canada Extradition Application: The Defendant's Perspective." Singleton filed this paper as an exhibit in his extradition hearing. The court "reluctantly" admitted the paper into evidence. I was also given access to notes

that Singleton has made about his case. He explains these notes: "I'm almost 73 years old and am a totally isolated pariah. I'd better get it down."

5. From Singleton's notes.

6. Marvin Singleton, letter to author, 9 December 2005.

7. Suzy Hamilton, "Client's ashes in box, cash gone: His clients are dead, but a retired lawyer is being sued over thousands of dollars they left behind," *The Province*, 27 February 1994, A28. Singleton disputes the "client's ashes" story (the ashes were those of Haroldine Copp). He says that the Copp ashes had not been abandoned in his office, but were in an expensive urn, waiting to be shipped for burial in the Copp family plot in Ontario.

8. Don Skogstad, telephone interview by Philip Slayton, 16 March 2005. There is personal animosity between Skogstad and Singleton. Singleton refers to Skogstad as his "frequent adversary" and says that he always beat Skogstad in court. In his 2004 paper, Singleton writes, "Skogstad, in the perspective of 100's of years of litigation, was simply the eternal Estates-aggrandizing litigator versus the Power-of-Attorney life-quality protector." Singleton blames Skogstad for promoting the "client's ashes" story.

9. Two charges were laid under section 334(a) (theft over $1,000), and two under section 380(1)(A) (fraud over $1,000).

10. Darren Davidson, "Nelson fugitive nabbed after 11-year hunt; Former local lawyer who allegedly misappropriated $800,000 arrested in Kansas, where he was living modestly as a part-time English professor and librarian," *Nelson Daily News*, 7 September 2004, 1.

11. Luc Quenneville, telephone interview by Philip Slayton, 29 April 2005.

12. An infant son died of hyaline membrane disease. Singleton says that one reason for his deep interest in President Kennedy is that one of Kennedy's own sons, Patrick Bouvier Kennedy, died in infancy from the same disease.

13. Solveig Singleton is a Senior Adjunct Fellow of the Progress and Freedom Foundation (PFF), specializing in technology law and policy, in Washington, D.C. The PFF describes itself as "a

market-oriented think tank that studies the digital revolution and its implications for public policy. Its mission is to educate policymakers, opinion leaders and the public about issues associated with technological change, based on a philosophy of limited government, free markets and individual sovereignty."

14. From Singleton's 2004 paper. A Justice Department investigation of the wrongful charging of Brandon Mayfield blamed sloppy paperwork by the FBI, and overconfidence in fingerprint identification technology. See David Stout, "Inquiry Says F.B.I. Erred in Implicating Man in Attack," *The New York Times*, 7 January 2006, A8.

15. From Singleton's notes.

16. In 1894, Alfred Dreyfus, a Jewish officer in the French army, was convicted of treason. He was innocent and was eventually pardoned by the president of France. The Dreyfus Affair was a major scandal in modern French history. In 1898, the writer Émile Zola published a famous newspaper article titled "J'accuse!" proclaiming the innocence of Dreyfus and attacking the process that led to his conviction.

17. In particular, Singleton believes that U.S. and Canadian authorities are seeking to disregard what is known in extradition law as the "principle of speciality." This principle provides that an extradited person may be tried only for the offence(s) stated in the extradition request.

18. Jim Cross, telephone interviews with Philip Slayton, 4 and 8 November 2005.

19. Marvin Singleton, letter to author, 2 March 2006.

20. Singleton's notes.

21. Scott Canon and Dawn Bormann, "Cheney touts economy in visit," *The Kansas City Star*, 7 January 2006, C1.

22. Marvin Singleton, letter to author, 28 January 2006.

23. Philip Slayton, "My Truman Capote Moment," *Canadian Lawyer*, May 2006, 43.

24. Marvin Singleton, letter to author, 24 June 2006.

25. Philip Slayton, letter to Marvin Singleton, 17 July 2006.

Fourteen: Guerrilla Fighters

1. Christina Finney, telephone interviews by Philip Slayton, December 2005 and January 2006.

2. Susan Semenak, "I was conned out of $300,000: teacher; Samir Badr swept Christina Finney off her feet. Then, she says, he bilked her," *The Gazette* (Montreal), 17 July 1994, A1. For some of the facts about the dispute between Christina Finney and Eric Belhassen, especially its early days, I rely on extensive coverage by Montreal's *Gazette*, particularly stories by Susan Semenak and Geoff Baker.

3. Later Jasson played the role of "guard" in the movie *Gothika*, starring Halle Berry. In 2005, he ran unsuccessfully for mayor of Lachine. Most recently, he played the role of "bodyguard" in a television film about Justice Louise Arbour.

4. See note 2.

5. See Geoff Baker, "Misconduct hearing bogs down," *The Gazette* (Montreal), 11 September 1995, A3.

6. See note 2.

7. See Geoff Baker, "Lawyer still unpunished," *The Gazette* (Montreal), 30 May 1998, A1.

8. *Barreau du Québec c. Belhassen*, [1994] D.D.A.N. no.115.

9. Geoff Baker, "Lawyer gets disciplinary hearing postponed," *The Gazette* (Montreal), 23 February 1995, E7.

10. See note 5.

11. *McCullock-Finney c. Barreau du Québec*, [1999] R.R.A. 83.

12. R.S.Q., c. C-26. Section 193 says this: "The syndics, assistant syndics, corresponding syndics, the investigators and experts of a professional inspection committee, the members of the Office, of a Bureau, of a committee on discipline, of a professional inspection committee or of a committee of inquiry established by a Bureau, and the members of a tribunal hearing an appeal from a decision by a committee on discipline or by a Bureau, shall not be prosecuted for acts done in good faith in the performance of their duties."

13. Allison Hanes, "10-year battle resumes: A schoolteacher, defending herself, takes lawsuit to appeal, claiming the Bar is

trying to 'smear' her," *The Gazette* (Montreal), 28 September 2001, B10.

14. *McCullock-Finney c. Barreau du Québec*, 2002 IIJCan 9255.

15. Guy Pratte, telephone interview by Philip Slayton, 4 November 2005.

16. *Finney v. Barreau du Québec*, [2004] 2 S.C.R. 17.

17. Mike King, "Bar association must pay, Supreme Court rules," *The Gazette* (Montreal), 11 June 2004, A8.

18. Beppi Crosariol, "Supreme Court decision puts watchdogs on high alert: Ruling puts onus on regulators to investigate complaints quickly, experts say," *The Globe and Mail*, 16 August 2004, B9.

19. At the end of the trial, Finney suddenly reduced the damages she was demanding, from $3.5 million to $75,000.

20. See *McCullock-Finney v. Gauthier*, [2006] J.Q. no. 2429, para 2.

21. The trial began by Finney asking the court to make available a French-English interpreter at no cost to her. The trial judge said that she was entitled to interpretation if she paid for it. Going to a judge of the Court of Appeal for leave to appeal this decision, Finney argued that the right to understand what is going on during a civil trial was part and parcel of her common law right to a full and fair hearing, embodied in the Constitution of Canada. She asserted that the provincial government had the constitutional obligation, at its expense, to ensure that all who appeared before the courts had the means to understand all that is said during the course of a trial. Justice Hilton, denying leave to appeal, noted that part of Finney's underlying claim was that in the previous trial that resulted in a Supreme Court of Canada judgment she was denied a fair hearing by the defendants' deliberately choosing to plead and testify in French. Said Justice Hilton, "If I was to grant leave to appeal the interlocutory judgment of the trial judge as requested by Mrs. Finney, this Court effectively would be called upon to decide one of the issues in the current trial without an adequate factual context and without the benefit of a reasoned judgment of the trial judge on the subject." *McCullock-Finney c. Quebec Bar Association*, [2006] Q.J. No. 220.

22. Finney was still busy before the discipline committee of the Quebec bar, and before the professions tribunal, pursuing unsuccessfully the lawyers who had represented the bar before the Supreme Court of Canada. In McCullock Finney c. Doray, 2006 QCTP 16, the professions tribunal rejected Finney's objections to certain procedures being followed in her misconduct complaint against Raymond Doray. The facts were similar, and the outcomes the same, in McCullock Finney c. Gauthier, 2006 QCTP 54, and McCullock Finney c. Houle, 2006 QCTP 55.

23. Christina Finney, telephone interview by Philip Slayton, 14 December 2005.

Fifteen: The Last Hope

1. "Famous lawyer ousted," The Province, 9 November 1989, 21.

2. Jack Lakey, "Toronto lawyer draws cheers from Bejing demonstrators," Toronto Star, 31 May 1989, A19.

3. Harry Kopyto, interview by Philip Slayton, Toronto, 27 September 2005. Several of the Kopyto quotations in this chapter come from this interview.

4. In March 1987, Antonio Borges, a Canadian citizen, came into Codina's Toronto office with Marguerida, his sister. Marguerida was in Canada on a tourist visa, but she wanted to live in Canada. There were six Borges siblings, all, except Antonio, living in Portugal, and all, except Marguerida, married. Antonio later said that he told Codina about his brothers and sisters, but she "told me whenever I went to the immigration to tell them that I didn't have anybody else in my family." In Codina's opinion, that would make Marguerida eligible for Canadian residency under an immigration program designed to favour the "last remaining single family member."

5. Rick Haliechuk, "Kopyto's luxury home for sale, Can't afford it, controversial lawyer admits," Toronto Star, 28 August 1989, A2.

6. Harry Kopyto separated from his wife, Sabina Kopyto, also known as Shirley Resnick or Reznick, in 1984, after he met Angie. They were divorced in 1990. In 1988, at Harry's urging,

Sabina mortgaged what had been the family home, where she still lived, for $230,000. Kopyto and Codina used the proceeds to purchase the house at 211 Dunvegan Road. In 1993, Sabina's litigation guardian attempted unsuccessfully to secure an interim injunction stopping the mortgagee from exercising a power of sale over her home. Evidence was given that Sabina suffered from schizophrenia. The judge said that "Mrs. Kopyto seemed to be a tool for her husband; what he wanted her to do, she did." But he did not grant the injunction, saying that "Mrs. Kopyto knew exactly what she was doing when she signed the mortgage." See *Kopyto (Litigation guardian of) v. Royal Bank of Canada*, [1993] O.J. No. 2168.

Kopyto never paid the child support required by the 1990 divorce judgment. In 1996, the Ontario Family Support Plan brought an action to enforce the child support order—*Ontario (Family Support Plan, Director) v. Kopyto*, [1996] O.J. No. 2095. Although Kopyto was technically in default, the judge found that he was meeting all his children's financial needs, and refused to make an order. The judge noted:

> The payor's evidence was that he has an association or relationship with another person, Ms. Codina, who seems to have taken over the role of his benefactor. Mr. Kopyto has made it clear repeatedly in his testimony that he has access to almost unlimited funds from her, sometimes without even the asking, not only to meet his own expenses, but to meet any and all the expenses of his children. This arrangement has been in effect for the last several years. Mr. Kopyto has stated in his evidence that Ms. Codina has voluntarily taken on the responsibility of meeting all his expenses and those of his children.

7. *R. v. Codina*, 1995 CanLII 572.

8. The judge failed to instruct the jury on whether the existence of married siblings in Portugal was a material fact for immigration officials. See note 4.

9. *R. v. Codina*, 1999 CanLII 2818.

10. *R. v. Codina*, [1997] O.J. No. 6429.

11. *Law Society of Upper Canada v. Codina*, [2002] L.S.D.D. No. 84. Codina had a long history of trouble with the law

society. When she was arrested in 1989 on immigration charges, the law society was already looking into allegations that she counselled Hong Kong clients to circumvent Canadian immigration hearings. Eventually this complaint was withdrawn. After her initial conviction for immigration fraud, the law society brought charges of conduct unbecoming a solicitor. This complaint was withdrawn when the Court of Appeal quashed the immigration fraud conviction. Codina sought to have Kopyto (as agent—he was now disbarred) represent her in disciplinary proceedings arising out of her immigration fraud conviction. A law society panel refused, saying that "the tribunal could not rely upon Mr. Kopyto's integrity, honesty and forthrightness, and ... therefore he is not competent properly to represent or to advise Ms. Codina before it." An application to the Divisional Court for judicial review of this decision was dismissed—*Codina v. Law Society of Upper Canada*, [1996] O.J. No. 3348.

In May 1989, Harry Kopyto defended Codina against law society charges that she had counselled clients in Hong Kong on how to avoid Canadian immigration law. Kopyto argued that the law society was harassing Codina because of her association with him. Unwittingly, the lawyer for the law society substantiated his argument. In a May 17, 1989, story, Rick Haliechuk of the Toronto Star described the disciplinary proceedings:

> Veteran Toronto lawyer Harry Kopyto created a poisoned atmosphere that likely led a younger solicitor into discipline trouble, a law society lawyer testified yesterday.
>
> A discipline charge against Angie Codina probably resulted from her professional and personal ties to Kopyto, Reg Watson told a Law Society of Upper Canada discipline panel....
>
> "You poisoned the atmosphere," Watson charged, noting that Codina and Kopyto share a Bay St. office, and have a personal relationship. "There was a close link between you professionally and personally, and that atmosphere was dishonest." ...
>
> Watson replied quickly when Kopyto challenged the assertion that he and Codina had a personal relationship.
>
> "I also saw you together in a nightclub downtown," Watson said. "In fact, when I was on the dance floor, you came over and spoke to me."

> Watson also said that during a meeting he held with
> the two lawyers, Kopyto repeatedly referred to Codina as
> "dear." Watson said that was unprofessional.

Rick Haliechuk, "Kopyto 'poisoned' lawyer's behaviour law society told," *Toronto Star*, 17 May 1989, A23.

12. For a full description of Codina's rejection of the charges against her, see David Gambrill, "Angie Inside," *Canadian Lawyer*, January 2001.

13. *Angie Codina v. The People of the State of New York*, 297 A.D. 2d 539 (2002).

14. Harry Kopyto and Angie Codina, "Hopes for human rights fade behind prison walls," *The Globe and Mail*, 10 September 1985, 7.

15. Gambrill, in *Canadian Lawyer*.

16. *Regina v. Kopyto*, 32 O.R. (2d) 585.

17. Vianney Carriere, "Lawyer takes Establishment as his wind-mill," *The Globe and Mail*, 25 March 1982, 1.

18. Bill Gladstone, "Life's work was 'labour of love,'" *The Globe and Mail*, 18 March 2002, R7.

19. An account of what happened, from Dowson's point of view, can be found in *Ross Dowson v. RCMP* (Forward Publications, 1980). In a foreword, well-known civil rights lawyer Clayton Ruby described the case as "a modern attempt at the suppression of freedom of thought."

20. Kirk Makin, "Ex-RCMP officers only doing job, Ontario judge decides," *The Globe and Mail*, 18 December 1985, A17.

21. Kirk Makin, "Thorn in side of legal system cited for contempt of court," *The Globe and Mail*, 10 February 1986, A11.

22. Kirk Makin, "Lawyer's case draws support," *The Globe and Mail*, 8 April 1985, A15.

23. Drew Fagan, "Contempt case puts courts on trial," *The Globe and Mail*, 23 September 1986, A16.

24. "Mr. Kopyto's offence," *The Globe and Mail*, 7 November 1986, A6.

25. *R. v. Kopyto*, [1987] O.J. No. 1052.

26. The law society had twice before disciplined Kopyto. In 1973, he was forced to retake his bar admission course after he was found cheating on exams. In 1984, he was reprimanded over the Chanukah Caper.

27. Jack Nagler, "Maverick lawyer does sudden switch, admits he overbilled Ontario Legal Aid," *The Globe and Mail*, 25 July 1989, 1. The law society now dropped the "Krazy Glue" charges as redundant (Kopyto later commented to *Toronto Star* reporter Rick Haliechuck, "They did an Al Capone on me.... They got him for tax evasion, but they wanted him for something else.").

28. Frances Kelly, "60 backers pledge 'love and support' for maverick lawyer, *Toronto Star*, 18 September 1989, A11.

29. One bencher, Thomas Carey, dissented and gave extensive reasons for his dissent. The reasons in part were as follows:

> Although estimating, the solicitor clearly believed in the essential truth of his accounts.... There was not one piece of evidence called by the Society's counsel to repudiate the Solicitor or to suggest that he acted dishonestly for a dishonest purpose. The Statement of Facts discloses no such motive.... The uncontradicted evidence is that the Solicitor worked exceedingly long hours almost continually, that he took work on vacation, that he was constantly on the phone (sometimes carrying on more than one conversation at once). Having heard the Solicitor give evidence I can accept that his phone conversations could be quite lengthy. In concluding that the Solicitor must be disbarred the Discipline Committee made numerous derogatory comments about the Solicitor calling him "histrionic, bombastic", "patently dishonest". The Committee suggested that the Solicitor wanted "to tear down and smash" the legal process.... [These remarks] illustrate a level of antagonism towards the Solicitor that was inconsistent with an objective detachment.

30. Kirk Makin, "Disbarred for false billings, Kopyto promises fight," *The Globe and Mail*, 9 November 1989, 1.

31. Kirk Makin, "Kopyto victimized public, law society says," *The Globe and Mail*, 14 November 1989, A10.

32. An appeal from the disbarment was dismissed by the Divisional Court—*Kopyto v. Law Society of Upper Canada*, [1993] O.J. No. 2550.

33. Scott Stinson, "Pluto's owner wins him back in court," *National Post*, 22 April 2005, A3.

34. See Natalie Alcoba, "Boy sues hockey body after coach and dad fight," *National Post*, 20 June 2005, A15.

35. But time may finally be running out for Harry. On May 1, 2007, the Access to Justice Act came into force in Ontario, giving the law society the power to license and regulate paralegals. The act says that only someone of good character may practise as a paralegal. It seems unlikely, at least in the eyes of the Law Society of Upper Canada, that Harry Kopyto (and other disbarred lawyers) will qualify.

Sixteen: The Search for Justice

1. See Philip Slayton, "Access to justice? Forget it!" *Canadian Lawyer*, January 2005.

2. See Statistics Canada, "Average income after tax by economic family types (1999 to 2003)," www40.statcan.ca/l01/cst01/famil21a.htm (accessed 31 August 2006).

3. Every province has a system of legal aid that, in limited circumstances, makes lawyers available to the indigent. As well, some attempts have recently been made in Canada to promote pro bono (free) legal representation of the poor and disadvantaged; witness, for example, the creation in 2002 of Pro Bono Law Ontario, a professional organization that doesn't provide free legal services itself, but supports "volunteerism in the legal sector" (a similar organization exists in British Columbia). Most commentators agree, however, that, for the moment at least, very few pro bono legal services are provided in Canada.

By contrast, the United States has a strong pro bono tradition. Rule 6.1 of the American Bar Association Model Rules states that "every lawyer has a professional responsibility to provide legal services to those unable to pay. A lawyer should aspire to render at least (50) hours of pro bono publico legal services per year." *The American Lawyer* newspaper reports that in 2002 the two hundred largest firms in the United States reported just over three million pro bono hours.

4. A number of U.S. lawyers have won the Horatio Alger Award, given by the Horatio Alger Association of Distinguished Americans to persons who have risen to prominence despite humble beginnings.

5 See Paul Seabright, *The Company of Strangers: A Natural History of Economic Life* (Princeton: Princeton University Press, 2004). Seabright writes that "most kinds of professional training, whether apprenticeship as a mechanic or studying for the bar or attending an off-site course as a chef, involve learning not just how to accomplish particular tasks but how to project yourself as a certain kind of person" (91). This is what Seabright means by "learning the narrative."

6. A famous 1973 New Yorker cartoon has a lawyer saying to his client, "You have a pretty good case, Mr. Pitkin. How much justice can you afford?"

7. Ward Just, *Forgetfulness* (New York: Houghton Mifflin, 2006).

8. Michael Gorra, "Imprisoned by History," *The New York Times Book Review*, 24 September 2006, 13.

9. At large New York firms, the annual salary of a first-year lawyer is about $150,000. See Ellen Rosen, "For New Lawyers, the Going Rate Has Gone Up," *The New York Times*, 1 September 2006, www.nytimes.com/2006/09/01/business/01legal.html?ei=5087%0A&en=3e084a47 (accessed 3 September 2006). In downtown Toronto the starting salary is about $100,000.

10. See Chapter 6.

11. Martin E.P. Seligman, *Authentic Happiness* (New York: Free Press, 2002), 181.

12. See Chapter 1.

13. Contingency fee arrangements tie a lawyer's fee to the outcome of a case. If the client wins the case, the client pays his or her lawyer a percentage or other agreed-on portion of the settlement. If a client loses, the client doesn't pay—the lawyer accepts the risk of not being paid when taking a case on a contingent basis. (See www.lsuc.on.ca/media/newconductoct3102.pdf [accessed 30 December 2006]). A class action is a lawsuit brought by one or more plaintiffs on behalf of a large group of

others who have a common interest; typically, class actions are fought on a contingency fee basis.

14. "Law Society approves new conduct rule for contingency fees," Law Society of Upper Canada press release, 31 October 2002.

15. *McIntyre (Estate) v. Ontario (Attorney General)*, 2002 CanLII 45046 (ON C. A.).

16. See "Ontario government improves access to justice for Ontarians," 1 October 2004 news release of the Ontario Ministry of the Attorney General.

17. The amendments require all contingency fee agreements to be made in writing; prohibit contingency fees in criminal, quasi-criminal, and family law matters; prohibit a lawyer from getting paid more than the client recovers; and set out specific protections for minors and incapable adults.

18. See, for example, the story of Martin Wirick in Chapter 12.

19. One might think that this is what happened to Harry Kopyto. See Chapter 15.

20. *The Future of Legal Services: Putting Consumers First*, presented to Parliament by the Secretary of State for Constitutional Affairs and Lord Chancellor, October 2005 (Cmd. 6679). See Chapter 1.

Sources and Acknowledgments

1. Donaldson and I were law partners for several years; I knew him fairly well when he resigned in disgrace from our law firm in 1991. Strother and I worked closely on several large files in the late nineties (representing different clients). I met with Dan Cooper twice, after which he no longer returned messages. I met Richard Shead only once, and he then decided not to cooperate further.

2. Pilzmaker was a student of mine at McGill University's law faculty in the seventies.

3. Professor Hofman drew my attention to the words celebrating Saint Ivo (1253–1303), the patron saint of lawyers, in a stained-glass window in the cathedral of Tréguier in Brittany:

Sanctus Ivo erat Brito,
Advocatus, et non latro
Res miranda populo.

Professor Hofman, who is a Latin scholar, among other things, offered this translation:

Saint Ivo was a Breton,
A lawyer, and not a thief
A thing of amazement to the people.

INDEX